AMERICAN
LEGAL
LITERATURE

AMERICAN LEGAL LITERATURE

A Guide to Selected Legal Resources

Bernard D. Reams, Jr.
James M. Murray
Margaret H. McDermott

1985
Libraries Unlimited, Inc.   **Littleton, Colorado**

Copyright © 1985
Bernard D. Reams, Jr., James M. Murray, Margaret H. McDermott
All Rights Reserved
Printed in the United States of America

No part of this publication may be reproduced, stored in a retrieval system, or transmitted, in any form or by any means, electronic, mechanical, photocopying, recording, or otherwise, without the prior written permission of the publisher.

LIBRARIES UNLIMITED, INC.
P.O. Box 263
Littleton, Colorado 80160-0263

Library of Congress Cataloging-in-Publication Data

Reams, Bernard D.
  American legal literature.

  Includes index.
  1. Law--United States--Bibliography. I. Murray, James M. II. McDermott, Margaret H. III. Title.
KF1.R42   1985   016.34973   85-20769
ISBN 0-87287-514-8   016.3473

Libraries Unlimited books are bound with Type II nonwoven material that meets and exceeds National Association of State Textbook Administrators' Type II nonwoven material specifications Class A through E.

To

Eloise Hickman Reams

and

*Clarence and Della Murray
and Linda Monthy-Murray*

and

Mary and Michael McDermott

"He that goes to law (as the proverb is) holds a wolf by the ear."

—Robert Burton
Anatomy of Melancholy: Democritus to the Reader
1621

CONTENTS

Preface xi

Introduction xiii

Acknowledgments xxi

Abbreviations Used in the Text xxiii

1 – Current Primary Legal Materials 1
    Comments 1
    Federal 5
    States and District of Columbia 6
    Outlying Territories 30

2 – Selected Legal Reference Sources 35
    Comments 35
    Outline of Reference Sources 37
    Annotations 38

3 – Selected Subject Bibliography of Law-related Monographs 75
    Comments 75
    Outline of Subject Headings 77
    Annotations 80

Appendixes
    A – Outline of the United States Court System 177
    B – Selected List of Law Book Publishers 179
    C – Selected List of Major Legal Research Texts 185
    D – Selected List of Online Database Files and Vendors 187

Author Index 189

Title Index 195

About the Authors 205

PREFACE

This work is an introduction to the corpus of contemporary American legal literature. It is designed to provide a survey of materials significant to the researcher seeking an overview of American legal literature. The bulk of the text consists of annotated titles to well over 550 selected American works on many areas of the law written between 1969 and 1984. The book is divided into three sections, the first providing information on primary legal materials available in the federal government, the District of Columbia, all the states, and outlying United States territories. The second chapter contains annotations to selected legal reference materials arranged by type of reference source and including legal dictionaries, indexes, and encyclopedias. The final chapter generally consists of selected annotations to law books arranged by subject, and is especially intended for individuals desiring introductory information on the law. Appendixes include a list of major legal publishers and their addresses, a chart of the federal court system, and a bibliography of leading legal research texts.

This book is intended to direct researchers to significant primary and secondary legal materials. Primary legal materials are those items which are mandated by some rule or regulation to be cited as legal authority. These include statutes, court reports, and administrative regulations. Secondary materials are texts and monographs that are regarded as persuasive authority. These items include hornbooks, practice manuals, and law review articles that explain or advocate a legal position. It is the authors' expectation that a variety of researchers will use this text as a compendium of major legal reference sources. As a bibliography of contemporary law materials, it should prove particularly helpful to those needing an introduction to the sources of legal information.

With the exception of the legal abbreviations used for primary materials in chapter 1, all citations follow *The Chicago Manual of Style,* 13th ed. (Chicago: University of Chicago Press, 1982). In chapters 2 and 3, we have added information about page numbers, indexes, glossaries, etc., to most citations. We have avoided the use of traditional legal citation forms because of their lack of complete bibliographical data. The *Chicago* form better meets the needs of the legal researcher seeking detailed bibliographic information.

INTRODUCTION

Origin and Purpose

A recent nationwide survey conducted by the Hearst Corporation revealed that the American public is surprisingly ignorant about important legal concepts,[1] and C. Thomas Ross, chairman of the American Bar Association Commission on Public Education About the Law, referring to his satisfying experiences as a volunteer working for bar associations in educating the public on legal matters, was prompted to say, "Ironically, this service has led to one of my biggest frustrations—recognizing the inescapable conclusion that the vast majority of the public continues to exhibit an alarming ignorance about the law and its constant impact on their lives."[2]

Concomitant with this perception of a lack of knowledge about law and the legal system, there has been an increasing demand in recent years from various segments of the population to improve understanding of the legal system by teaching the public about the law. A. Bartlett Giamatti, president of Yale University, and James O. Freedman, president of the University of Iowa, have both advocated including undergraduate-level courses on law as a means of expanding legal knowledge.[3] Already this educational process is well under way as evidenced by the National Institute for Citizen Education in the Law, a nonprofit Washington, D.C.-based organization set up by Edward L. O'Brien—with a staff of fifteen people—promoting a program of law-related education (LRE) in which lawyers are providing instruction in public schools throughout all fifty states.[4]

Another response to the increased interest in law has been the emergence of self-help legal publishers, who are briefly discussed in the introduction to chapter 3 (in fact, a recent article indicates that self-help legal publishing is expanding[5]). Along these same lines, a law professor recently stated that there have been parts of some areas traditionally controlled by the legal profession (e.g., divorce, real estate, probate, bankruptcy, and debt collection) that could more appropriately be handled by nonlawyer specialists.[6]

Even though the legal profession is charged by statute with the responsibility for rendering legal services and continues to exercise a kind of monopoly on the giving of legal advice, access to legal information—as distinguished from legal services and advice—is not restricted by law and can be freely provided by public and private libraries and institutions. Access to legal information for persons without legal training should be encouraged as a means of furthering an understanding of personal rights and legal institutions.

In addition to the legal profession's monopoly—and economic cutbacks—various other factors have contributed to the increased demand for legal information by the citizenry. The major stimulus has been the growth of consumer awareness and advocacy. This broad movement has encouraged individual interest and the use of self-help measures where personal rights (e.g., civil liberties) and community interests (e.g., environmental concerns) are at stake.

Along the broad spectrum of legal problems, a large number are found to require no legal services or advice for their resolution. The economic interests of the legal profession itself are best served when citizens with access to legal information can deal effectively with their own legal difficulties. By the same token, the interests of the public are best served when it is recognized that self-help does not resolve all legal problems.

This bibliographic work fills a void in the current literature by bringing coherence to the scattered efforts aimed at improving access to legal information. Legal researchers should be able to determine appropriate primary materials by referring to the first chapter; chapters 2 and 3 provide information on secondary resources or materials suitable for additional collection needs. The preliminary "Comments" to chapter 1 provide a definition of primary resources (e.g., case and statutory laws). Secondary resources are essentially all other legal materials such as treatises, hornbooks, and encyclopedias. These secondary resources provide explanations, interpretations, and information about the law.

Historical Background

Prior to 1960, there were few books on law useful to the generalist. Since that time, especially within the last fifteen years, there has been a proliferation of books for citizens interested in knowing about their legal rights and responsibilities. This bibliography provides a representative sampling of the wealth of available American legal material, on both a technical and an informative level.

There are five works previously published in the United States that could be partial precedents for this publication.

Andrews, Joseph L. *The Law in the United States of America: A Selective Bibliographic Guide.* New York: New York University Press, 1965.

Besterman, Theodore. *Law and International Law: A Bibliography of Bibliographies.* Totowa, N.J.: Rowman and Littlefield, 1971.

Howell, Margaret A. *A Bibliography of Bibliographies of Legal Material.* 2 vols. with 1969-71 suppl. Woodbridge, N.J.: New Jersey Appellate Printing, 1969.

Mersky, Roy M. *Law Books for Non-Law Libraries and Laymen: A Bibliography.* Dobbs Ferry, N.Y.: Oceana, 1969.

Sloan, Richard, ed. *Recommended Law Books.* Chicago: American Bar Association, Committee on Business Law Libraries, 1969.

The Andrews bibliography was compiled at the request of the International Association of Law Libraries (I.A.L.L.), and was intended primarily for the use of law librarians in countries other than the United States. However, the Andrews bibliography has had a much wider audience. Its simple subject arrangement and highly selective content have made it a convenient reference for anyone wishing to identify the leading sources in a given field of U.S. law without undertaking extensive bibliographic research. The Andrews bibliography has been widely used by public and academic librarians both in the United States and abroad as an aid in selecting basic U.S. legal materials.

The Besterman bibliography (it is annotated in chapter 2 under the heading "Bibliographies") consists of a listing of bibliographies throughout the world. It is not only dated, but it also is international in scope, listing many sources unavailable in most libraries.

The Howell bibliography was developed out of the considered need of students, faculty, and patrons of the Law Library of Rutgers, the State University at Newark, N.J., for a working resource comprising the body of legal literature necessary to research given problem areas. The bibliography is broad in scope and international in coverage, including references to legal bibliographies published up to 1971.

The Mersky bibliography resembles this work more than the other bibliographies do. Directed primarily at public libraries and lawyers (in spite of its title), the Mersky text includes chapters addressing prelaw students, chapters listing professional nonlaw reading for lawyers, and chapters dealing with writing and language skills for lawyers. Other chapters concentrate on recommended law books for public libraries. Thus, the content and scope of the Mersky work differs significantly from those of this work.

Finally, the Sloan bibliography was intended for use by law firm libraries and provides a comprehensive selection of law books and other legal authority of interest to practicing lawyers.

All of the above works are now out-of-date and of little practical value, and it is not known whether any plans exist to reissue any of them. In any case, this work is unique, and addresses an important area of bibliographic concern not previously dealt with in a comprehensive way in the United States.

Scope

This publication includes few foreign materials. Emphasis is on American law and resources published in the United States. With the exception of primary materials listed in chapter 1 and selected reference materials in chapter 2, we have avoided including in this work items of a continuing nature (e.g., looseleafs, periodicals, etc.) for several reasons: most legal materials available to the American lay public are in the form of single volume books or monographs, and reasonable space and time considerations supported our choice to exclude periodical publications. Nevertheless, we feel it is appropriate to mention some of the many other historical and current bibliographic resources which interested individuals and institutions may wish to consult.

Additional Resources

The following sources (a number of these works have been annotated in chapter 2 under the heading "Bibliographies") provide information on reviews, catalogs, books, and items of a continuing nature, such as periodicals and looseleafs.

Abstracts of Book Reviews in Current Legal Periodicals. Provo, Utah: Law Library, J. Reuben Clark Law School, 1976- . Published semimonthly.

Annual Legal Bibliography. 21 vols. Cambridge, Mass.: Harvard Law School Library, 1961-1981.

Bibliographic Guide to Law. Boston: G.K. Hall, 1969- . Called *Law Book Guide* prior to 1975.

Books in Print. New York: R.R. Bowker, 1948- . Annual publication with bimonthly issues of *Forthcoming Books.*

Bowker's Law Books and Serials in Print Update. See *Law Information . . .,* below.

Buckwalter, Robert L., ed. and comp. *Law Books in Print.* 4th ed. 5 vols. Dobbs Ferry, N.Y.: Glanville, 1982.

_____. *Law Books Published.* Dobbs Ferry, N.Y.: Glanville, 1969- . Publication updating *Law Books in Print* published three times annually.

Card Catalogs of the Harvard Law School Library 1817-1981. (Microfiche) New York: K. G. Saur., 1983. Updates since 1981 are also available.

Chiang, W. S., and L. E. Dickson. *Legal Bibliography Index.* Baton Rouge, La.: Publications Institute, Paul M. Herbert Law Center, Louisiana State University, 1978- . Annual publication of legal bibliographies similar to Howell's *A Bibliography of Bibliographies of Legal Material.*

Current Publications in Legal and Related Fields. Littleton, Colo.: Fred B. Rothman, 1953- . Published monthly with annual cumulations.

Dictionary Catalog of the Columbia University Law Library. 28 vols. Boston: G. K. Hall, 1969. 11 volume supplement to 1977.

Eis, Arlene L., ed. and comp. *Legal Looseleafs in Print.* New York: Infosources, 1981- . Annual publication.

_____. *Legal Newsletters in Print.* New York: Infosources, 1985- . Annual publication.

Hein, William S., Jr., Kevin M. Marmion, and Ilene N. Hein. *Hein's Legal Periodical Check List.* Buffalo: William S. Hein, 1977- .

Law Books, 1876-1981. 4 vols. New York: R.R. Bowker, 1981.

Law Books in Review: A Quarterly Journal of Review in Current Publications in Law and Related Fields. Dobbs Ferry, N.Y.: Glanville, 1973- .

Law Books Recommended for Libraries. 6 vols. Littleton, Colo.: Fred B. Rothman, 1967- . 4 volume supplement to 1976.

Law Information . . . New York: R.R. Bowker, 1982- . Annual publication continuing *Law Books, 1876-1981;* kept up to date by *Bowker's Law Books and Serials Update,* a companion service issued ten times a year and called *Law Information Update* before 1984.

Pimsleur, Meira G. *Checklists of Basic American Legal Publications.* Littleton, Colo.: Fred B. Rothman, 1962- .

Schwartz, Mortimer D., and Dan F. Henke, eds. and comps. *Anglo-American Law Collections: University of California Law Libraries Berkeley and Davis with Library of Congress Class K Added.* 10 vols. Littleton, Colo.: Fred B. Rothman, 1970. 9 volume supplement to 1979.

Taylor, Betty W., and Robert J. Monroe. *American Law Publishing, 1860-1900: Historical Readings & Bibliography.* 4 vols. Dobbs Ferry, N.Y.: Glanville, 1984.

Tseng, Henry P. *Complete Guide to Legal Materials in Microform.* Arlington, Va.: University Publications of America, 1976.

Ward, Peter D., ed. *National Legal Bibliography: Recent Acquisitions of Major Legal Libraries.* Buffalo: William S. Hein, 1984- . Monthly issues and bound cumulative annual.

Wypysky, Eugene M. *Legal Periodicals in English.* 4 vols. Dobbs Ferry, N.Y.: Glanville, 1976- .

In addition to hard copy bibliographic guides, automation now provides bibliographers with resources for information. Legal research databases are briefly discussed in the "Comments" to chapter 2, and a selected list of online files and vendors is located in the appendixes.[7] The following vendors rank among the leading sources for online bibliographic information relating to acquisition and cataloging of legal materials:

OCLC (Online Computer Library Center)
6565 Frantz Road
Dublin, Ohio 43017
Phone: (614) 764-6000

RLG/RLIN (Research Libraries Group/Research Libraries Information
   Network)
Jordan Quadrangle
Stanford University
Stanford, California 94305
Phone: (415) 328-0920

WLN (Western Library Network)
Washington State Library, AJ-11
Olympia, Washington 98504
Phone: (206) 459-6518

One of the best sources for information on law books of general interest is *Library Journal,* published twenty times a year by R.R. Bowker. "The Book Review" section of this magazine regularly publishes reviews on law-related books under the heading of "Social Science," subheading "Law & Criminology."

There are numerous other resources, but we have neither the space nor the specific need to list the myriad that exist. We would like to point out, however, that individuals, librarians, institutions, and organizations should find what they require with a little incentive and some assistance from law librarians. For example, information exists on what consists of a core legal collection in the states of Indiana, Kentucky, Michigan, and Ohio.[8] There are also bibliographies published by law libraries, listing their holdings;[9] there are articles on recommended law books in social science libraries[10] and legal reference works for Missouri public libraries.[11] The information is available, and the resources only need to be tapped.

Trends

In addition to increasing litigation[12] in recent years, we have witnessed a growing public desire to remedy a lack of knowledge of legal issues. By way of example, a nonprofit organization located in Washington, D.C., called HALT (Help Abolish Legal Tyranny), was founded in 1978 by two Rhodes Scholars disenchanted with the legal system;[13] it now has over 135,000 members with an annual budget around $1.3 million.[14] However, no matter how educated the citizenry becomes, there will always be a need for the legal profession in appropriate circumstances. This fact is well underscored by John Naisbitt, the author of *Megatrends,* who appropriately concludes:

> Just as we have begun to look after our own health and diet, nutrition, exercise and home test kits for blood pressure or pregnancy, so too will we be more inclined to do our own simple legal procedures—wills, name changes, adoptions and even divorces and bankruptcies—often assisted by a clerk or self-help manual. . . . But as other transactions between people (and their machines) become more complex, the demand for attorneys to assist in sorting out the implications of these complicated dealings will increase. . . .[15]

Introduction / xix

While we realize the value of legal materials to the researcher, these works alone cannot cover every legal contingency. The purpose of these resources is to inform citizens, and provide insight on how to avoid or approach litigation in the least expensive manner. There is no substitute for well-informed citizens who have an idea what the law is, know when to utilize a lawyer, and understand how to assert their rights within the framework of society. If we have contributed to this end, this book has satisfied its primary purpose.

Notes

[1] Lynne Reaves, "Ignorance of Law: Poll Finds Public Ill-Informed," *American Bar Association Journal* 70 (March 1984): 47.

[2] Robert S. Peck and Charles J. White, eds., *Understanding the Law: A Handbook on Educating the Public* (Chicago: American Bar Association Commission on Public Understanding About the Law, 1983), 9.

[3] "Yale President Calls for Teaching about Law in Colleges," *American Bar Association Journal* 70 (February 1984): 88.

[4] Kathleen Sylvester, "Attorneys Who Teach 'Street Law,'" *The National Law Journal,* Monday, 20 June 1983, 1.

[5] Kathleen Sylvester, "The People vs. Lawyers: More Groups Cash In on Hatred of Attorneys," *The National Law Journal,* Monday, 9 January 1984, 48.

[6] Deborah L. Rhode, "Policing the Professional Monopoly: A Constitutional and Empirical Analysis of Unauthorized Practice Prohibitions," *Stanford Law Review* 34 (November 1981): 89.

[7] Appendix D.

[8] Kathy Joyce Welker, ed., *Core Legal Collection* (Columbus, Ohio: Ohio State Bar Association, 1982-).

[9] See, for example: Bruce S. Johnson, Steven M. Barkan, and Mary C. Wilson, *Secondary Legal Sources: A Subject Bibliography of Selected Treatises, Looseleaf Services and Formbooks,* 4th ed. (Ann Arbor, Mich.: University of Michigan Law Library, 1980); Frank G. Houdek and James E. Hambleton, comps., *The Freedom of Information Act: A Comprehensive Bibliography of Law Related Materials* (Austin, Tex.: Tarlton Law Library, School of Law, University of Texas at Austin, 1981).

[10] Anita K. Head, "Law Books for Social Science Libraries," *Special Libraries* 70 (January 1979): 1.

[11] Larry De Piesse, "Basic Legal Reference Books for Missouri Public Libraries," *Show-Me Libraries* 30 (June 1979): 9.

[12] Tom Pauken, "Open Forum: Reforms in the Law: The Age of Litigation," *Detroit College of Law Review* 1983 (Winter): 1393, 1395.

[13] Sylvester, "The People vs. Lawyers," 46.

[14] Ibid.

[15] John Naisbitt, "Megatrends for Lawyers and Clients," *American Bar Association Journal* 70 (June 1984): 47.

ACKNOWLEDGMENTS

We would like to express our appreciation to those individuals who have assisted us. Marian G. Gallagher, Law Librarian and Professor of Law Emerita, University of Washington, contributed insight and preliminary comments at the outset of this project. Bonnie Fischer, Research Assistant, spent long hours gathering information on the state and federal primary legal authority found in the first chapter. We would especially like to thank Marlene C. McGuirl and her fine staff of the American-British Law Division in the Library of Congress Law Library for their help in the same chapter with verifying primary legal authority for the outlying United States territories. We also extend a note of thanks to Nina Melechen and Denise Rogers of the Freund Law Library staff, who contributed their support and time to portions of the book, in addition to soliciting complimentary copies of materials for inclusion in the text.

We want to extend our recognition to Bengt Dalemar and Joanna Bartow, Student Assistants, for their efforts on the final chapter and appendixes. A special note of appreciation is due Mary C. Schelling and the Washington University School of Law word processing department for their contribution in typing the manuscript for publication. Finally, we are indebted to those publishers who provided review copies of books that have been included in this work.

ABBREVIATIONS USED IN THE TEXT*

Parts of Publications

app., apps. (appendix, appendixes)
bib., bibs. (bibliography, bibliographies)
comp., comps. (compiler, compilers)
ed. (edition)
ed., eds. (editor, editors)
fig., figs. (figure, figures)
fms. (forms)
glos., gloss. (glossary, glossaries)
ill. (illustrated)

ind., inds. (index, indexes)
ns. (notes)
p., pp. (page, pages)
pl., pls. (plate, plates)
rev. (revised)
suppl., suppls. (supplement, supplements)
tbl., tbls. (table, tables)
vol., vols. (volume, volumes)

States and Territories

Ala. (Alabama)
Alas. (Alaska)
Ariz. (Arizona)
Ark. (Arkansas)
Calif. (California)
C.Z. (Canal Zone)
Colo. (Colorado)
Conn. (Connecticut)
D.C. (District of Columbia)
Del. (Delaware)
Fla. (Florida)
Ga. (Georgia)
Gu. (Guam)
Haw. (Hawaii)
Ida. (Idaho)
Ill. (Illinois)

Ind. (Indiana)
Ia. (Iowa)
Kans. (Kansas)
Ky. (Kentucky)
La. (Louisiana)
Md. (Maryland)
Mass. (Massachusetts)
Mich. (Michigan)
Minn. (Minnesota)
Miss. (Mississippi)
Mo. (Missouri)
Mont. (Montana)
Nebr. (Nebraska)
Nev. (Nevada)
N.H. (New Hampshire)
N. J. (New Jersey)

---

*Abbreviations are used in chapters 2 and 3 and are taken from, or modeled after, those found in Rules 9.12, 9.13 and 9.38 of the U.S. Government Printing Office *Style Manual,* rev. ed. (Washington, D.C.: U.S. G.P.O., 1973), pp. 150-51, 154.

N. Mex. (New Mexico)
N.Y. (New York)
N.C. (North Carolina)
N. Dak. (North Dakota)
Oh. (Ohio)
Okla. (Oklahoma)
Oreg. (Oregon)
Pa. (Pennsylvania)
P.R. (Puerto Rico)
R.I. (Rhode Island)
S.C. (South Carolina)

S. Dak. (South Dakota)
Tenn. (Tennessee)
Tex. (Texas)
Ut. (Utah)
Vt. (Vermont)
Va. (Virginia)
V.I. (Virgin Islands)
Wash. (Washington)
W. Va. (West Virginia)
Wis. (Wisconsin)
Wyo. (Wyoming)

1 CURRENT PRIMARY LEGAL MATERIALS

Comments

In this chapter we provide a list of current primary resources available for researching laws of the federal government, all the states, and U.S. territories. Primary legal authority consists of written constitutions, enactments of legislatures (i.e., session laws and statutes) and written opinions of courts.[1] With an exception for the U.S. territories—which are discussed in depth below—we have listed only current sources: developing case law and statutory material presently compiled, printed, or published either by governmental bodies or private publishers. Individuals or organizations interested in obtaining a retrospective, as well as a more detailed and exhaustive, listing of primary and selected secondary resource materials for the fifty states may also want to consult Leah F. Chanin's informative two-part bibliography.[2] Other publications also provide current information. Cohen and Berring's *How to Find the Law* includes "Primary Legal Sources for the States."[3] Twice a year—in April and October—James Tsao compiles a checklist of current federal, state, and Canadian publications.[4] This checklist also includes some secondary legal materials, but it does not appear in the annually published cumulation. Additionally, descriptions and explanations of federal and state primary and secondary legal authority, and the distinction between statutory authority and case law, may be found in one or more of the legal research texts annotated in chapter two (see note 6 below).

Although our emphasis is upon current primary law materials, we have included "Finding Aids," or secondary authority, to assist researchers in the location of primary resources. With federal materials, we have named current federal digests[5] for the location of case law, and we have noted leading, selected resources for locating federal legislation and legislative histories of statutes.[6] For the states[7] and U.S. territories, only digests are listed as "Finding Aids." For the most part, digests are useful tools for locating case authority through several means, such as by case name, descriptive word, topic, or words and phrases.[8]

We have only listed digests that exist for the United States and each particular state or territory. General and regional digests[9] have not been included since our emphasis is upon specific resources available for each particular jurisdiction. Furthermore, the sheer bulk of these larger digests inhibits efficient research for case authority from each governmental entity. However, regional and general digests should be kept in mind because they provide access to cases of those states—such as Delaware and Utah—that do not have digests.[10]

We have divided legal materials for the United States and each of the states and outlying territories into three general categories: "Cases," "Statutes," and "Finding Aids." Where there is no available publication within one of these three categories, we indicate "No Formal Compilation" or insert a similar clarifying remark. "Cases" includes published reports for the highest court of each jurisdiction as well as intermediate courts or courts of appeal. "Statutes" includes session laws (current session laws are also available in microfiche from William S. Hein & Co., which is named in the selected list of publishers found in appendix B), session law services, statutory codes or compilations, administrative codes, rules, or regulations, and administrative registers. Administrative registers update the rules and regulations, providing currency and notice of changes in administrative codes.[11] Administrative codes have the same force as law and are considered primary authority because they are enacted by federal and state agencies pursuant to enabling legislation.[12] We have also included U.S. Presidential Proclamations and Executive Orders within the category of federal administrative materials because of the importance and legal impact of Presidential documents.[13]

Our list of federal, state, and territorial administrative codes and registers is gathered primarily from the most current compilation published annually by the National Association of Secretaries of State.[14] Elyse H. Fox has also drawn up a helpful list of state administrative codes and registers.[15] Furthermore, we have consulted the work of Tseng and Pedersen, who have drafted an excellent summary listing available state and territorial administrative codes and registers; and they have provided information on such matters as price, whether the material is available in microform, and where to write or call for information.[16]

Included within parentheses after each named resource under "Cases," "Statutes," and "Finding Aids" are the recommended, or most appropriate, *bluebook* abbreviations for use in citing legal authority taken from *A Uniform System of Citation*,[17] commonly called the *"Bluebook."* After the abbreviations follow the name of the publisher, printer, or compiler. Where a state agency or body is the only (or major) publisher, printer, or distributor of a work, the notation "State of . . ." has been made. In those cases where the federal government and outlying territories are the publishers, the letters U.S.G.P.O. (United States Government Printing Office) and the name of the territorial agency have been used, respectively. Individuals are cautioned to consult the *Bluebook*[18] for the complete citation forms to be used when formally referring to primary legal authority. Abbreviations are not given for digests and some federal resources listed under "Finding Aids" since these are classified as books of index. Books of index include legal resources such as digests, *Shepard's Citations*,[19] and other titles that aid in locating primary legal sources. Books of index are not cited; the primary legal material located by the book is cited.

Readers may notice that we have not listed every possible resource for locating case authority. For example, the *Supreme Court Bulletin*, published by Commerce Clearing House, was not named in section B under "United States Supreme Court" as a case reporter. We have also not listed those West Publishing Company state reporters that are merely recompilations of the regional reporting system. Several reasons exist for this. First, we have sought to include only those leading case materials discussed in the *Bluebook*. More importantly, it has been our desire to keep the listing simple and straightforward so as to eliminate possible confusion and misinterpretation by lay readers.

As indicated above, we have referred to retrospective as well as current legal authority for the U.S. territories. The nature of territorial possessions, their location outside of the geographical United States, and the rather difficult task of locating past and current primary legal authority led us to the conclusion that our readers—as well as interested librarians—would be best served and less confused by a fairly simple complete listing of available materials, including volumes and dates where appropriate. With this exception, the content is the same as that in the preceding annotations.

As far as we can tell, our listing of primary resources for United States territories is the most current and comprehensive compilation available at this time. Jacobstein and Mersky have a useful discussion of "Legal Research in Territories of the United States" where both primary and other legal research materials are briefly discussed.[20] We have decided not to include the Panama Canal Zone as a territory since this area is no longer a permanent United States possession; it is under the jurisdiction of the United States Panama Canal Commission pursuant to the Panama Canal Treaty of 1977, which expires on 31 December 1999.[21] We also have not included unincorporated territories (e.g., Johnston Atoll, Midway Islands, and Wake Island) since they are subject to federal jurisdiction and are administered by the U.S. Armed Services.[22] Other lesser known territorial possessions are not discussed because of the paucity of available primary legal materials.

The most troublesome and confusing U.S. territory or possession in terms of understanding what legal resources apply and are available is the Trust Territory of the Pacific Islands. Since 1978 the Trust Territory has been undergoing major changes. The Northern Mariana Islands are in the process of becoming a commonwealth in union with the United States, and the Marshall Islands, the Federated States of Micronesia, and the Republic of Palau have been negotiating for the status of free association with the federal government.[23] One should keep in mind that primary legal authority for the Trust Territory is still controlling where not specifically changed by one of the four governmental entities because these governments are still legally subject to the jurisdiction of the Trust Territory system until its termination.[24]

There are relatively few specific digests for the outlying territories, but we want to emphasize that published cases reaching the federal district and circuit courts may be found in *West's Federal Practice Digest 3d*. Likewise, cases reaching the United States Supreme Court may be located in one of the two published Supreme Court digests.[25]

Notes

[1] J. Myron Jacobstein and Roy M. Mersky, *Fundamentals of Legal Research*, 3d ed. (Mineola, N.Y.: Foundation Press, 1985), 2-3.

[2] Leah F. Chanin, "Developing a State Law Collection: Part 1," *Legal Reference Services Quarterly* 2 (Fall 1982): 47; and "Developing a State Law Collection: Part 2," *Legal Reference Services Quarterly* 2 (Winter 1982): 3.

[3] Morris L. Cohen and Robert C. Berring, *How to Find the Law*, 8th ed. (St. Paul: West, 1983), appendix B, 715.

4 / Current Primary Legal Materials

[4] James Tsao, "Checklist of Current State, Federal and Canadian Publications," Section 3, *Current Publications in Legal and Related Fields* (Littleton, Colo.: Fred B. Rothman, 1953-).

[5] Cohen and Berring, *How to Find*, 115-17.

[6] These particular materials may be explored in depth by referring to legal research texts noted herein, or by consulting additional materials annotated in chapter 2 under the heading "Guides to Legal Research."

[7] Cohen and Berring, *How to Find*, 115, 117-18.

[8] Miles O. Price, Harry Bitner, and Shirley Raissi Bysiewicz, *Effective Legal Research*, 4th ed. (Boston: Little, Brown, 1979), 205-12.

[9] Cohen and Berring, *How to Find*, 106, 115, 117.

[10] Ibid., 117.

[11] Ibid., 336-39, 371-72.

[12] Ibid., 333, 370-71.

[13] Jacobstein and Mersky, *Fundamentals*, 240.

[14] *Administrative Codes and Registers 1983 State/Federal Survey* (Austin, Tex.: Administrative Codes and Registers Committee, 1983).

[15] Elyse H. Fox, "Status of State Administrative Codes and Registers," *Legal Reference Services Quarterly* 2 (Winter 1982): 77.

[16] Henry P. Tseng and Donald B. Pedersen, "Acquisition of State Administrative Rules and Regulations—Update 1983," *Administrative Law Review* 35 (Summer 1983): 349.

[17] *A Uniform System of Citation*, 13th ed. (Cambridge, Mass.: Harvard Law Review Association, 1981), 133-76.

[18] Ibid.

[19] Cohen and Berring, *How to Find*, 249.

[20] Jacobstein and Mersky, *Fundamentals*, appendix C, 683.

[21] Ibid., 604. See also, Tseng and Pedersen, "Acquisition . . . Update 1983," 387.

[22] *Statesman's Yearbook*, 119th ed. (New York: St. Martin's Press, 1982-83), 1,571.

[23] Ibid., 1570.

[24] Ibid.

[25] Price, Bitner, and Bysiewicz, *Effective*, 212-16.

Federal

Cases
  United States Supreme Court
    United States Law Week (U.S.L.W.; Bureau of National Affairs)
    United States Reports (U.S.; U.S.G.P.O.)
    Supreme Court Reporter (S.Ct.; West)
  United States Courts of Appeals
    Federal Reporter (F.2d; West)
  United States District Courts
    Federal Supplement (F.Supp.; West)

Statutes
  Statutory Compilation
    United States Code (U.S.C.; U.S.G.P.O.)
    United States Code Annotated (U.S.C.A. (West); West)
    United States Code Service (U.S.C.S. (Law. Co-Op.); Lawyers Co-Op.)
  Session Laws
    United States Code Service, Advance (U.S.C.S. Adv. (Law. Co-Op.); Lawyers Co-Op.)
    United States Statutes at Large (Stat.; U.S.G.P.O.)
  Administrative
    Code
      Code of Federal Regulations (C.F.R.; U.S.G.P.O.)
    Register
      Federal Register (Fed. Reg.; U.S.G.P.O.)
    Presidential Proclamations and Executive Orders
      Code of Federal Regulations (C.F.R.; U.S.G.P.O.)
      Federal Register (Fed. Reg.; U.S.G.P.O.)
      Weekly Compilation of Presidential Documents (Weekly Comp. Pres. Doc.; U.S.G.P.O.)

Finding Aids
  Cases
    United States Supreme Court Digest (West)
    United States Supreme Court Reports Digest, Lawyer's Edition (Lawyers Co-Op.)
    West's Federal Practice Digest 3d (West)
  Legislation and Legislative History
    Congressional Index (Commerce Clearing House)
    CIS Annual (Congressional Information Service)
    Congressional Record (Cong. Rec.; U.S.G.P.O.)
    Congressional Record. Index. History of Bills and Resolutions (Cong. Rec.; U.S.G.P.O.)
    Cumulative Index of Congressional Committee Hearings (U.S.G.P.O.)
    Digest of Public General Bills and Resolutions (U.S.G.P.O.)
    Monthly Catalog of Government Publications (U.S.G.P.O.)
    Shepard's Acts and Cases by Popular Name (Shepard's/McGraw-Hill)
    United States Code Congressional and Administrative News (U.S. Code Cong. & Ad. News; West)

States and District of Columbia

1. ALABAMA
    Cases
       Supreme Court, Court of Civil and Criminal Appeals
          Southern Reporter (S.2d; West)
    Statutes
       Statutory Compilation
          Code of Alabama (Ala. Code; Michie)
       Sessions Laws
          Acts of Alabama (Ala. Acts; Skinner)
       Administrative
          Code
             Alabama Administrative Code (Ala. Admin. Code; State of Alabama)
             Formal Compilation in Preparation
          Register
             Alabama Administrative Monthly (Ala. Admin. Reg.; State of Alabama)
    Finding Aid:
       West's Alabama Digest (West)

2. ALASKA
    Cases
       Supreme Court, Court of Appeals
       Pacific Reporter (P.2d; West)
    Statutes
       Statutory Compilation
          Alaska Statutes (Alaska Stat.; Michie)
       Session Laws
          Alaska Session Laws (Alaska Sess. Laws; State of Alaska)
          Alaska Statutes Advanced Legislative Service (Alaska Adv. Legis. Serv.; Michie)
       Administrative
          Code
             Alaska Administrative Code (Alaska Admin. Code; Book Publishing)
          Register
             Alaska Register (Alaska Admin. Reg.; Book Publishing)
    Finding Aid:
       Alaska Digest (West)

3. ARIZONA
    Cases
       Supreme Court, Court of Appeals
          Arizona Reports (Ariz.; West)
          Pacific Reporter (P.2d; West)

Statutes
　Statutory Compilation
　　Arizona Revised Statutes Annotated (Ariz. Rev. Stat. Ann.; West)
　Session Laws
　　Session Laws, State of Arizona (Ariz. Sess. Laws.; State of Arizona)
　　Arizona Legislative Service (Ariz. Legis. Serv.; West)
　Administrative
　　Code
　　　Arizona Official Compilation of Administrative Rules and Regulations (Ariz. Admin. Comp. R.; State of Arizona)
　　Register
　　　Arizona Administrative Digest (Ariz. Admin. Dig.; State of Arizona)
Finding Aid:
　West's Arizona Digest (West)

4. ARKANSAS
　Cases*
　　Supreme Court
　　　Arkansas Reports (Ark.; Democrat Printing and Lithographing)
　　　Southwestern Reporter (S.W.2d; West)
　　Court of Appeals
　　　Arkansas Appellate Reports (Ark. App.; Democrat Printing and Lithographing)
　　　Southwestern Reporter (S.W.2d; West)
　Statutes
　　Statutory Compilation
　　　Arkansas Statutes Annotated (Ark. Stat. Ann.; Michie)
　　Session Laws
　　　General Acts of Arkansas (Ark. Acts.; General Publishing)
　　Administrative
　　　Code
　　　　No Formal Compilation
　　　Register
　　　　Arkansas Register (Ark. Admin. Reg.; State of Arkansas)
　Finding Aid:
　　West's Arkansas Digest (West)

5. CALIFORNIA
　Cases
　　Supreme Court
　　　California Reports (Cal.3d; Bancroft-Whitney)
　　　Pacific Reporter (P.2d; West)
　　　California Reporter (Cal. Rptr.; West)

---

*Arkansas Supreme and Appellate court cases are currently reported in the same volume of each regularly printed official state publication, but the same cases are arranged under the appropriate courts and cited accordingly.

Court of Appeals
  California Appellate Reports (Cal. App. 3d; Bancroft-Whitney)
  Pacific Reporter (P.2d; West)
  California Reporter (Cal. Rptr.; West)
Appellate Departments of the Superior Court
  California Appellate Reports Supplement (Cal. App. 3d; Bancroft-Whitney)
  California Reporter (Cal. Rptr.; West)
Statutes
  Statutory Compilation
    West's Annotated California Code (Cal. Code; West)
    Deering's Annotated California Code (Cal. Code; Bancroft-Whitney)
  Session Laws
    Statutes of California (Cal. Stat.; State of California)
    California Legislative Service (Cal. Legis. Serv.; West)
    California Advance Legislative Service (Cal. Adv. Legis. Serv.; Bancroft-Whitney)
Administrative
  Code
    California Administrative Code (Cal. Admin. Code; State of California)
  Register
    California Administrative Register (Cal. Admin. Reg.; State of California)
Finding Aids:
  West's California Digest 2d (West)
  California Digest of Official Reports, 3d Series (Bancroft-Whitney)

6. COLORADO
   Cases
     Supreme Court, Court of Appeals
       Pacific Reporter (P.2d; West)
   Statutes
     Statutory Compilation
       Colorado Revised Statutes (Colo. Rev. Stat.; Bradford)
     Session Laws
       Session Laws of Colorado (Colo. Sess. Laws; Bradford)
   Administrative
     Code
       Code of Colorado Regulations (Colo. Admin. Code; Public Record Corp.)
     Register
       Colorado Register (Colo. Admin. Reg.; Public Record Corp.)
   Finding Aid:
     West's Colorado Digest (West)

7. CONNECTICUT
    Cases
        Supreme Court
            Connecticut Reports (Conn.; State of Connecticut)
            Atlantic Reporter (A.2d; West)
        Superior Court
            Connecticut Supplement (Conn. Supp.; State of Connecticut)
            Atlantic Reporter (A.2d; West)
        Circuit Court
            Atlantic Reporter (A.2d; West)
    Statutes
        Statutory Compilation
            General Statutes of Connecticut (Conn. Gen. Stat.; State of
                Connecticut)
            Connecticut General Statutes Annotated (Conn. Gen. Stat. Ann.; West)
        Session Laws
            Connecticut Public and Special Acts (Conn. Acts; State of Connecticut)
            Connecticut Legislative Service (Conn. Legis. Serv.; West)
        Administrative
            Code
                Regulations of Connecticut State Agencies (Conn. Agencies Regs.;
                    State of Connecticut)
            Register
                Connecticut Law Journal (Conn. L.J.; State of Connecticut)
        Finding Aid:
            West's Connecticut Digest (West)

8. DELAWARE
    Cases
        Supreme Court, Court of Chancery, Superior Court, Family Court
            Atlantic Reporter (A.2d; West)
    Statutes
        Statutory Compilation
            Delaware Code Annotated (Del. Code Ann.; Michie)
        Session Laws
            Laws of Delaware (Del. Laws; State of Delaware)
        Administrative
            Code
                Register of Regulations (Del. Reg. of Regs.; State of Delaware)
            Register
                Delaware Documentation (Del. Doc.; State of Delaware)
        Finding Aids:
            No Formal Compilation

9. DISTRICT OF COLUMBIA
    Cases
        Court of Appeals
            Atlantic Reporter (A.2d; West)

10 / Current Primary Legal Materials

        United States Court of Appeals for the District of Columbia Circuit
           Federal Reporter (F.2d; West)
           United States Court of Appeals Reports (U.S. App. D.C.; West)
    Statutes
        Statutory Compilation
           District of Columbia Code Annotated (D.C. Code Ann.; Michie)
        Session Laws
           United States Statutes At Large (Stat.; U.S.G.P.O.)
           District of Columbia Register (D.C. Reg.; District of Columbia)
        Municipal Regulations
           Code
               District of Columbia Municipal Regulations (D.C. Mun. Regs.; District of Columbia)
           Register
               District of Columbia Register (D.C. Admin. Reg.; District of Columbia)
    Finding Aid:
        West's District of Columbia Digest (West)

10. FLORIDA
    Cases
        Supreme Court, District Court of Appeal
           Southern Reporter (S.2d; West)
        Lower Courts of Record and State Commissions
           Florida Supplement (Fla. Supp. 2d; South Publishing)
    Statutes
        Statutory Compilation
           Florida Statutes (Fla. Stat.; State of Florida)
           Florida Statutes Annotated (Fla. Stat. Ann.; Harrison)
           Florida Statutes Annotated (Fla. Stat. Ann.; West)
        Session Laws
           Laws of Florida (Fla. Laws; State of Florida)
           Florida Session Law Service (Fla. Sess. Law Serv.; West)
        Administrative
           Code
               Florida Administrative Code Annotated (Fla. Admin. Code Ann.; Harrison)
           Register
               Florida Administrative Weekly (Fla. Admin. Weekly; State of Florida)
    Finding Aid:
        West's Florida Digest (West)

11. GEORGIA
    Cases
        Supreme Court
           Georgia Reports (Ga.; Darby)
           Southeastern Reporter (S.E.2d; West)

Court of Appeals
  Georgia Appeals Reports (Ga. App.; Harrison)
  Southeastern Reporter (S.E.2d; West)
Statutes
  Statutory Compilation
    Code of Georgia Annotated (Ga. Code Ann.; Harrison)
    Official Code of Georgia Annotated (Ga. Official Code Ann.; Michie/Bobbs-Merrill)
  Session Laws
    Georgia Laws (Ga. Laws; State of Georgia)
    Georgia Annotated Code Advance Codification (Ga. Ann. Code Adv. Codif.; Harrison)
  Administrative
    Code
      Official Compilation Rules and Regulations of the State of Georgia (Ga. Admin. Comp.; State of Georgia)
    Register
      Georgia Official and Statistical Register (Ga. Admin. Reg.; State of Georgia)
Finding Aid:
  West's Georgia Digest (West)

12. **HAWAII**
  Cases
    Supreme Court
      Hawaii Reports (Hawaii; Fisher Printing)
      Pacific Reporter (P.2d; West)
    Intermediate Court of Appeals
      Hawaii Intermediate Court of Appeals Reports (Hawaii Ct. App.; Fisher Printing)
      Pacific Reporter (P.2d; West)
  Statutes
    Statutory Compilation
      Hawaii Revised Statutes (Hawaii Rev. Stat.; State of Hawaii)
    Session Laws
      Session Laws of Hawaii (Hawaii Sess. Laws; State of Hawaii)
    Administrative
      Code
        No Formal Compilation
      Register
        No Formal Compilation
  Finding Aid:
    West's Hawaii Digest (West)

13. **IDAHO**
  Cases
    Supreme Court, Court of Appeals
      Idaho Reports (Idaho; West)
      Pacific Reporter (P.2d; West)

Statutes
   Statutory Compilation
      Idaho Code Annotated (Idaho Code; Michie)
   Session Laws
      Session Laws, Idaho (Idaho Sess. Laws; Caxton Printers)
   Administrative
      Code
         No Formal Compilation
      Register
         No Formal Compilation
Finding Aid:
   West's Idaho Digest Annotated (West)

14. ILLINOIS
   Cases
      Supreme Court
         Illinois Reports (Ill.2d; Pantagraph Printing)
         Northeastern Reporter (N.E.2d; West)
      Appellate Court
         Illinois Appellate Court Reports (Ill. App. 3d; Pantagraph Printing)
         Northeastern Reporter (N.E.2d; West)
      Court of Claims
         Illinois Court of Claims Reports (Ill. Ct. Cl.; State of Illinois)
   Statutes
      Statutory Compilation
         Illinois Revised Statutes (Ill. Rev. Stat.; West)
         Smith-Hurd Illinois Annotated Statutes (Ill. Ann. Stat.; West)
      Session Laws
         Laws of Illinois (Ill. Laws; State of Illinois)
         Illinois Legislative Service (Ill. Legis. Serv.; West)
      Administrative
         Code
            Illinois Administrative Code (Ill. Admin. Code; State of Illinois)
            Formal Compilation in Preparation
         Register
            Illinois Register (Ill. Admin. Reg.; State of Illinois)
   Finding Aids:
      West's Illinois Digest 2d (West)
      Callaghan's Illinois Digest 3d (Callaghan)

15. INDIANA
   Cases
      Supreme Court
         Indiana Reports (Ind.; Western Newspaper)
         Northeastern Reporter (N.E.2d; West)
      Court of Appeals
         Indiana Court of Appeals Reports (Ind. App.; Western Newspaper)
         Northeastern Reporter (N.E.2d; West)

Statutes
   Statutory Compilation
      Indiana Code (Ind. Code; State of Indiana)
      Burns Indiana Statutes Annotated Code (Ind. Code Ann.; Michie/
          Bobbs-Merrill)
      West's Annotated Indiana Code (Ind. Code Ann.; West)
   Session Laws
      Acts, Indiana (Ind. Acts; Central Publishing)
      Burns Indiana Statutes Annotated Advanced Legislative Service
          (Ind. Adv. Legis. Serv.; Michie/Bobbs-Merrill)
      Indiana Legislative Service (Ind. Legis. Serv.; West)
   Administrative
     Code
        Indiana Administrative Code (Ind. Admin. Code; State of Indiana)
     Register
        Indiana Register (Ind. Admin. Reg.; State of Indiana)
Finding Aid:
   West's Indiana Digest (West)

16. IOWA
   Cases
     Supreme Court, Court of Appeals
       Northwestern Reporter (N.W.2d; West)
   Statutes
     Statutory Compilation
       Code of Iowa (Iowa Code; State of Iowa)
       Iowa Code Annotated (Iowa Code Ann.; West)
     Session Laws
       Acts and Joint Resolutions of the State of Iowa (Iowa Acts; State of
           Iowa)
       Iowa Legislative Service (Iowa Legis. Serv.; West)
     Administrative
       Code
         Iowa Administrative Code (Iowa Admin. Code; State of Iowa)
       Register
         Iowa Administrative Bulletin (Iowa Admin. Bull.; State of Iowa)
   Finding Aid:
     West's Iowa Digest (West)

17. KANSAS
   Cases
     Supreme Court
       Kansas Reports (Kan.; State of Kansas)
       Pacific Reporter (P.2d; West)
     Court of Appeals
       Kansas Court of Appeals Reports (Kan. App. 2d; State of Kansas)
       Pacific Reporter (P.2d; West)

14 / Current Primary Legal Materials

Statutes
Statutory Compilation
Kansas Statutes Annotated (Kan. Stat. Ann.; State of Kansas)
Vernon's Kansas Statutes Annotated (Kan. Ann. (Vernon); West)
Session Laws
Session Laws of Kansas (Kan. Sess. Laws; State of Kansas)
Administrative
Code
Kansas Administrative Regulations (Kan. Admin. Regs.; State of Kansas)
Register
Kansas Register (Kan. Admin. Reg.; State of Kansas)
Finding Aid:
West's Kansas Digest (West)

18. KENTUCKY
Cases
Supreme Court, Court of Appeals
Southwestern Reporter (S.W.2d; West)
Statutes
Statutory Compilation
Baldwin's Kentucky Revised Statutes Annotated (Ky. Rev. Stat. Ann. (Baldwin); Banks-Baldwin)
Kentucky Revised Statutes Annotated (Ky. Rev. Stat. Ann. (Bobbs-Merrill); Bobbs-Merrill)
Session Laws
Kentucky Acts (Ky. Acts; State of Kentucky)
Kentucky Revised Statutes and Rules Service (Ky. Rev. Stat. & R. Serv.; Banks-Baldwin)
Administrative
Code
Kentucky Administrative Regulations Service (Ky. Admin. Reg.; State of Kentucky)
Register
Administrative Register of Kentucky (Ky. Admin. Reg.; State of Kentucky)
Finding Aid:
West's Kentucky Digest (West)

19. LOUISIANA
Cases
Supreme Court, Court of Appeals
Southern Reporter (So.2d; West)
Statutes
Statutory Compilation
West's Louisiana Revised Statutes Annotated (La. Rev. Stat. Ann.; West)
West's Louisiana Civil Code Annotated (La. Civ. Code Ann.; West)

Current Primary Legal Materials / 15

      West's Louisiana Code of Civil Procedure (La. Code Civ. Proc.; West)
      West's Louisiana Code of Criminal Procedure (La. Code Crim. Proc.; West)
    Session Laws
      State of Louisiana; Acts of Legislature (La. Acts; State of Louisiana)
      Louisiana Session Law Service (La. Sess. Law Serv.; West)
    Administrative
      Code
        Louisiana Administrative Code (La. Admin. Code; State of Louisiana)
        Formal Compilation in Preparation
      Register
        Louisiana Register (La. Admin. Reg.; State of Louisiana)
  Finding Aid:
    West's Louisiana Digest (West)

20. MAINE
    Cases
      Supreme Judicial Court
        Atlantic Reporter (A2d; West)
    Statutes
      Statutory Compilation
        Maine Revised Statutes Annotated (Me. Rev. Stat. Ann.; West)
      Session Laws
        Laws of the State of Maine (Me. Laws; State of Maine)
        Acts, Resolves and Constitutional Resolutions of the State of Maine (Me. Acts; State of Maine)
        Maine Legislative Service (Me. Legis. Serv.; West)
    Administrative
      Code
        No Formal Compilation
      Register
        No Formal Compilation
    Finding Aid:
      Maine Key Number Digest (West)

21. MARYLAND
    Cases
      Court of Appeals
        Maryland Reports (Md.; Michie)
        Atlantic Reporter (A.2d; West)
      Court of Special Appeals
        Maryland Appellate Reports (Md. App.; Michie)
        Atlantic Reporter (A.2d; West)
    Statutes
      Statutory Compilation
        Annotated Code of Maryland (Md. Code Ann.; Michie)
      Session Laws
        Laws of Maryland (Md. Laws; State of Maryland)

16 / Current Primary Legal Materials

        Administrative
           Code
              Code of Maryland Regulations (Md. Admin. Code; State of Maryland)
           Register
              Maryland Register (Md. Admin. Reg.; State of Maryland)
        Finding Aid:
           West's Maryland Digest (West)

22.   MASSACHUSETTS
        Cases
           Supreme Judicial Court
              Massachusetts Report (Mass.; Bateman and Slade)
              Northeastern Reporter (N.E.2d; West)
           Appeals Court
              Massachusetts Appeals Court Reports (Mass. App. Ct.; Bateman and Slade)
              Northeastern Reporter (N.E.2d; West)
           District Court
              Appellate Decisions (Mass. App. Dec.; Wilson-Hill)
        Statutes
           Statutory Compilation
              Massachusetts General Laws Annotated (Mass. Gen. Laws Ann.; West)
              Annotated Laws of Massachusetts (Mass. Ann. Laws; Lawyers Co-Op.)
           Session Laws
              Acts and Resolves of Massachusetts (Mass. Acts; State of Massachusetts)
              Massachusetts Advance Legislative Service (Mass. Adv. Legis. Serv.; Lawyers Co-Op.)
              Massachusetts Legislative Service (Mass. Legis. Serv.; West)
           Administrative
              Code
                  Code of Massachusetts Regulations (Mass. Admin. Code; State of Massachusetts)
              Register
                  Massachusetts Register (Mass. Admin. Reg.; State of Massachusetts)
        Finding Aid:
           West's Massachusetts Digest Annotated (West)

23.   MICHIGAN
        Cases
           Supreme Court
              Michigan Reports (Mich.; Lawyers Co-Op.)
              Northwestern Reporter (N.W.2d; West)
           Court of Appeals
              Michigan Appeals Reports (Mich. App.; Lawyers Co-Op.)
              Northwestern Reporter (N.W.2d; West)

Statutes
　Statutory Compilation
　　Michigan Compiled Laws (Mich. Comp. Laws; State of Michigan)
　　Michigan Compiled Laws Annotated (Mich. Comp. Laws Ann.; West)
　　Michigan Statutes Annotated (Mich. Stat. Ann.; Callaghan)
　Session Laws
　　Public and Local Acts of the Legislature of the State of Michigan (Mich. Pub. Acts; State of Michigan)
　　Michigan Legislative Service (Mich. Legis. Serv.; West)
　　Michigan Statutes Annotated, Current Materials–Statutes (Mich. Stat. Ann., Current; Callaghan)
　Administrative
　　Code
　　　Michigan Administrative Code (Mich. Admin. Code R.; State of Michigan)
　　Register
　　　Michigan Register (Mich. Admin. Reg.; State of Michigan)
　Finding Aid:
　　West's Michigan Digest (West)

24. MINNESOTA
　Cases
　　Supreme Court
　　　Northwestern Reporter (N.W.2d; West)
　Statutes
　　Statutory Compilation
　　　Minnesota Statutes (Minn. Stat.; State of Minnesota)
　　　Minnesota Statutes Annotated (Minn. Stat. Ann.; West)
　　Session Laws
　　　Laws of Minnesota (Minn. Laws; State of Minnesota)
　　　Minnesota Session Law Service (Minn. Sess. Law Serv.; West)
　　Administrative
　　　Code
　　　　Minnesota Rules (Minn. Admin. R.; State of Minnesota)
　　　Register
　　　　Minnesota State Register (Minn. Admin. Reg.; State of Minnesota)
　Finding Aid:
　　West's Minnesota Digest (West)

25. MISSISSIPPI
　Cases
　　Supreme Court
　　　Southern Reporter (S.2d; West)
　Statutes
　　Statutory Compilation
　　　Mississippi Code Annotated (Miss. Code Ann.; Harrison, Lawyers Co-Op.)

Session Laws
General Laws of Mississippi (Miss. Laws; State of Mississippi)
Administrative
Code
No Formal Compilation
Register
Mississippi Register (Miss. Admin. Reg.; State of Mississippi)
Finding Aid:
West's Mississippi Digest (West)

26. MISSOURI
Cases
Supreme Court, Court of Appeals
Southwestern Reporter (S.W.2d; West)
Statutes
Statutory Compilation
Missouri Revised Statutes (Mo. Rev. Stat.; State of Missouri)
Vernon's Annotated Missouri Statutes (Mo. Ann. Stat.; West)
Session Laws
Laws of Missouri (Mo. Laws; State of Missouri)
Missouri Legislative Service (Mo. Legis. Serv.; West)
Administrative
Code
Missouri Code of State Regulations (Mo. Admin. Code; State of Missouri)
Register
Missouri Register (Mo. Admin. Reg.; State of Missouri)
Finding Aid:
West's Missouri Digest 2d (West)

27. MONTANA
Cases
Supreme Court
Montana Reports (Mont.; State Publishing Company)
Pacific Reporter (P.2d; West)
Statutes
Statutory Compilation
Montana Code Annotated (Mont. Code Ann.; State of Montana)
Session Laws
Laws of Montana (Mont. Laws; State of Montana)
Administrative
Code
Administrative Rules of Montana (Mont. Admin. R.; State of Montana)
Register
Montana Administrative Register (Mont. Admin. Reg.; State of Montana)
Finding Aid:
West's Montana Digest Annotated (West)

28. NEBRASKA
    Cases
      Supreme Court
        Nebraska Reports (Neb.; Gant)
        Northwestern Reporter (N.W.2d; West)
    Statutes
      Statutory Compilation
        Revised Statutes of Nebraska (Neb. Rev. Stat.; State of Nebraska)
      Session Laws
        Laws of Nebraska (Neb. Laws; State of Nebraska)
      Administrative
        Code
          Nebraska Administrative Rules and Regulations (Neb. Admin. R.; State of Nebraska)
        Register
          No Formal Compilation
    Finding Aid:
      West's Nebraska Digest (West)

29. NEVADA
    Cases
      Supreme Court
        Nevada Reports (Nev.; State of Nevada)
        Pacific Reporter (P.2d; West)
    Statutes
      Statutory Compilation
        Nevada Revised Statutes (Nev. Rev. Stat.; State of Nevada)
        Nevada Revised Statutes Annotated (Nev. Rev. Stat. Ann.; Michie—Scheduled for February, 1986)
      Session Laws
        Statutes of Nevada (Nev. Stat.; State of Nevada)
      Administrative
        Code
          Nevada Administrative Code (Nev. Admin Code; State of Nevada)
        Register
          No Formal Compilation
    Finding Aid:
      Nevada Digest (State of Nevada)

30. NEW HAMPSHIRE
    Cases
      Supreme Court
        New Hampshire Reports (N.H.; Equity)
        Atlantic Reporter (A.2d; West)
    Statutes
      Statutory Compilation
        New Hampshire Revised Statutes Annotated (N.H. Rev. Stat. Ann.; Equity)
      Session Laws
        Laws of the State of New Hampshire (N.H. Laws; Equity)

Administrative
Code
New Hampshire Code of Administrative Rules (N.H. Admin. Code; State of New Hampshire)
Formal Compilation in Preparation
Register
New Hampshire Rulemaking Register (N.H. Admin. Reg.; State of New Hampshire)
Finding Aid:
West's New Hampshire Digest (West)

31. NEW JERSEY
Cases
Supreme Court
New Jersey Reports (N.J.; West)
Atlantic Reporter (A.2d; West)
Superior Court
New Jersey Superior Court Reports (N.J. Super.; West)
Atlantic Reporter (A.2d; West)
Statutes
Statutory Compilation
New Jersey Revised Statutes (N.J. Rev. Stat.; Gann Law Books)
New Jersey Statutes Annotated (N.J. Stat. Ann.; West)
Session Laws
Laws of New Jersey (N.J. Laws; State of New Jersey)
New Jersey Session Law Service (N.J. Sess. Law; West)
Administrative
Code
New Jersey Administrative Code (N.J. Admin. Code; State of New Jersey)
Register
New Jersey Register (N.J. Admin. Reg.; State of New Jersey)
Finding Aid:
West's New Jersey Digest

32. NEW MEXICO
Cases
Supreme Court, Court of Appeal
New Mexico Reports (N.M.; West)
Pacific Reporter (P2d; West)
Statutes
Statutory Compilation
New Mexico Statutes Annotated (N.M. Stat. Ann.; Michie)
Session Laws
Laws of New Mexico (N.M. Laws; Bishop Printing and Litho.)
Administrative
Code
No Formal Compilation
Register
No Formal Compilation
Finding Aid:
West's New Mexico Digest (West)

Current Primary Legal Materials / 21

33. NEW YORK
    Cases
        Court of Appeals
            New York Reports (N.Y.2d; Lenz and Riecker)
            Northeastern Reporter (N.E.2d; West)
            New York Supplement (N.Y.S.2d; West)
        Supreme Court, Appellate Division
            Appellate Division Reports (A.D.2d; Lenz and Riecker)
            New York Supplement (N.Y.S.2d; West)
        Other Lower Courts
            New York Miscellaneous Report (Misc.2d; Lenz and Riecker)
            New York Supplement (N.Y.S.2d; West)
    Statutes
        Statutory Compilation
            Consolidated Laws Service (N.Y. Law (Consol.); Lawyers Co-Op.)
            McKinney's Consolidated Laws (N.Y. Law (McKinney); West)
        Session Laws
            Advance Legislative Service for the Consolidated Laws Service (N.Y. Adv. Legis. Serv. (Consol.); Lawyers Co-Op.)
            Consolidated Laws Service. Session Laws (N.Y. Sess. Laws (Consol.); Lawyer's Co-Op.)
            Laws of New York (N.Y. Laws; State of New York)
            McKinney's Session Law News of New York (N.Y. Sess. Law News (McKinney); West)
        Administrative
            Code
                Official Compilation of Codes, Rules and Regulations of the State of New York (N.Y. Admin. Code; Lenz and Riecker)
            Register
                New York State Register (N.Y. Admin. Reg.; State of New York)
    Finding Aid:
        West's New York Digest 3d (West)

34. NORTH CAROLINA
    Cases
        Supreme Court
            North Carolina Reports (N.C.; State of North Carolina)
            Southeastern Reporter (S.E.2d; West)
        Court of Appeals
            North Carolina Court of Appeals Reports (N.C. App.; State of North Carolina)
            Southeastern Reporter (S.E.2d; West)
    Statutes
        Statutory Compilation
            General Statutes of North Carolina (N.C. Gen. Stat.; Michie)
        Session Laws
            Session Laws of North Carolina (N.C. Sess. Laws; Hunter Publishing)
            Advance Legislative Service to the General Statutes of North Carolina (N.C. Adv. Legis. Serv.; Michie)

22 / Current Primary Legal Materials

        Administrative
           Code
                North Carolina Administrative Code (N.C. Admin. Code; State of North Carolina)
           Register
               No Formal Compilation
        Finding Aid:
           West's North Carolina Digest (West)

35.   NORTH DAKOTA
        Cases
           Supreme Court
               Northwestern Reporter (N.W.2d; West)
        Statutes
           Statutory Compilation
               North Dakota Century Code (N.D. Cent. Code; Allen Smith)
           Session Laws
               Laws of North Dakota (N.D. Sess. Laws; State of North Dakota)
        Administrative
           Code
               North Dakota Administrative Code (N.D. Admin. Code; State of North Dakota)
           Register
               No Formal Compilation
        Finding Aid:
           West's Dakota Digest (West)

36.   OHIO
        Cases*
           Supreme Court
               Ohio State Reports (Ohio St. 3d; Anderson)
               Northeastern Reporter (N.E.2d; West)
           Court of Appeals
               Ohio Appellate Reports (Ohio App.3d; Anderson)
               Northeastern Reporter (N.E.2d; West)
           Other Law Courts
               Ohio Miscellaneous (Ohio Misc.2d; Anderson)
               Northeastern Reporter (N.E.2d; West)
        Statutes
           Statutory Compilation
               Ohio Revised Code Annotated (Ohio Rev. Code Ann. (Page); Anderson)
               Ohio Revised Code Annotated (Ohio Rev. Code Ann. (Baldwin); Banks-Baldwin)

**Ohio Official Reports* have been published since 1982 and consolidate all reported Ohio court cases into a single volume where cases are arranged under the appropriate courts and cited accordingly.

Session Laws
　　State of Ohio: Legislative Acts Passed and Joint Resolutions
　　　　Adopted (Ohio Laws; National Graphics)
　　Ohio Legislative Bulletin (Ohio Legis. Bull. (Anderson); Anderson)
　　Ohio Legislative Service (Ohio Legis. Serv. (Baldwin); Banks-Baldwin)
Administrative
　　Code
　　　　Ohio Administrative Code (Ohio Admin. Code; Banks-Baldwin)
　　Register
　　　　Ohio Monthly Record (Ohio Monthly Rec.; Banks-Baldwin)
Finding Aid:
　　West's Ohio Digest (West)

37. OKLAHOMA
Cases
　　Supreme Court, Court of Criminal Appeals, Court of Appeals
　　　　Pacific Reporter (P.2d; West)
Statutes
　　Statutory Compilation
　　　　Oklahoma Statutes (Okla. Stat.; West)
　　　　Oklahoma Statutes Annotated (Okla. Stat. Ann.; West)
　　Session Laws
　　　　Oklahoma Session Laws (Okla. Sess. Laws; West)
　　　　Oklahoma Session Law Service (Okla. Sess. Law Serv.; West)
Administrative
　　Code
　　　　No Formal Compilation
　　Register
　　　　Oklahoma Register (Okla. Admin. Reg.; State of Oklahoma)
Finding Aid:
　　West's Oklahoma Digest (West)

38. OREGON
Cases
　　Supreme Court
　　　　Oregon Reports (Or.; State of Oregon)
　　　　Pacific Reporter (P.2d; West)
　　Court of Appeals
　　　　Oregon Reports, Court of Appeals (Or. App.; State of Oregon)
　　　　Pacific Reporter (P.2d; West)
　　Land Use Board of Appeals
　　　　Oregon LUBA Decisions (Or. LUBA Dec.; Butterworth)
　　Tax Court
　　　　Oregon Tax Reports (Or. T. R.; State of Oregon)
Statutes
　　Statutory Compilation
　　　　Oregon Revised Statutes (Or. Rev. Stat.; State of Oregon)
　　　　Oregon Revised Statutes Annotated (Butterworth - *in preparation*)

Session Laws
    Oregon Laws and Resolutions (Or. Laws; State of Oregon)
    Oregon Laws and Resolutions. Advance Sheets (Or. Laws Adv. Sh.; State of Oregon)
Administrative
    Code
        Oregon Administrative Rules (Or. Admin. R.; State of Oregon)
    Register
        Administrative Rules Bulletin (Or. Admin. R. Bull.; State of Oregon)
Finding Aid:
    West's New Oregon Digest (West)

39. PENNSYLVANIA
    Cases
        Supreme Court
            Pennsylvania State Reports (Pa.; West)
            Atlantic Reporter (A.2d; West)
        Superior Court
            Pennsylvania Superior Court Reports (Pa. Super.; West)
            Atlantic Reporter (A.2d; West)
        Commonwealth Court
            Pennsylvania Commonwealth Court Reports (Pa. Commw.; Murrelle Printing)
            Atlantic Reporter (A.2d; West)
        Other Lower Courts
            Pennsylvania District and County Reports (D. & C.3d; Legal Intelligencer)
            Pennsylvania Fiduciary Reporter (Pa. Fiduc.2d; Geo. T. Bisel)
    Statutes
        Statutory Compilation
            Pennsylvania Consolidated Statutes (Pa. Cons. Stat.; State of Pennsylvania)
            Pennsylvania Consolidated Statutes Annotated (Pa. Cons. Stat. Ann. (Purdon); Geo. T. Bisel, West)
        Session Laws
            Laws of the General Assembly of the Commonwealth of Pennsylvania (Pa. Laws; State of Pennsylvania)
            Pennsylvania Legislative Service (Pa. Legis. Serv. (Purdon); Geo. T. Bisel, West)
        Administrative
            Code
                Pennsylvania Code (Pa. Admin. Code; Shepard's)
            Register
                Pennsylvania Bulletin (Pa. Admin. Bull.; State of Pennsylvania)
    Finding Aid:
        West's Pennsylvania Digest 2d (West)

Current Primary Legal Materials / 25

40. RHODE ISLAND
    Cases
        Supreme Court
            Rhode Island Reports (R.I.; Lashin Publishing)
            Atlantic Reporter (A.2d; West)
    Statutes
        Statutory Compilation
            General Laws of Rhode Island (R.I. Gen. Laws; Michie)
        Session Laws
            Public Laws of Rhode Island (R.I. Pub. Laws; William R. Brown)
        Administrative
            Code
                No Formal Compilation
            Register
                No Formal Compilation
    Finding Aid:
        West's Rhode Island Digest (West)

41. SOUTH CAROLINA
    Cases
        Supreme Court
            South Carolina Reports (S.C.; R. L. Bryan)
            Southeastern Reporter (S.E.2d; West)
    Statutes
        Statutory Compilation
            Code of Laws of South Carolina 1976 Annotated (S.C. Code Ann. (Law. Co-op.); Lawyers Co-Op.)
        Session Laws
            Acts and Joint Resolutions, South Carolina (S.C. Acts; State of South Carolina)
        Administrative
            Code
                Code of Laws of South Carolina 1976 Annotated. Vols. 23-26 (S.C. Code Ann. (Law. Co-op.); Lawyers Co-Op.)
            Register
                South Carolina State Register (S.C. Admin. Reg.; State of South Carolina)
    Finding Aid:
        West's South Carolina Digest (West)

42. SOUTH DAKOTA
    Cases
        Supreme Court
            Northwestern Reporter (N.W.2d; West)
    Statutes
        Statutory Compilation
            South Dakota Codified Laws Annotated (S.D. Codified Laws Ann.; Allen Smith)
        Session Laws
            Laws of South Dakota (S.D. Sess. Laws; State of South Dakota)

Administrative
Code
Administrative Rules of South Dakota (S.D. Admin. R.; State of South Dakota)
Register
South Dakota Register (S.D. Admin. Reg.; State of South Dakota)
Finding Aid:
West's Dakota Digest (West)

43. TENNESSEE
Cases
Supreme Court, Court of Appeals, Court of Chancery Appeals, Court of Criminal Appeals
Southwestern Reporter (S.W.2d; West)
Statutes
Statutory Compilation
Tennessee Code Annotated (Tenn. Code Ann.; Michie)
Session Laws
Public Acts of the State of Tennessee (Tenn. Pub. Acts; State of Tennessee)
Private Acts of the State of Tennessee (Tenn. Priv. Acts; State of Tennessee)
Tennessee Code Annotated. Advanced Legislative Service (Tenn. Adv. Legis. Serv.; Michie)
Administrative
Code
Official Compilation—Rules and Regulations of the State of Tennessee (Tenn. Admin. Comp.; State of Tennessee)
Register
Tennessee Administrative Register (Tenn. Admin. Reg.; State of Tennessee)
Finding Aid:
West's Tennessee Digest (West)

44. TEXAS
Cases
Supreme Court, Court of Civil Appeals, Court of Criminal Appeals
Southwestern Reporter (S.W.2d; West)
Statutes
Statutory Compilation
Texas Codes Annotated (Tex. Code Ann. (Vernon); West)
Texas Statutes Annotated (Tex. Stat. Ann. (Vernon); West)
Texas Revised Civil Statutes Annotated (Tex. Rev. Civ. Stat. Ann. (Vernon); West)
Session Laws
General and Special Laws of the State of Texas (Tex. Gen. Laws; State of Texas)
Texas Session Law Service (Tex. Sess. Law Serv. (Vernon); West)

Administrative
    Code
        Official State of Texas Administrative Code (Tex. Admin. Code;
            Hart Information Systems)
    Register
        Texas Register (Tex. Admin. Reg.; State of Texas)
Finding Aid:
    West's Texas Digest 2d (West)

45. UTAH
    Cases
        Supreme Court
            Utah Advance Reports (Utah Adv.; Code Co.)
            Pacific Reporter (P.2d; West)
    Statutes
        Statutory Compilation
            Utah Code (Utah Code; Code Co.)
            Utah Code Annotated (Utah Code Ann.; Allen Smith)
        Session Laws
            Laws of Utah (Utah Laws; State of Utah)
        Administrative
            Code
                Administrative Rules of the State of Utah (Utah Admin. R.;
                    State of Utah)
            Register
                State of Utah Bulletin (Utah Admin. Bull.; State of Utah)
    Finding Aid:
        No Formal Compilation

46. VERMONT
    Cases
        Supreme Court
            Vermont Reports (Vt.; Equity)
            Atlantic Reporter (A.2d; West)
    Statutes
        Statutory Compilation
            Vermont Statutes Annotated (Vt. Stat. Ann.; Equity)
        Session Laws
            Laws of Vermont (Vt. Acts; State of Vermont)
        Administrative
            Code
                Vermont Administrative Code (Vt. Admin. Code; State of
                    Vermont)
            Register
                Vermont Administrative Procedures Bulletin (Vt. Admin. Bull.;
                    State of Vermont)–*irregular*
    Finding Aid:
        West's Vermont Key Number Digest (West)

28 / Current Primary Legal Materials

47. VIRGINIA
    Cases
        Supreme Court
            Virginia Reports (Va.; State of Virginia)
            Southeastern Reporter (S.E.2d; West)
    Statutes
        Statutory Compilation
            Code of Virginia (Va. Code; Michie)
        Session Laws
            Acts of the General Assembly of the Commonwealth of Virginia
                (Va. Acts; State of Virginia)
        Administrative
            Code
                No Formal Compilation
            Register
                No Formal Compilation
    Finding Aid:
        West's Virginia and West Virginia Digest (West)

48. WASHINGTON
    Cases
        Supreme Court
            Washington Reports (Wash.2d; State of Washington)
            Pacific Reporter (P.2d; West)
        Court of Appeals
            Washington Appellate Reports (Wash. App.; State of Washington)
            Pacific Reporter (P.2d; West)
    Statutes
        Statutory Compilation
            Revised Code of Washington (Wash. Rev. Code; State of Washington)
            Revised Code of Washington Annotated (Wash. Rev. Code Ann.; West)
        Session Laws
            Laws of Washington (Wash. Laws; State of Washington)
            Washington Legislative Service (Wash. Legis. Serv.; West)
        Administrative
            Code
                Washington Administrative Code (Wash. Admin. Code R.; State
                    of Washington)
            Register
                Washington State Register (Wash. Admin. Reg.; State of
                    Washington)
    Finding Aid:
        West's Washington Digest Annotated (West)

49. WEST VIRGINIA
    Cases
        Supreme Court of Appeals
            West Virginia Reports (W.Va.; State of West Virginia*)
            Southeastern Reporter (S.E.2d; West)

West Virginia Reports was last published in 1974 but has not been officially discontinued; S.E.2d has not been adopted as the official reporter.

Current Primary Legal Materials / 29

    Statutes
        Statutory Compilation
            West Virginia Code (W. Va. Code; Michie)
        Session Laws
            Acts of the Legislature of West Virginia (W. Va. Acts; BJW Printers)
        Administrative
            Code
                No Formal Compilation
            Register
                No Formal Compilation Available for Distribution
    Finding Aid:
        West's Virginia and West Virginia Digest (West)

50. WISCONSIN
    Cases
        Supreme Court, Court of Appeals
            Wisconsin Reports (Wis.2d; Callaghan)
            Northwestern Reporter (N.W.2d; West)
    Statutes
        Statutory Compilation
            Wisconsin Statutes (Wis. Stat.; State of Wisconsin)
            Wisconsin Statutes Annotated (Wis. Stat. Ann.; West)
        Session Laws
            Laws of Wisconsin (Wis. Laws; State of Wisconsin)
            Wisconsin Legislative Service (Wis. Legis. Serv.; West)
        Administrative
            Code
                Wisconsin Administrative Code (Wis. Admin. Code; State of Wisconsin)
            Register
                Wisconsin Administrative Register (Wis. Admin. Reg.; State of Wisconsin)
    Finding Aid:
        West's Wisconsin Key Number Digest (West)

51. WYOMING
    Cases
        Supreme Court
            Pacific Reporter (P.2d; West)
    Statutes
        Statutory Compilation
            Wyoming Statutes (Wyo. Stat.; Michie)
        Session Laws
            Session Laws of Wyoming (Wyo. Sess. Laws; State of Wyoming)
        Administrative
            Code
                No Formal Compilation Available for Distribution
            Register
                No Formal Compilation
    Finding Aid:
        West's Wyoming Digest (West)

Outlying Territories

1. AMERICAN SAMOA
    Cases
        American Samoa Reports. 4 vols. 1900-1975 (Am. Samoa; Equity)
        American Samoa Reporter. 1975-*. (Am. Samoa 2d; High Court of American Samoa)
    Statutes
        Statutory Compilation†
            American Samoa Code. 2 vols. 1973 (Am. Samoa Code; Equity)
            American Samoa Code Annotated. 1 vol. Current (Am. Samoa Code Ann.; Book Publishing)
        Session Laws
            American Samoa Session Laws and Digest (Am. Samoa Sess. Laws; Legislative Reference Bureau)
        Administrative
        Code
            American Samoa Administrative Code. 1 vol. (Am. Samoa Admin. Code; Book Publishing)
        Register
            No Formal Compilation
    Finding Aid:
        American Samoa Digest. 1 vol. 1900-1975 (Equity)
        No Formal Compilation since 1975

2. GUAM
    Cases
        Guam Reports. 1 vol. 1955-1979 (Guam; Equity)
        Guam Reports. vol. 2. 1979- (Guam; Department of Law, Compiler of Laws Division)
    Statutes
        Statutory Compilation**
            Guam Code. 8 vols. Various Codes. 1970 ed. Supplemented to 1974 (Guam Code; Department of Law, Compiler of Laws Division)
            Guam Code Annotated. 5 vols. Various titles. Current (Guam Code Ann.; Department of Law, Compiler of Laws Division)

---

*Selective Publication of cases with Precedential Value

†A 1949 and 1961 code were published, but little information is available on these codes, which are most likely unavailable and out of print.

**Prior to 1970, statutes and codes were published, leading to the 1970 Compilation of the Guam Code. In 1952 a one-volume *Statutes and Amendments to the Codes of the Territory* was published. In 1952 the *Government Code* was published, and in 1961 a revised two-volume *Government Code* was published. In 1953, civil, penal, civil procedure, and probate codes were published. This material was updated to 1964 by pocket parts. The compiler was John A. Bohn, Walnut Creek, CA. These are most likely unavailable and no longer in print.

Session Laws
: Guam Session Laws. 1951-1975 (Guam Sess. Laws; Guam
Legislature)
Formal Compilation Now Incomplete and Unavailable
Guam Session Laws. 1975- . (Guam Sess. Laws; Department of Law,
Compiler of Laws Division)

Administrative
: Code
: The Administrative Rules and Regulations of the Government of
Guam. 3 vols. (Guam Admin. R.; Department of Law,
Compiler of Laws Division)

Register
: *No Formal Compilation*

Finding Aid:
: Guam Federal Digest. 1 vol. 1950-1984*. (Department of Law,
Compiler of Laws Division)

3. (COMMONWEALTH OF) PUERTO RICO

Cases
: Decisiones de Puerto Rico (D.P.R.; Equity)
Official Translations of the Opinions of the Supreme Court of Puerto
Rico. 10 vols. 1973-1981 (P.R. Op.; Supreme Court of Puerto
Rico, Bureau of Translations)
Puerto Rico Reports. 100 vols. 1900-1972 (P.R.R.; Equity)

Statutes
: Statutory Compilation
: Laws of Puerto Rico Annotated (P.R. Laws Ann.; Equity)
Session Laws
: Puerto Rico Session Laws (P.R. Laws; Equity)

Administrative
: Code
: Commonwealth of Puerto Rico Rules and Regulations. 15 vols.
1957-73 (P.R.R. & Regs.; Equity)
No Current Formal Compilation Prepared**

Register
: Puerto Rico Register. Ceased with vol. 12 (P.R. Admin. Reg.,
Equity)
No Current Formal Compilation Prepared**

Finding Aid:
: Digesto de Puerto Rico (Equity)

---

*Includes only published cases decided in United States Federal Courts.

**Equity Publishing Company has published a one-volume *General Guide to Rules and Regulations (Guia General de Reglas y Reglamentos de Puerto Rico)* covering the period 1972-1983. Escrutinio Legislativo, Inc. publishes a two-volume *Catalog of Regulations* along with a weekly bulletin entitled *Escrutinio Ejectivo*. None of these works include the full text of administrative rules. These publications are useful for brief descriptions of regulations, subject access to regulations, updating regulations since 1972, and so forth.

32 / Current Primary Legal Materials

4. TRUST TERRITORY OF THE PACIFIC ISLANDS
    Cases
        Trust Territory Reports. 7 vols. 1951-1978 (Trust Terr.; Equity)
        No Formal Compilation since 1978
    Statutes
        Statutory Compilation
            Code of the Trust Territory of the Pacific Islands. 1970 (Trust Terr. Code; Book Publishing)
            Trust Territory Code. 2 vols. 1980 Current (Trust Terr. Code; Michie)*
        Session Laws
            Laws and resolutions. Congress of Micronesia. 1965-1978 (Trust Terr. Laws; Publications Division of the Trust Territories)
            No Formal Compilation since 1978
        Administrative
        Code
            Trust Territory Code of Public Regulations. 1 vol. 1966- (Trust Terr. Admin. Code; Publications Division of the Trust Territories)
        Register
            Territorial Register (Trust Terr. Reg.; Bureau of Public Affairs)
            No Formal Compilation since 1978
    Finding Aid:
        No Formal Compilation

4a. (COMMONWEALTH OF) THE NORTHERN MARIANA ISLANDS
    Cases
        No Formal Compilation
            See "Trust Territory . . . "
    Statutes
        Statutory Compilation
            Northern Mariana Islands. Commonwealth Code. 2 vols. 1984. (N. Mariana Code; Law Revision Commission)
        Session Laws
            No Formal Compilation
                See "Trust Territory . . . "
        Administrative
        Code
            Commonwealth Register. 6 vols. (N. Mariana Regs.; Registrar of Corporation, Office of the Attorney General).
        Register
            See "Code."**
    Finding Aid:
        No Formal Compilation

---

*This material is sold out of Saipan by the Publications Division of the Trust Territories.

**The *Commonwealth Register* serves a dual function as both a code and register where both early and final versions of administrative rules are filed. An index provides subject access.

4b. FEDERATED STATES OF MICRONESIA
    Cases
        No Formal Compilation
           See "Trust Territory . . . "
    Statutes
        Statutory Compilation
           Code of the Federated States of Micronesia. 2 vols. 1982- (Micro. Code; Book Publishing)
        Session Laws
           No Formal Compilation
               See "Trust Territory . . . "
        Administrative
           Code
               No Formal Compilation
                   See "Trust Territory . . . "
           Register
               No Formal Compilation
                   See "Trust Territory . . . "
    Finding Aid:
        No Formal Compilation

4c. MARSHALL ISLANDS
    Cases
        No Formal Compilation
           See "Trust Territory . . . "
    Statutes
        Statutory Compilation
           Marshall Islands Code. 1 vol. 1976 (M.I. Code; Office of the Legislative Counsel)
               No Formal Compilation since 1976
                   See "Trust Territory . . . "
        Session Laws
           No Formal Compilation
               See "Trust Territory . . . "
        Administrative
           Code
               No Formal Compilation
                   See "Trust Territory . . . "
           Register
               No Formal Compilation
                   See "Trust Territory . . . "
    Finding Aid:
        No Formal Compilation

4d. REPUBLIC OF PALAU (BELAU)*
  Cases
    No Formal Compilation
      See "Trust Territory ... "
  Statutes
    Statutory Compilation
      Formal Compilation in Preparation
    Session Laws
      No Formal Compilation
        See "Trust Territory ... "
    Administrative
      Code
        No Formal Compilation
          See "Trust Territory ... "
      Register
        No Formal Compilation
          See "Trust Territory ... "
  Finding Aid:
    No Formal Compilation

5. VIRGIN ISLANDS OF THE UNITED STATES
  Cases
    Virgin Island Reports (V.I.; Equity)
  Statutes
    Statutory Compilation
      Virgin Islands Code Annotated (V.I. Code Ann.; Equity)
    Session Laws
      Virgin Islands Session Laws (V.I. Acts; Equity)
    Administrative
      Code
        Virgin Islands Rules and Regulations (V.I.R. & Regs.; Equity)
      Register
        Virgin Islands Register (V.I. Admin. Reg.; Equity)
  Finding Aid:
    No Formal Compilation

---

*Also called Belau.

2 SELECTED LEGAL REFERENCE SOURCES

Comments

Legal reference materials, while generally falling into the same categories as sources in other disciplines, are unique in some ways because of the specialized needs of the legal profession. This chapter gathers a representative collection of these reference materials, and is a brief introduction to basic legal reference sources. More detailed discussion of many of the sources mentioned may be found in the major texts listed in appendix C and under "Guides to Legal Research" in this chapter.

Emphasis has been placed on titles from 1970 to the present; however, a few older titles of particular interest have been included. Bibliographies, directories, and indexes covering materials in various areas of the social sciences, which might be expected to be found in a comprehensive general reference collection have not been included; however, sources such as *Social Sciences Citation Index, Public Affairs Information Service Bulletin,* and *Congressional Quarterly Weekly Report* may be useful resources in further legal research.

In addition to the reference materials cited in this chapter, computerized legal retrieval services have become important resources for reference service. The two major legal services, LEXIS and WESTLAW, permit full-text searching of selected federal and state court decisions, the *United States Code,* the *Code of Federal Regulations,* the *Federal Register,* and various administrative materials by key words and phrases. WESTLAW also permits searching by West Digest Topics and Key Numbers. For a discussion of the two services, see Price, Bitner, and Bysiewicz's *Effective Legal Research*[1] and Cohen and Berring's *How to Find the Law.*[2] Specialized subject files such as tax and trade regulation, major legal treatises, and law reviews are also available through both systems. Auxiliary components allow the user to Shepardize cases, i.e., to verify citations, and to obtain parallel citations or citations to cases directly affecting the validity of a case.

A number of law and law-related files are available from the commercial suppliers listed in appendix D of this work. *Legal Resource Index,* Congressional Information Service (CIS), the National Criminal Justice Reference Service (NCJRS), *Federal Index,* and numerous social science files are available through Dialog Information Services. The Electronic Legislative Search System (ELSS), which helps trace the current status of both state and federal legislation, is available from Commerce Clearing House (CCH). Special automated government files, such as FLITE (Federal Legal Information Through Electronics) from the U.S. Air Force, and JURIS (Judicial Retrieval and Inquiry System) from the U.S. Department of Justice, are legal databases available to federal agencies and departments. A comprehensive list of databases available in all subject areas may be found in Martha E. Williams, *Computer-Readable Databases: A Directory and Data Sourcebook*,[3] the quarterly *Directory of Online Databases*,[4] published by Cuadra Associates, and *The Federal Data Base Finder*.[5] General discussions of the application of social science databases to legal research are also available.[6]

Legal research requires accessing a variety of information sources. It is our hope that this chapter will provide the starting point for individuals unfamiliar with the methods, materials, and technology involved in legal research.

Notes

[1] Miles O. Price, Harry Bitner, and Shirley Raissi Bysiewicz, *Effective Legal Research*, 4th ed. (Boston: Little, Brown, 1979), 459-68.

[2] Morris L. Cohen and Robert C. Berring, *How to Find the Law*, 8th ed. (St. Paul: West, 1983), 693-703.

[3] Martha E. Williams, ed., *Computer-Readable Databases: A Directory and Data Sourcebook* (Washington, D.C.: American Society for Information Science, 1982).

[4] Cuadra Associates, *Directory of Online Databases* (Santa Monica, Calif.: Cuadra Associates, 1979-).

[5] Sharon Zarozny and Monica Horner, *The Federal Data Base Finder: A Directory of Free and Fee-Based Files Available from the Federal Government* (Potomac, Md.: Information U.S.A., 1984).

[6] Terry Appenzellar, "Non-Legal Databases: Informing Clientele of the Existence and Application of Online Services," *Law Library Journal* 73 (Fall 1980): 867-81; and James A. Sprowl, "Dialog, LEXIS, and WESTLAW: Using the Computer to Search through Legal and Technological Data Bases," *APLA Quarterly Journal* 11 (Winter-Spring 1983): 90-101.

Outline of Reference Sources

Abstracts and Indexes 38
    Periodicals
    Government Documents and Legislative Histories
    Court Opinions, Statutes, Treaties

Bibliographies 42
    Government Publications
    International Law
    Legislative Histories
    Library Catalogs
    Periodicals and Looseleaf Services
    Special Subjects
    Trade Bibliographies

Biographical Sources 47
    Judges
    Law Teachers and Librarians
    Lawyers and Law Firms

Dictionaries 52
    General/Legal
    Abbreviations
    Foreign Language
    Quotations
    Specialized
    Thesaurus

Directories 59

Encyclopedias 62

Formbooks and Style Manuals 64

Guides to Legal Information 65
    Government Publications and the Legislative Process
    Courts
    Legal Careers

Guides to Legal Research 67

Handbooks and Manuals 71

Annotations

Abstracts and Indexes

Periodicals

2-1 **Criminal Justice Abstracts.** V. 1 - . Hackensack, N.J.: National Council on Crime and Delinquency, 1968- . quarterly.

Abstracting books, articles, reports, and studies in the field of criminal justice, this service covers research on policies and theories as well as practical program evaluations. Broadly interpreting "criminal justice," it includes such areas as correctional systems, police agencies, crime prevention, and juvenile justice. Intended not only for the practitioner, it could prove useful in many disciplines within the social sciences. The abstracts are detailed and discuss findings, implications, and recommendations. This title includes a subject and geographic index as well as an author index. Previously titled *Information Review on Crime and Delinquency* and *Crime and Delinquency Literature.*

2-2 **The Criminal Justice Periodical Index.** V. 1 - . Ann Arbor, Mich.: Indexing Services, University Microfilms International, 1975- . three times a year.

An index to approximately one hundred periodicals broadly covering the field of criminal justice. Areas covered include criminal law, prisons, police, forensic science, and juvenile justice. With author and subject indexes, main entries provide complete bibliographic information. Indications are made if the periodical is available in microform or if articles may be ordered from University Microfilms International. CJPI is published three times a year, with the third issue being the annual cumulation.

2-3 **Current Law Index.** V. 1 - . Menlo Park, Calif.: Information Access Corporation, 1980- . monthly with quarterly and annual cumulations.

Indexing over seven hundred legal periodicals selected by the Committee on Indexing of Periodical Literature of the American Association of Law Libraries, CLI is available in paper copy and on microfilm. The film copy, *Legal Resources Index* (LRI) is completely cumulated every month, and uses a reader sent to subscribers. CLI is published monthly with quarterly and annual cumulations. Both formats have subject and author/title indexes, as well as Tables of Cases and Statutes. Using Library of Congress subject headings with some modification, the entries have complete bibliographic information at all access points. This index is searchable by computer using the approaches available for searching the paper copy, as well as free text searching. Access to the online file is available from Dialog Information Service.

2-4 **Federal Tax Articles: Income, Estate, Gift, Excise, Employment Taxes.** Chicago: Commerce Clearing House, 1962- . monthly.

A looseleaf index to periodical articles from 1954 to the present, dealing with federal taxes found in law reviews, tax publications, and accounting periodicals. Citations are arranged by Internal Revenue Code Section and indexed by topic and author.

Selected Legal Reference Sources / 39

2-5   Goldstein, Gersham, comp. **Index to Federal Tax Articles.** Boston: Warren, Gorham & Lamont, 1975- . updated by cumulative supplements.

An index to articles since 1913, dealing with federal income, estate, and gift taxes found in legal periodicals and in accounting and economics journals. Indexing is by topic and author.

2-6   **Index to Legal Periodicals.** V. 1 - . New York: H.W. Wilson, 1908- . monthly with annual cumulations.

ILP is one of the major indexes for legal periodicals published in the U.S., Canada, and Great Britain. Although the subject headings are broad and the five page minimum for articles eliminates some items, the library user should feel comfortable with the format of this typical Wilson index. Regularly indexing over 450 legal periodicals of high quality, issues are published monthly and cumulated quarterly, annually, and triennially. Entries are arranged by author and subject, with separate sections for case names, statutes, and book reviews. The subject and author section provides bibliographic information only under subject, forcing the user doing an author search to move back and forth between authors and subjects. Another Wilson index, *Social Sciences Index,* should also prove useful for those interested in law-related areas such as criminology and public administration.

2-7   **Index to Periodical Articles Related to Law.** V. 1.- . Dobbs Ferry, N.Y.: Glanville, 1958- . quarterly with annual cumulations.

This index supplements *Current Law Index, Index to Legal Periodicals,* and *Index to Foreign Legal Periodicals* by covering periodicals not included in those indexes. Entries are arranged by broad subject with a separate author index. Covering over 150 journals from the social and behavioral sciences, it includes law-oriented articles in such fields as business, political science, psychiatry, economics, and philosophy. Useful for developing areas outside of but related to law, and therefore of interest to the legal researcher. There is a ten-year cumulation for 1958-1968, and there are five-year cumulations for 1969-1973 and 1974-1978.

2-8   **Index to U.S. Government Periodicals.** V. 1 - . Chicago: Infordata International, 1970- . quarterly with annual cumulations.

This index provides access to approximately 170 periodicals published by over one hundred agencies of the federal government. Utilizing a specially developed thesaurus of fairly narrow headings and subheadings, each entry under both subject and author provides complete bibliographic information, as well as a microfiche identification number for ordering the periodical from the publisher. A useful tool for a wide range of users and any library with a documents collection.

2-9   **Shepard's Law Review Citations: A Compilation of Citations to Law Reviews and Legal Periodicals.** 3d ed. Colorado Springs, Colo.: Shepard's, 1979. 1,131 pp. kept up to date by cumulative supplements.

A citator to articles since 1957 in over 180 law reviews and legal periodicals that have been cited by the United States Supreme Court or by lower federal courts in decisions reported in *Federal Reporter, Second Series, Federal Supplement,* or *Federal Rules Decisions,* or by state courts in cases reported in state reports or the various units of the National Reporter System. In addition, the volume provides citations appearing in articles in numerous law reviews and periodicals. Footnotes indicate recently added periodicals and the year inclusion began. *Shepard's Federal Law Citations in Selected Law Reviews* goes in the opposite direction, with prominent law reviews as the citing source and federal court decisions and rules as the cited source.

Government Documents and Legislative Histories

2-10 **CIS Abstract/Index**. Washington, D.C.: Congressional Information Service, 1970- . monthly.

Published monthly with annual and quinquennial cumulations, this abstract/index provides access to Congressional committee hearings, documents, prints, and reports. The abstract section, which is organized by CIS accession number, provides complete bibliographic information and an abstract for the Congressional publication. The index section contains subject, title, bill number, report number, and document number indexes, with reference to the abstract/accession number. The annual abstract volume also contains a legislative history section, which brings together all CIS entries as well as references in the *Congressional Record* and the *Weekly Compilation of Presidential Documents* pertaining to a particular public law. CIS is available as a computerized database and is searchable online through several commercial sources. An indispensable tool for any medium or large reference collection regardless of whether the library subscribes to the companion microfiche collection of Congressional publications available from the same publisher.

2-11 **CIS U.S. Congressional Committee Hearings Index**. Washington, D.C.: Congressional Information Service, 1981- .

An index to Congressional hearings published from the early 1800's through 1969 contained in the *CIS U.S. Congressional Committee Hearings on Microfiche Full Collection*. Published in eight parts covering various Congresses (23rd-91st Congress), indexing is by subject, organization, personal name, title, bill number, Superintendent of Documents classification number, and report or document number. Companion indexes include the *CIS U.S. Serial Set Index* covering all numbered Congressional reports and documents issued from 1789 through 1969, and the *CIS U.S. Congressional Committee Prints Index*, which indexes committee prints issued from the early 1800's through 1969.

2-12 **Congressional Index**. Chicago: Commerce Clearing House, 75th Congress - . 1937-38 - . biennial with weekly updates.

A looseleaf service designed to enable the user to trace the status and history of legislation introduced in Congress. Bills and resolutions are listed, summarized, and indexed by subject, principal author, sponsor, companion, and identical bill number. New laws are indexed using the same approaches, as well as by public law number. References to hearings are arranged by committee and subcommittee and include all the dates hearings were held. The section on roll call votes reports votes on bills, resolutions, nominations, and treaties, and selectively indicates how each member voted. Updated weekly when Congress is in session, this looseleaf can prove invaluable in determining the status of current legislation and when doing historical legislative research.

2-13   **CSI Federal Index.** Washington, D.C.: Capitol Services, 1983- . monthly with annual cumulations.

An index to the *Congressional Record, Federal Register, The Weekly Compilation of Presidential Documents,* and *U.S. Law Week.* Divided into eight different sections, citations are indexed by federal agency, department, and federal court as well as by government function, Standard Industrial Classification Code (SIC), Congressman's name, and Congressional committee. A Calendar of Legislation, helpful in tracking the latest action on bills, is also included.

2-14   **Index to the Code of Federal Regulations.** V. 1 - . Bethesda, Md.: Congressional Information Service, 1978- . annual.

This annual index attempts to provide access to regulations throughout all fifty titles of the *Code of Federal Regulations.* The main portion of the index is organized by a controlled vocabulary of over 20,000 terms created especially for this work. The topics are specific with even more detailed subtopics and numerous cross references. The geographic indexes provide access to regulations concerning activities within states, cities, counties, and foreign countries as well as regulations concerning national parks, monuments, rivers, and harbors. Other portions of the index include a list of all the descriptive headings officially assigned to each title, subtitle, chapter, subchapter, part or subpart in effect that year. Useful for anyone doing research on federal regulations. Beginning with 1984, CIS also began publishing a weekly index to the *Federal Register.*

2-15   Nabors, Eugene. **Legislative Reference Checklist: The Key to Legislative Histories from 1789-1903.** Littleton, Colo.: Fred B. Rothman, 1982. 440 pp.

This checklist provides access to the bill and joint resolution numbers of legislation that became law from the first Congress (1789) through the fifty-seventh Congress (1903). As the author explains in the introduction, no bill numbers were used in the *Statutes at Large* prior to 1903, thus making it difficult for the legislative historian to trace legislation. This collection of tables fills a need by providing bill numbers for public laws and resolutions.

Court Opinions, Statutes, Treaties

2-16   Blandford, Linda A. and Patricia R. Evans, eds. **Supreme Court of the United States, 1789-1980: An Index to Opinions Arranged by Justice.** Millwood, N.Y.: Kraus International, 1983. 2 vols. apps.

An index to all Supreme Court opinions published from 1789 through the October, 1979, term. The opinions are arranged by justice and classified into seven categories: majority opinions, concurring opinions, dissenting opinions, separate opinions, opinions announcing judgment, opinions as Circuit Justice, and statements made by the justices through the Reporter of Decisions. Not only useful in doing research on a particular justice, this index also provides verification of the title and citation of opinions between 1789 and 1980. Appendices include a list of members of the Supreme Court with pertinent dates and a Table of Succession of the Justices of the Supreme Court.

2-17   Chapman, Mary R. **Bibliographical Index to the State Reports Prior to the National Reporter System.** Dobbs Ferry, N.Y.: Trans-Media, 1977. 66 pp.

An index to over four hundred report series on eleven hundred reels of microfilm included in the collection entitled *State Reports Prior to the National Reporter System*, edited by Erwin C. Surrency and published by Trans-Media Publishing Company. This index is arranged in two parts: first by jurisdiction, and then alphabetically by report series. Within each jursidiction the reports are arranged in chronological order. Each entry for a series of reports includes the number of volumes in the series, the time period covered, and the reel number. The alphabetical index gives the user the abbreviation for the report series and the page in the jurisdictional index where the series appears.

2-18   Kavass, Igor, and Adolf Sprudzs, comps. **Current Treaty Index,** 2d ed. Buffalo: William S. Hein, 1983. 428 pp.

An index to recent treaties and other international agreements (available only in slip form) to which the United States is a party. The entries are arranged numerically, chronologically, geographically, and by subject. This is the same arrangement followed by the authors in *UST Cumulative Indexing Service,* a looseleaf service in which the entries in *Current Treaty Index* will eventually be indexed once the treaty or agreement appears in the bound volumes of the *United States Treaties and Other International Agreements* (UST) series.

2-19   Schultz, Jon S. **Comparative Statutory Sources.** 2d ed. Buffalo: William S. Hein, 1978. 68 pp.

An index to comparative statutory studies, which are updated or revised frequently enough to be useful to the researcher attempting to compare statutes on a particular topic. For this reason, most of the references included are to "comparative statutory studies which are revised or supplemented annually or more frequently and those which are published in loose-leaf services." The subject headings are general (employment practices, bankruptcy, environment) and each entry provides a brief description of the comparative statutory study.

Bibliographies

Government Publications

2-20   Browne, Cynthia E., comp. **State Constitutional Conventions: From Independence to the Completion of the Present Union, 1776-1959: A Bibliography.** Westport, Conn.: Greenwood Press, 1973. 250 pp.

A bibliography of "all publications of state constitutional conventions, commissions, and legislative or executive committees, and all publications for or relating to these conventions and commissions issued by other agencies of state governments." The entries, which are arranged by state and then chronologically, provide full bibliographic information and occasionally include a brief description or contents note. This bibliography has been supplemented by *State Constitutional Conventions, Commissions, and Amendments, 1959-1978: An Annotated Bibliography* (Washington, D.C.: Congressional Information Service, 1981), which is a guide to *State Constitutional Conventions, Commissions, and Amendments on Microfiche* available from Congressional Information Service.

2-21 Fisher, Mary L., ed. **Guide to State Legislative Materials**. rev. ed. Littleton, Colo.: Fred B. Rothman, 1983. looseleaf.

A comprehensive guide to the publication and availability of state legislative and administrative documents. Information pertaining to availability, format, and frequency is provided for bills, hearings, committee reports, slip laws, session laws, codes, Attorney General Opinions, Executive Orders, and administrative regulations. The looseleaf format allows for easy updating.

2-22 **Monthly Catalog of United States Government Publications**. Washington, D.C.: Government Printing Office, 1895- . monthly. inds.

The major bibliography of publications issued by all branches of the federal government. Entries include bibliographic information, paging, price, and Superintendent of Documents numbers. Monthly, semi-annual, and annual author, title, subject, series/report, contract number, stock number, and title/keyword indexes are included. A serials supplement, which lists federal publications issued three or more times per year as well as a few annual publications, is issued yearly.

International Law

2-23 Besterman, Theodore. **Law and International Law: A Bibliography of Bibliographies**. Totowa, N.J.: Rowman and Littlefield, 1971. 436 pp.

A collection of all the titles dealing with law and international law found in the fourth edition of Besterman's monumental *A World Bibliography of Bibliographies*. Arranged by general topics and numerous subtopics, this bibliography lists major bibliographies in all areas of law.

2-24 Doimi di Delupis, Ingrid. **Bibliography of International Law**. New York: R.R. Bowker, 1975. 670 pp. ind.

This selective bibliography is intended to lead the researcher to major books and journal articles in all areas of international law. Divided into fourteen topics with various subtopics and cross references, each entry provides complete bibliographical information but no annotations. An author index is included.

2-25 Kleckner, Simone-Marie. **International Legal Bibliography**. Dobbs Ferry, N.Y.: Oceana, 1983. 57 pp.

A bibliography that includes primary and subsidiary sources such as treaties, customs, general principles, judicial decisions, and writings on international law and organizations. Periodicals, yearbooks, and other secondary sources are also included. Intended as a guide for libraries wishing to build a sizeable collection in international law, this bibliography is divided into two main parts: part 1, which deals with Public International Law and international organizations, and part 2, which deals with International Trade Law.

Legislative Histories

2-26   Johnson, Nancy P., comp. **Sources of Compiled Legislative Histories: A Bibliography of Government Documents, Periodical Articles, and Books, 1st Congress - 94th Congress.** Littleton, Colo.: Fred B. Rothman, 1979. (AALL Publication Series, no. 14). inds.

A useful tool for identifying previously compiled legislative histories for federal statutes. The entries for the legislative histories, which are arranged by Congress and within each Congress by public law number, provide complete bibliographic information, and, when applicable, Superintendent of Documents numbers and microfiche code numbers. Other portions include a listing of major compilations of legislative histories arranged by publisher, as well as an author/title index. The bibliography has a looseleaf format for updating.

2-27   **Union List of Legislative Histories, 47th Congress, 1881-93rd Congress, 1974.** Compiled by Law Librarians Society of Washington, D.C. Littleton, Colo.: Fred B. Rothman, 1979. 375 pp.

An important tool for locating legislative histories of federal laws. The fourth edition of this union list has been expanded to include the holdings of fifty participating libraries and provides a list of libraries subscribing to the "Legislative Histories on Microfiche" series. The main portion of the list (part C) is arranged by Congress and public law number, and indicates holding libraries by a number code. The number code refers the user to part A, which contains the address, phone number, hours, and borrowing policy for each participating library.

Library Catalogs

2-28   Columbia University. Libraries. Law Library. **Dictionary Catalog of the Columbia University Law Library.** Boston: G.K. Hall, 1969. 28 vols. 1st suppl., 1973. 7 vols.; 2d suppl., 1977. 4 vols.

Entries in the catalog of Columbia University's Law Library, approximately 470,000 volumes, from its establishment as a separate catalog through 1966. Supplements have been published covering 1967-1972 and 1972-1975.

2-29   Schwartz, Mortimer and Dan F. Henke, eds. and comps. **Combined Catalog, Anglo-American Law Collections, University of California Law Libraries, Berkeley and Davis, with Library of Congress Class K Added.** South Hackensack, N.J.: Fred B. Rothman, 1970. 10 vols. suppl., 1979. 9 vols.

A catalog of the holdings of the University of California at Davis and the University of California at Berkeley Law Libraries. The catalog includes titles classified as American law, the majority of which are monographs and treatises, federal and state government documents, pamphlets, and some serials. Materials in foreign languages have been included only if they relate directly to American law.

Periodicals and Looseleaf Services

2-30   **Legal Looseleafs in Print.** New York: Infosources, 1981- . annual. ind.

A subject and title guide to over 2,100 looseleafs covering all areas of law. Consisting of three major sections, this bibliography includes a directory of publishers with names, addresses, and telephone numbers; a title list that provides complete bibliographic information including price, frequency of supplementation, and Library of Congress card number; and a subject index that utilizes Library of Congress subject headings.

2-31   Mersky, Roy M., Robert C. Berring, and James K. McCue. **Author's Guide to Journals in Law, Criminal Justice, and Criminology.** New York: Haworth Press, 1979. 243 pp. ind.

A guide "intended to assist the prospective author in deciding on an appropriate journal to which to submit his/her article by providing as much information as possible about the journals and their policies." Journals were chosen from those included in the *Index to Legal Periodicals, Criminal Justice Periodical Index, Crime and Delinquency Abstracts,* and *Ulrich's International Periodicals Directory.* The periodical listings are divided into four parts: general law school law reviews, specialized law school law reviews, association publications, and periodicals by commercial publishers. The entries for approximately four hundred journals give brief descriptions of the types of articles and specialized subject areas included in the journal, review period, acceptance rate, and style requirements. The introduction provides a brief overview of periodicals in law, criminal law, and criminal justice. Indexing is by subject, title, and keyword.

2-32   Oxbridge Communications. **Legal and Law Enforcement Periodicals: A Directory.** New York: Facts on File, 1981. 238 pp. ind.

A directory of 3,800 law and law-related periodical publications arranged by some fifty broad subjects. Entries include full bibliographic information as well as subscription rates, circulation, distribution of readership, and a description of editorial content.

Special Subjects

2-33   Foster, Lynn and Carol Boast. **Subject Compilations of State Laws: Research Guide and Annotated Bibliography.** Westport, Conn.: Greenwood Press, 1981. 473 pp. inds.

This research guide and bibliography will be of great value to anyone doing research involving state statutes. Part 1 is a research guide, which discusses the tools and methodology required for both doing and locating a subject compilation of state laws. Part 2 is a bibliography of compilations of state statutes arranged by subject and covering the period 1960 to 1979. Covering a broad range of subjects from abortion to zoning, the bibliography includes references to treatises, reference books, periodical articles, government documents, and looseleaf services. Both parts have their own indexes, and a directory and index of publishers is also included. A 1984 expansion of this text authored by Cheryle Nyberg and Carol Boast covers 1979-1983.

2-34   Gasaway, Laura N., James L. Hoover, and Dorothy M. Warden. **American Indian Legal Materials: A Union List.** Stanfordville, N.Y.: E.M. Coleman, 1980. 152 pp. ind.

A union list of materials dealing with all aspects of American Indian law held in fifty-six law libraries across the United States. Included in the bibliography are monographs, government documents, and serials. Specific periodical articles are not included. Complete bibliographic information is provided for each entry, and no entries are annotated. Items are arranged alphabetically by main entry with Library of Congress cataloging and indexing by subject, geographical designation, and tribe. Helpful for the legal historian and interlibrary loan librarian.

2-35   Tompkins, Dorothy Campbell, comp. **Court Organization and Administration: A Bibliography.** Berkeley, Calif.: Institute of Governmental Studies, University of California, 1973. 200 pp. ind.

A bibliography of 3,179 items dealing with the organization, reorganization, and administration of American courts published between 1957 and 1973. Generally materials on the United States Supreme Court and juvenile or traffic courts have not been included. The bibliography does include courts of general and limited jurisdiction such as magistrate, family, mayor's, and police courts, as well as federal and appellate courts. Also included is a list of periodicals and an index by author and subject.

Trade Bibliographies

2-36   Buckwalter, Robert L., ed. **Law Books in Print: Books in English Published throughout the world and in Print through 1981.** 4th ed. Dobbs Ferry, N.Y.: Glanville, 1982. 5 vols.

A bibliography combining entries from *Law Books in Print* compiled by J. Myron Jacobstein and Meira G. Pimsleur, and editions of *Law Books Published* from 1975 through 1981. Entries are organized by author/title, subject, and publishers' series; and include author, title, edition, publisher date, pagination, Library of Congress card number, ISBN, subject headings, and price. Also included is a section entitled "Publisher's Price List," which organizes entries by publisher's name. Each volume contains its own directory of publishers.

2-37   **Law Books, 1876-1981: Books and Serials on Law and Its Related Subjects.** New York: R.R. Bowker, 1981. 4 vols.

A major bibliographic tool that brings together law-related titles from the *American Book Publishing Record,* the *National Union Catalog,* and MARC tapes. Organized by Library of Congress subject headings, the entries contain complete bibliographic information, including LC classification number, Dewey Decimal classification number, and tracings. Author and title indexes are included, as well as serials, subject and title indexes. The set is supplemented by *Law Information* and *Bowker's Law Books and Serials in Print Update.*

2-38 **Law Books Published.** V. 1 - . Dobbs Ferry, N.Y.: Glanville, 1969- . issued three times a year with an annual cumulation.

Produced from the same database as *Law Books in Print,* the title serves as a supplement to the four-volume set, and is organized in a similar manner.

2-39 Ward, Peter D., ed. **National Legal Bibliography: Recent Acquisitions of Major Legal Libraries.** Buffalo: William S. Hein, 1984- . monthly with quarterly and annual cumulations.

A bibliography of monographs, serials, documents, and dissertations cataloged within the last thirty to ninety days by participating law libraries. Organized by broad subject and within the subject by jurisdiction, entries provide complete bibliographic information as well as locations.

Biographical Sources

Judges

2-40 **Almanac of the Federal Judiciary.** Chicago: Law Letters, 1984- . semi-annual suppls. ind.

A useful source of information on all active U.S. district judges. Entries include not only information on education and previous professional experience, but also noteworthy rulings, comments from lawyers, and any special guidelines required by the judge.

2-41 **The American Bench: Judges of the Nation.** 2d ed. Minneapolis: Reginald Bishop Forster and Associates, 1979. 2,117 pp. ind. glos.

This biographical directory provides information on both federal and state judges as well as descriptions and information about the structure and jurisdiction of federal, state, and local courts. Organized into fifty-two sections, each section includes a description of the court structure, biographical information on the judges, and maps indicating geographical jurisdictions. Although dated, it is a valuable reference work for an academic reference collection.

2-42 Barnes, Catherine A. **Men of the Supreme Court: Profiles of the Justices.** New York: Facts on File, 1978. 221 pp. ill. bib. ind.

This volume provides three- to five-page biographies on the twenty-six justices who served on the Supreme Court between 1945 and 1976. Each profile describes the justice's educational background and training, as well as his judicial philosophy and position on various types of cases. Any notable opinions are discussed and each entry has a full page portrait. Additional material includes an excellent essay covering major trends on the Supreme Court since 1945, an extensive bibliography organized by subject, and summaries of significant decisions for the period. A valuable source of background information on the Court, and a handy companion volume to Friedman and Israel's *The Justices of the United States Supreme Court, 1789-1969.*

48 / Selected Legal Reference Sources

2-43   Chase, Harold, et al., comps. **Biographical Dictionary of the Federal Judiciary**. Detroit: Gale Research, 1976. 381 pp. app.

This biographical directory includes entries for federal judges with lifetime tenure and covers 1789 to 1974. When available, biographies were reproduced from *Who's Who* and *Who Was Who*. However, when no information was available from Marquis Who's Who, Inc., entries were compiled by the publisher. Tables provide statistics on occupation at the time of nomination, religious preference, and years of service in the federal executive branch of government. An appendix arranges the judges by appointing president. Helpful for anyone needing biographical information on a federal judge.

2-44   Friedman, Leon and Fred L. Israel, eds. **The Justices of the United States Supreme Court 1789-1969: Their Lives and Major Opinions**. New York: Chelsea House in association with Bowker, 1969-1978. 5 vols. apps. ind.

An invaluable source of biographical information and background material on Supreme Court justices and the Court from 1789 to 1978. Each article is signed and contains a "Selected Bibliography" and list of representative opinions. The pieces are scholarly and should provide a good starting point for anyone doing research on the justices and the Court. The appendix includes statistics on age and length of service, as well as lists of acts declared unconstitutional by the Court, and Supreme Court decisions overruled by subsequent decisions. Volume 5 covers the Burger Court, 1969-1978.

2-45   Judicial Conference of the United States. Bicentennial Committee. **Judges of the United States**. 2d ed. Washington, D.C.: Government Printing Office, 1983. 681 pp. tbls. inds.

A biographical directory of judges of the United States from before the adoption of the Constitution to December 31, 1981. Entries provide basic information concerning employment, publications, memberships, and family. Indexes by appointing president and year of appointment provide access to the entries.

Law Teachers and Librarians

2-46   **Biographical Directory of the American Association of Law Libraries**. 4th ed. St. Paul: West, 1984. 170 pp.

A directory of biographical information on American Association of Law Libraries members who responded to a questionnaire from the association. Entries include information on education, professional work experience, and publications.

2-47   **Directory of Law Teachers**. St. Paul: West, 1922- . biennial. inds.

A biographical directory of law teachers that provides vital statistics and data on the faculty members' education, professional career, and publications. Included are lists of law teachers by school and subject area, a list of Canadian law teachers by school, and a directory of law schools in both the United States and Canada.

2-48   **Who's Who in American Law**. 3d ed. Chicago: Marquis Who's Who, 1983. 863 pp. ind.

The third edition of this biographical directory provides information on approximately 20,000 individuals practicing law or working in a variety of law-related fields. This is a reduction from the approximately 34,000 entries included in the second edition, which is reviewed in *ARBA* 81. Nevertheless, this is a valuable source for biographical information on lawyers, judges, deans and faculty of law schools, officials of bar associations, legal historians, and law librarians. The entries are brief and contain data on education, professional experience, professional memberships, and writings. An index by field of practice and area of interest is included. Valuable for any public or academic library.

Lawyers and Law Firms

2-49 **The American Bar, the Canadian Bar, the International Bar.** Minneapolis: Reginald Bishop Forster and Associates, 1918- . annual. ind.

An excellent source for information on individual attorneys and leading law firms. *The American Bar,* according to the foreword "includes only lawyers and law firms in each city as determined by the above-described annual surveys made among leading firms by representatives of the publishers. Its purpose is to make readily and conveniently available to lawyers and their clients everywhere the names and biographical data on lawyers qualified and situated to perform any legal work required." *The Canadian Bar* is compiled using the same criteria. Additional portions of the volume are devoted to attorneys in Mexico and the international bar. Entries for law firms include names and biographical information on members of the firm, as well as areas of specialization, and a list of representative clients. The *American Bar Reference Handbook,* a companion volume, is a condensation of the larger volume and includes abbreviated entries consisting of the firm name, members, location, address, and telephone number.

2-50 **The American Lawyer Guide to Leading Law Firms, 1983-84.** 2d ed. New York: Am-Law, 1983. 2 vols. inds.

A directory which provides information on 240 law firms in twenty-one major U.S. cities. The profiles include data on size, billing rates, and age of partners, as well as information on the history, governance, and structure of the firm, and names of key clients.

2-51 **Directory of the Legal Profession: Major Firms, Specialty Firms, and Corporate Legal Departments.** New York: New York Law, 1984. 1,111 pp. ind.

A directory providing profiles of over six hundred law firms throughout the United States. While the major firm section is limited to firms of at least fifty lawyers, specialty firms of fewer than fifty lawyers have been included when considered prominent. Profiles provide information on the personnel, administration, clients, and areas of specialization of the firms. In addition to the profiles of major firms, similar information is provided in separate sections for selected specialty firms and corporate legal departments. An appendix includes *National Law Journal's Survey of the 250 Largest Law Firms.*

2-52 **The Insurance Bar: A Directory of Eminent Lawyers and the Selective Digest of the Law of Insurance and Related Topics.** Chicago: Bar List, 1926- . annual. ind.

A directory of attorneys specializing in insurance practice. Biographical data includes law school attended and year of admission to practice, as well as insurance specialties, and representative clients. The volume also contains an index of insurers and a digest of state insurance laws.

2-53 **Law and Business Directory of Corporate Counsel.** New York: Harcourt Brace Jovanovich, 1980- . annual. inds.

This title is the most comprehensive directory to the personnel of corporate legal departments available to libraries. The compilation includes names and biographical information on more than 24,000 attorneys in more than 5,000 companies. Including predominantly American companies, there are cross-references between parent companies and subsidiaries, and old and new names. The directory includes indexes by geographic location, individual name, and corporate name. Useful for special libraries requiring a comprehensive listing of corporate legal departments.

2-54 **Law and Business Directory of Major U.S. Law Firms, 1984-85.** Clifton, N.J.: Law and Business/Harcourt Brace Jovanovich, 1984. 2 vols. inds.

A guide to five hundred leading U.S. law firms. Organized geographically, the profiles describe areas of specialization, clients represented, approach to practice, firm organization, and history. The statements, which were furnished by the firms, vary greatly in the amount of data included.

2-55 **Lawyer's Register by Specialties and Fields of Law: A National Directory of Lawyers Listed by Fields of Law.** Solon, Ohio: Lawyer's Register, 1978- . annual.

A biographical directory that organizes attorneys into 191 fields of specialization. Data includes name, address, phone number, and, when available, information on education, work history, and publications. Also included is a section on corporate counsel.

2-56 Lewis, William Draper, ed. **Great American Lawyers.** Philadelphia: John C. Winston, 1907: repr. South Hackensack, N.J.: Rothman Reprints, 1971. 8 vols.

Covering the eighteenth and nineteenth centuries, this reprint of a 1907 biographical encyclopedia includes lengthy biographical sketches on ninety-six prominent judges and lawyers. Biographies include judges like Marshall and Story, and lawyers like Webster and Benjamin, as well as some who never attained national prominence. The entries, written by law professors, justices, and practicing attorneys, also contain portraits.

2-57 **Martindale-Hubbell Law Directory.** Summit, N.J.: Martindale-Hubbell, 1931- . annual.

An annual listing of the Bar of both the United States and Canada. The most comprehensive directory of its kind, it is geographically organized and provides the present address and educational background of each attorney. The more extensive biographical section, which lists subscribers, includes the same information plus a description of the type of practice and clients, and additional personal details. Special sections include the names of lawyers registered to practice Patent Law, a section on foreign attorneys, a digest of the laws of the fifty states, and a digest of the laws of Canada, the Canadian provinces, and other countries of the world. Many Uniform and Model Acts and the texts of International Conventions that the United States has ratified are also reprinted.

2-58   Naifeh, Steven W. and Gregory White Smith. **The Best Lawyers in America.** Vol. 1, New York: Seaview/Putnam, 1983. 248 pp.; Vol. 2, New York: Woodward/White, 1983. 360 pp.

These two volumes represent a nonscholarly attempt at a consumer guide for those selecting an attorney. Entries were obtained by interviewing and soliciting names from prominent attorneys of colleagues they felt were outstanding. They cover a broad range of specialties, from Domestic Relations, Trusts and Estates, and Creditor and Debtors' Rights, to Corporate, Labor, Real Estate, and Tax Law. Each specialty is arranged geographically and the only information provided is the name and address of the attorney.

2-59   **Nelson's Law Office Directory.** Minnetonka, Minn.: Nelson, 1968- .

A directory of U.S. law offices that have been rated highly by attorneys in the area. Arranged by state and city, information includes the name, address, and phone number of the attorney or law firm.

2-60   **Parker Directory of California Attorneys.** Los Angeles: Parker and Son, 1980- . annual.

A popular example of an annual state legal directory, which includes names and addresses for federal, state, and county government officials, officers of professional legal associations, and attorneys and law firms in California. Although most of the information could be obtained from other sources, it provides a handy source of information about the California legal community.

2-61   Tarlow, Barry, ed. **National Directory of Criminal Lawyers.** Los Angeles: University Publishers, 1979. 189 pp. ind.

A directory of criminal lawyers throughout the United States. Organized by state, this biographical directory provides information on the education and professional experience of criminal attorneys. Selection was based upon inquiries sent to over 25,000 criminal defense lawyers throughout the country.

2-62   **United States Lawyers Reference Directory.** Dallas: Legal Directories, 1977- .

Organized by state, this biographical directory provides data on attorneys and law firms who purchased space in the volume. Also included are the names of major state officials, a description of the state and county court systems, and the names of judges and other court personnel. The federal section provides names and addresses for the judicial, executive, and legislative branches of government, as well as independent departments and agencies.

Dictionaries

General/Legal

2-63 Ballentine, James A. **Ballentine's Law Dictionary, with Pronunciations**. 3d ed. Edited by William S. Anderson. Rochester, N.Y.: Lawyers Cooperative, 1969. 1,429 pp. glos.

A standard one-volume legal dictionary defining over 30,000 terms. The definitions are based on the construction of the term by courts of last resort and citations are given to the page of the opinion on which the definition appears. Pronunciation is given for difficult words. A glossary of abbreviations for legal reports, treatises, and phrases is also included.

2-64 Black, Henry C. **Black's Law Dictionary: Definitions of the Terms and Phrases of American and English Jurisprudence, Ancient and Modern.** 5th ed. rev. St. Paul: West, 1979. 1,511 pp. apps. tbls.

Probably the most popular single-volume legal dictionary available. Covering all areas of law, the entries include pronunciation for difficult terms and phrases, case and statutory references as well as references to other West publications. Numerous *see* and *see also* references are included. Of particular value are the table of legal abbreviations and the time chart of the United States Supreme Court, which comprise two of the appendices. Indispensible for any library.

2-65 Gifis, Steven H. **Dictionary of Legal Terms: A Simplified Guide to the Language of Law.** Woodbury, N.Y.: Barron's Educational Series, 1983. 511 pp. app.

A legal dictionary intended for the researcher who requires simple basic definitions for legal terms and phrases. Based on the author's *Law Dictionary* (1975), the definitions have been rewritten in lay terms and citations to authority have been deleted. Examples are provided for many of the definitions, and numerous cross references are included. The appendix, which is entitled "Consumer's Guide to Law and Lawyers," briefly covers such areas as wills, divorce, and buying or selling a home.

2-66 Gordon, Frank S., and Thomas Hemnes, comps. **The Legal Word Book.** Boston: Houghton Mifflin, 1978. 296 pp.

Intended as a guide to the spelling of legal terms and the preparation of legal forms and documents, this dictionary includes 20,000 terms that are in common use but have a specific legal meaning. Each entry divides the word into syllables and indicates which syllables are stressed. Also included is a list of abbreviations for court reports and journals, and a directory that provides addresses for federal courts, U.S. embassies and consulates, and county seats of the states of the United States.

2-67 Hemphill, Charles F., Jr., and Phyllis D. Hemphill. **The Dictionary of Practical Law**. Englewood Cliffs, N.J.: Prentice-Hall, 1979. 231 pp.

Intended for law students, legal secretaries, and students in the administration of justice who need legal definitions in simple, everyday language. Containing approximately 2,500 terms, the dictionary emphasizes new terms used by attorneys and the courts. Latin terms presently being used and selected foreign terms are also defined.

2-68 Oran, Daniel. **Law Dictionary for Non-Lawyers**. St. Paul: West, 1975. 333 pp. bib. apps.

A basic dictionary that provides simple, comprehensive definitions for English and Latin words and phrases. Appendices include a section on additional sources of information, a guide to pronunciation, and a section on "Lawyer Talk," which discusses technical, vague, and worthless words one might encounter when talking to an attorney.

2-69 Osborn, Percy George. **Osborn's Concise Law Dictionary**. 6th ed. London: Sweet and Maxwell, 1976. 396 pp.

The sixth edition of a standard legal dictionary first introduced in 1927. Noted for its precise and concise definitions, this edition has updated and expanded its coverage of constantly changing fields such as family law, commerce, taxation, planning and land use, and criminal law. Also included is a list of law reports and their abbreviations, as well as a table of regnal years of English Sovereigns.

2-70 Rothenberg, Robert E., ed. **The Plain-Language Law Dictionary**. New York: Penguin Books, 1981. 430 pp. app.

A dictionary of over 6,500 legal terms with simple and understandable definitions intended for the layman. Most definitions include capitalized words referring to other entries in the dictionary. No pronunciations are provided, even for the selectively included Latin terms and phrases. The appendix is a collection of data such as marriage and divorce information for each state, names of the federal judiciary, how to become a U.S. citizen, and descriptions of various Social Security programs.

2-71 **Webster's Legal Speller**. Springfield, Mass.: G. and C. Merriam, 1978. 348 pp.

A guide to the spelling and division of about 28,000 legal words and words that occur frequently in legal contexts. Also included are some of the more common British legal terms and historical terms that are likely to be found in older legal reports and records. Intended primarily for legal secretaries, this dictionary is useful for anyone transcribing legal material and who needs to know which variant spelling is the most widely used, whether a compound word is hyphenated or not, and at what point a word may be divided at the end of a line. Also included is a list of abbreviations, and a section on forms of address for federal, state, and local judiciaries.

54 / Selected Legal Reference Sources

2-72   **Words and Phrases.** St. Paul: West, 1940- . 90 vols.

The most comprehensive and detailed of all legal dictionaries, this multi-volume set includes words and phrases which have been defined by state and federal courts since 1658. Breaking broader topics into subheadings, the definitions provide official and unofficial citations to the cases as well as the page on which the definition appears. Updated annually with pocket parts, the set includes numerous *see* and *see also* references. Useful for anyone doing legal research.

Abbreviations

2-73   Bieber, Doris M., comp. **Current American Legal Citations.** With 2,100 examples. Buffalo: William S. Hein, 1983. 342pp.

This dictionary is intended as an aid for lawyers and law students in citing American legal authorities according to the rules stated in *A Uniform System of Citation*. The entire work is arranged in two columns, the left column listing the full name of privately published legal periodicals and legal publications of all U.S. jurisdictions, and the right column providing the corresponding citation form. The citation forms are accompanied by numerous examples, some 2,100 in all.

2-74   Bieber, Doris M., comp. **Dictionary of Legal Abbreviations Used in American Law Books.** 2d ed. Buffalo: William S. Hein, 1985. 490pp.

One of the more helpful tools available for those doing legal research, this dictionary defines abbreviations, acronyms, and symbols found in American legal literature. Containing over 20,000 entries, foreign abbreviations are included when they are frequently used in American legal publications and government documents. Essential for anyone using legal materials.

2-75   Bryson, William H. **Dictionary of Sigla and Abbreviations to and in Law Books before 1607.** Charlottesville, Va.: University Press of Virginia, 1975. 179 pp. glos. ind.

This dictionary is intended as a guide for legal historians and other researchers who come across unfamiliar citations, and includes "Roman law, medieval, civil, canon, and customary law on the continent, and the common law of England up to 1607." Part 1 covers the standard methods of legal citation, and Part 2 is the actual dictionary of sigla and abbreviations. Also included is a glossary of name variations, which gives nicknames, Latin forms of names, various spellings of names, and name changes that popes made upon their election.

2-76   Raistrick, Donald. **Index to Legal Citations and Abbreviations.** Abingdon, Great Britain: Professional Books, 1981. 326 pp.

A comprehensive guide to over 20,000 frequently encountered legal abbreviations and acronyms used in the United Kingdom, the Commonwealth, the United States, and the Common Market countries. Entries provide the dates for law reports and legal treatises as well as the country of origin of the abbreviation if not England or U.K.

Foreign Language

2-77   Anderson, Ralph J.B. **Anglo-Scandinavian Law Dictionary of Legal Terms Used in Professional and Commercial Practice**. Prepared under the auspices of the Royal Norwegian Ministry of Justice. Oslo: Universitetsforlaget; distributed New York: Columbia University Press, 1977. 137 pp.

This dictionary is intended as a quick reference list of current legal terms in the law relating to contractual obligations used in professional and commercial practice. Entries are given in English, Norwegian, Swedish, and Danish. Divided into four parts, one for each language, every entry provides a definition and equivalents in the other three languages. Frequently entries include comments and examples. When no equivalent exists, the absence of an equivalent is indicated. American legal terminology is not included, and English and Scandinavian terms in maritime and criminal law and procedure have been deleted. The introduction includes a brief outline of the civil law system of each of the four countries.

2-78   Beseler, Dora Hedwig von. **Law Dictionary: Technical Dictionary of the Anglo-American Legal Terminology, English-German**. 3d ed. New York: W. de Gruyter, 1976. 888 pp.

The English-German companion to the German-English dictionary published in 1971. Going from English to German, this dictionary attempts to provide German equivalents for major English legal terms. It includes legal terms from all areas of law as well as from the military, tax, customs, insurance, business, finance, and banking. When there is no German equivalent, the author attempts to provide terms that are as nearly equivalent as possible. When concepts exist only in Great Britain or the United States, entries are annotated with a *GB* or *USA*. Numerous examples of current usage are provided as well as variations in spelling and synonyms.

2-79   Egbert, Lawrence D., and Fernando Morales-Macedo. **Multilingual Law Dictionary: English, Francais, Espanol, Deutsch**. Dobbs Ferry, N.Y.: Oceana, 1978. 551 pp. bib. ind. app.

The main portion of this dictionary consists of vertical lists of English legal terms followed by their French, Spanish, and German equivalents. When there is no counterpart in French, German, or Spanish, a brief explanation is provided in each of these languages. Indexes in French, Spanish, and German allow access to the English equivalent when it is unknown. Appendixes include a brief list of English legal terms and their meanings, a bibliography of bilingual and multilingual dictionaries, and a list of members of the United Nations. An update of Egbert's *Law Dictionary* published in 1949, this new edition is intended for interpreters and anyone working with foreign legal terms.

2-80   Gilbertson, Gerard. **Harrap's German and English Glossary of Terms in International Law**. London: Harrap, 1980. 355 pp. ind.

A glossary designed for translators, interpreters, legal experts, and those involved in politics and international business. Divided into three parts, the main portion

56 / Selected Legal Reference Sources

is the German-English section that contains German words and their English equivalents, derived phrases, and contextual examples. Abbreviations are provided for treaties, conventions, and statutes used as sources for the contextual examples. Part 2 is a collection of extracts from a variety of international instruments, and Part 3 is a register of English words and phrases with references to other parts of the glossary.

2-81   Paenson, Issac. **English-French-Spanish-Russian Manual of the Terminology of Public International Law (Law of Peace) and International Organizations.** Brussels: Bruylant for Graduate Institute of International Studies and Intercentre, 1983. 846 pp. inds. bibs.

A monumental manual, which may almost be described as a treatise on international law rather than a dictionary. In attempting to define and explain concepts and themes in international law, Paenson's manual provides synonyms as well as references and cross-references. In addition to the alphabetical index, there are indexes of bi- or multilateral transactions, declarations and resolutions of international organizations, international conferences, cases, and Latin terms.

2-82   Quemner, Thomas A. **Dictionnaire juridique francais-anglais, [anglais-francais].** 6th rev. ed. Paris: Editions de Navarre, 1976. 323 pp.

Divided into both French-English and English-French portions, this dictionary provides meanings for terms commonly used in law, finance, commerce, customs, and insurance. When no exact meaning exists, the entry indicates that the meaning given is the meaning nearest to a term or notion in the other language.

Quotations

2-83   Gerhart, Eugene C. **Quote It! Memorable Legal Quotations: Data, Epigrams, Wit, and Wisdom from Legal and Literary Sources.** New York: C. Boardman, 1969. 766 pp. inds.

A collection of legal quotations from treatises, novels, plays, and judicial decisions. The quotations, organized by broad subject, are indexed by author and key word.

Specialized

2-84   Cartwright, John M. **Glossary of Real Estate Law.** Rochester, N.Y.: Lawyers Co-Operative, 1972. 1,027 pp.

A glossary of real estate terms and legal concepts intended for the person engaged in the real estate business and anyone involved in the sale or purchase of real property. Definitions provide complete citations to cases and *see also* references to related topics in other Lawyers Co-Operative publications.

2-85   **Dictionary of Criminal Justice Data Terminology: Terms and Definitions Proposed for Interstate and National Data Collection and Exchange.** 2d ed. Washington, D.C.: Department of Justice, 1981. 257 pp. bib. app.

A comprehensive dictionary, which provides definitions and descriptive annotations for criminal justice statistical terminology. It is intended as a basic reference work for those involved in compiling and using criminal justice statistics. Included are the specialized vocabularies of national statistical programs as well as technical terms that are not quantitative in nature, but must be understood to interpret data. Entries contain a definition, special defining features, an annotation providing information about usages, related terms, and cross references. Appendixes include a grouping by subject of statistical terms in the dictionary, the Uniform Crime Reports offense categories, and the National Crime Information Center's Uniform Offense Classifications code structure outline. A depository item, which should prove helpful to anyone using criminal justice data.

2-86   Haensch, Günther. **Dictionary of International Relations and Politics.** Munich: Marx Huber Verlag, 1975. 781 pp. ind.

This dictionary is divided into ten parts covering such areas as international law, politics, treaties, courts, and organizations. The terms are organized by topics and subtopics and provide the German, French, Spanish, and English equivalent of the word. Alphabetical indexes are included for each of the four languages, which refer the user to the appropriate page.

2-87   Hieb, Elizabeth A., ed. **Employee Benefit Plans: A Glossary of Terms.** 4th ed. Brookfield, Wis.: International Foundation of Employee Benefit Plans, 1982. 89 pp.

This book is designed as a guide to terminology used in the employee benefit field. It is not intended to be definitive, but only to provide interpretive assistance or act as a resource for terms utilized in a rapidly changing field. It is a useful companion work to Levin's *Guidelines for Ficuciaries of Taft-Hartley Trusts: An ERISA Manual,* discussed in chapter 3 under the topic "Labor Law."

2-88   Jowitt, William Allen, and Clifford Walsh. **Jowitt's Dictionary of English Law.** London: Sweet & Maxwell, 1977. 2 vols. bib.

These two volumes are intended "to provide a really comprehensive lexicon covering English law from earliest times to the present day, giving a definition and an explanation of every legal term old and new." The definitions are lengthy and contain citations to statutes, cases, and legal texts as well as numerous *see* and *see also* references.

2-89   Martin, Julian A. **Law Enforcement Vocabulary.** Springfield, Ill.: Charles C. Thomas, 1973. 255 pp.

Covering the field of criminal justice with emphasis in law enforcement, this alphabetically arranged text includes words, phrases, and slang terms. Legal terms as well as juvenile slang are defined, along with words used in gambling, narcotics, and in jails and penitentiaries. Medical and computer terminology is described along with names of narcotics and drugs. This interesting work, although somewhat dated, should prove useful to police officers, corrections personnel, lawyers, and judges.

2-90   Rice, Michael Downey. **Prentice-Hall Dictionary of Business, Finance, and Law.** Englewood Cliffs, N.J.: Prentice-Hall, 1983. 362 pp.

Intended for both the businessman and the lawyer, this dictionary covers a wide range of subjects falling within the scope of business law. Terms used in corporate law, taxation, contracts, securities regulation, antitrust, bankruptcy, and labor law are defined, and references to periodicals, the Internal Revenue Code, the *IRS Bulletin,* the *CFR, Federal Register,* and the *United States Code* are provided.

2-91 Rush, George E. **Dictionary of Criminal Justice.** Boston: Holbrook Press, 1977. 374 pp.

A dictionary that covers major terms used in law enforcement, courts, probation, parole, and corrections. The preface indicates that the dictionary, while making no attempt to be comprehensive, "combines medical, legal, forensic, sociological, anthropological, psychological, and selected management terms commonly used in the broad, interdisciplinary field of criminal justice." Definitions contain a code referring the user to one of twenty-five other specialized dictionaries, encyclopedias, or treatises. Legal citations are provided selectively, and brief biographies are included. No attempt has been made to provide pronunciation or etymology.

2-92 Vasan, R.S., ed. **Latin Words and Phrases for Lawyers.** New York: Datender S. Sodhi for Law and Business Publications (Canada), 1980. 355 pp. ind.

A one-volume compilation of Latin words, phrases, and maxims that are currently in use or are of historical significance. For most entries, the source of the word, phrase, or maxim is provided. Also included is a cross-reference index, which organizes Latin maxims by subject.

2-93 Williams, Howard R., and Charles J. Meyers. **Oil and Gas Terms: Annotated Manual of Legal Engineering Tax Words and Phrases.** 6th ed. New York: Matthew Bender, 1984. 985pp.

A dictionary of terms for those concerned with any aspect of the oil and gas industry. Intended for engineers, attorneys, accountants, and investors, this glossary provides clear, concise definitions as well as citations to major treatises, articles, statutes, and cases.

Thesaurus

2-94 Burton, William C. **Legal Thesaurus.** New York: Macmillan, 1980. 1,058 pp. ind.

This thesaurus contains "words that are strictly legal, words that are not strictly legal but which are commonly used by members of the legal profession, and those words that are not legal and not widely used by lawyers, but are sufficiently sophisticated to warrant their use by attorneys." The introduction cautions that a wide range of words are included for each term, some of which are not exact synonyms; therefore, use of a legal dictionary in conjunction with the thesaurus is recommended. Entries include associated and foreign phrases when applicable. The tool is valuable for law students and attorneys when writing, doing research, and searching computerized legal databases.

Directories

2-95   **American Bar Association Directory.** Chicago: American Bar Association. annual. inds.

Referred to as the *Redbook,* this directory outlines the organization of the ABA and gives the names of individuals in leadership positions. It also includes a directory of state and local bar associations, and lists of both related and affiliated organizations. Indexing is by name, state, and committee.

2-96   **Civil Rights Directory.** rev. ed. Washington, D.C.: U.S. Commission on Civil Rights, 1981. 549 pp.

A directory of federal, state, and private organizations whose responsibilities are directly related to civil rights. The information provided includes the name of the director, the address, and a brief statement regarding the purpose and responsibilities of the agency. Of particular value is a list of the major civil rights authorities under which the agencies operate.

2-97   **Directory of Juvenile and Adult Correctional Departments, Institutions, Agencies, and Paroling Authorities, United States and Canada.** College Park, Md.: American Correctional Association, 1975/76- . annual. inds.

A directory, which provides ready reference information and an organizational description of the adult and juvenile correctional system of each state, territory, the federal government, and Canada. Included is data on approximately 1,600 institutions involved in correctional service. Although local agencies are not covered, an indication is made when such a service exists. Also included are statistics on such things as recidivism, incarceration by race, sex, and age, and imprisonment rate by geographical area. This directory is one in a series of three published by the ACA. Other titles in the series include the *National Jail and Adult Detention Directory* and the *Probation and Parole Directory.*

2-98   **Directory of Law Libraries.** Chicago: American Association of Law Libraries, 1965- . annual. ind.

The major source for addresses, phone numbers, and names of library personnel for law libraries in the United States. The entries also include job function codes for library staff, and a classification code for the size of the library collection. Additional sections cover Canadian and foreign law libraries. Indexing is provided by personal name.

2-99   **Directory of Law-Related Education Projects.** 4th ed. Chicago: American Bar Association, 1982. 153 pp.

A directory describing over three hundred national and local educational programs predominantly concerned with the study of law and the legal system. The directory is arranged alphabetically by state and includes any local program with more than one teacher. For states with a multitude of programs, entries are limited to centralized projects, which direct one to local programs and to projects that utilize a particularly novel approach. The remainder of the directory describes national law-related educational projects. Each entry includes program sponsor, address, activities, materials that have been developed, publications, and source of funding.

2-100   **Directory of Lawyer Referral Services**. Chicago: American Bar Association, Standing Committee on Lawyer Referral Services. annual.

A geographically organized directory providing the names, addresses, and phone numbers of statewide and county lawyer referral services. A handful of addresses for Canadian referral services are also included.

2-101   **The Directory of Legal Aid and Defender Offices in the United States**. Washington, D.C.: National Legal Aid and Defender Association, 1957- . annual.

Divided into two sections, this directory supplies names, addresses, and phone numbers for approximately 2,600 offices that provide civil legal assistance to persons unable to retain private counsel. Part 1 is organized by state and then city, and part 2 organizes both civil legal services and legal aid offices by specialized area of the law. Also included is a list and brief description of organizations that provide support services to legal aid and defender attorneys.

2-102   **Federal Court Directory**. Washington, D.C.: WANT. annual.

A directory, which provides names, addresses, and phone numbers for the U.S. Supreme Court and lower federal court judges and clerks of the court. There is also a section on state courts that gives the name, address, and phone number for the Chief Justice, the Clerk, and the Court Administrator for the highest court in each state. Part of a three-directory set that includes a *U.S. Government Directory* and a *State-Local Government Directory*.

2-103   **Federal Regulatory Directory**. Washington, D.C.: Congressional Quarterly, 1979/80- . annual.

An excellent general guide to the responsibilities, powers, and authority of federal administrative agencies. Indexed by subject, agency, and personnel, the directory is most helpful in obtaining names, addresses, and ordering information for publications available from the various agencies.

2-104   **Federal Yellow Book**. Washington, D.C.: Washington Monitor, 1976- . Looseleaf for updating.

A comprehensive directory that provides names, addresses, and telephone numbers for over 29,000 employees in the executive branch of the federal government. The looseleaf format allows for updates reflecting major organizational changes.

2-105   **Human Rights Organizations and Periodicals Directory**. 5th ed. Berkeley, Calif.: Meiklejohn Civil Liberties Institute, 1983. 247 pp. inds.

A guide with over seven hundred entries describing human rights organizations and periodicals. The entries chosen are headquartered in the United States and are national in scope. The major portion of the directory is arranged alphabetically and includes an address and descriptive annotation. Subject, periodical, and geographical indexes are included.

2-106   **International Directory of Bar Associations.** 4th ed. Chicago: American Bar Foundation, 1983. 49 pp.

This international directory includes information on seven international bar associations and ninety-one national or regional bar associations. Each entry includes the official name, address, name of the chief executive officer, membership qualifications, total membership, association activities and powers, publications, and affiliations with international bar associations. Generally only national associations are included for each country; however, in a few cases important regional or local associations have been added.

2-107   **Kime's International Law Directory.** London: Kime's International Law Directory, 1892- . annual. app. inds.

A list of attorneys and law firms throughout the world. Organized by continent, country, and then city, the entries provide an address, telephone number, and in some instances a telex number for the attorney or law firm. The appendix includes a brief country-by-country summary of the laws governing enforcement and execution of foreign judgments and an international list of law societies and bar associations.

2-108   **The National Directory: Law Enforcement Administrators, Prosecutors, Correctional Institutions, and Related Agencies.** Milwaukee: National Police Chiefs and Sheriffs Information Bureau, 1965- . annual. ind.

Divided into four sections, this directory provides names, addresses, and telephone numbers for county, municipal, state, and federal officials involved in law enforcement. It includes county sheriffs, county and regional prosecutors, municipal and county police chiefs, state and federal correctional and penal institutions, and the offices of U.S. Attorneys and U.S. Marshalls. A useful directory with broad coverage.

2-109   **The National Directory of State Agencies.** Washington, D.C.: Information Resources Press, 1974/75- . biennial.

This directory organizes state agencies into 102 functional categories, and provides a name, address, and telephone number for each agency. Part 1 organizes the agencies by state, and part 2 organizes them by function. A basic tool for any reference department.

2-110   **Probation and Parole Directory.** College Park, Md.: American Correctional Association, 1981- . biennial. glos. bib.

A sourcebook for data on federal, state, county, and municipal probation and parole services. The directory first presents data on the federal probation system, providing names, addresses, telephone numbers, as well as statistics on salary, personnel, and client caseloads. The state section provides the same information for state, county, and municipal services. The directory also includes a glossary of probation and parole terms as well as policy statements and information on the organizational structure and publications of the American Correctional Association.

62 / Selected Legal Reference Sources

2-111   Tseng, Henry P. **The Law Schools of the World.** Buffalo: William S. Hein, 1977. 419 pp.

A directory that includes basic information on law schools throughout the world. Part 1 of the directory includes a summary of the philosophy and system of legal education of each country included in the volume. Part 2, which is also arranged by country, provides the official title of the school, address, telephone number, degrees offered, information on admission of foreign students, the primary language spoken, the admissions officer, the dean and the law librarian. Although the same information could be obtained from other sources, it could prove to be a handy one-volume source for addresses and background on the systems of legal education throughout the world.

2-112   **United States Court Directory.** Washington, D.C.: Administrative Office of the U.S. Courts, 1979- . semiannual.

A directory that provides the names, addresses, and telephone numbers of justices, judges, clerks, and other key officials of federal courts throughout the United States.

2-113   Wasserman, Paul, and Marech Kasgulski, eds. **Law and Legal Information Directory.** Detroit: Gale Research, 1980- . biennial. inds.

Covering a wide range of organizations and services, this directory includes addresses for federal and state courts, state and local bar associations, legal publishers and periodical publications, and law schools and law libraries. The lengthy introduction describes the methodology and organization of each of the sixteen sections in a fairly detailed manner, and each of the sections contains its own index. Although not comprehensive, this handy directory should prove extremely useful for any library, particularly one without the sources that would provide the same or more complete information.

2-114   **World Legal Directory.** Washington, D.C.: World Peace through Law Center, 1974- .

A directory of judges, lawyers, law professors, law schools, law libraries, and bar associations throughout the world. Information is brief and, in most cases, simply includes an address.

Encyclopedias

2-115   **American Jurisprudence: A Modern Comprehensive Text Statement of American Law, State and Federal.** 2d ed. rev. Rochester, N.Y.: Lawyers Co-Operative, 1962- . 101 vols. bibs. ind. tbls. ill. fms.

This is one of the major legal encyclopedias available to attorneys and other researchers. The set contains an eight-volume general index, which provides subject access to the articles. In addition, each volume has its own index to articles found in that particular volume. Each article has its own table of contents as well as a description of the scope of the topic and cross-references to related topics. While more selective than *Corpus Juris Secundum* in providing citations to relevant cases, the articles provide citations to the annotated reporters (*American Law Reports* and *American Law Reports, Federal*) also published by Lawyers Co-Op. The volumes are updated by pocket parts and new topics are introduced in the "New Topic Service" binder. The *Am Jur 2d Desk Book,* a collection of documents, charts, statistics, and tabulations, accompanies the set.

2-116 **Corpus Juris Secundum: A Complete Restatement of the Entire American Law as Developed by All Reported Cases: 1658 to Date.** St. Paul: West, 1936- . 155 vols. bibs. ind. tbls. ill. fms. pls.

This major legal encyclopedia is part of the West Publishing Company's collection of publications and utilizes the West topics and key numbers also found in their reports and digests. *Corpus Juris Secundum* attempts "to provide a complete encyclopedic treatment of the law, which means that it must be based upon all the reported cases." Therefore, the articles include numerous footnotes, which at times overshadow the text. A five-volume general index and individual indexes for each volume provide access to the articles. Each article contains a description of the scope as well as an analysis of the key numbers within the topic. Legal definitions are also included throughout the set, and each volume contains a list of words, phrases, and maxims defined in that volume. Volumes are updated annually by pocket parts.

2-117 **Encyclopedia of Crime and Justice.** Edited by Sanford H. Kadish. New York: Free Press, 1983. 4 vols. bibs. ind. glos. pls.

This encyclopedia attempts to bring together in one place information on criminal behavior from a variety of disciplines. It covers the nature and causes of crime as well as its prevention and the punishment and treatment of offenders. Intended for the professional and the lay user alike, the signed articles are written by sociologists, law professors, criminologists, and attorneys. Articles provide complete citations to cases and statutes, and contain bibliographies of primary and secondary sources. The first volume includes a "Guide to Legal Citations" and a list of legal abbreviations accompanied by the full title and a brief explanation. Volume 4 contains a table of cases, an index by legal document, and a general index by name and subject.

2-118 **The Guide to American Law: Everyone's Legal Encyclopedia.** St. Paul: West, 1983- . 12 vols. (in progress) pls. apps. inds. bibs.

This is one of the first legal encyclopedias intended for nonlawyers. Covering over 5,000 subjects, the articles discuss major principles and concepts in American law. Also included in the set are discussions of important acts, landmark cases, and biographies of prominent individuals. The articles are written in plain English and provide complete citations to cases and statutes. Well illustrated throughout and containing numerous sample forms, the articles include definitions, bibliographies, and cross-references. Each volume has its own set of appendixes, which index sample forms, special topics, quotations, names, and subjects found in the volume. A good starting point for the nonlawyer to begin research.

2-119   **Lawyers' Medical Cyclopedia of Personal Injuries and Allied Specialties.** 3d ed. Indianapolis: A. Smith, 1981- . 9 vols. apps. bibs. glos. inds. pls. tbls.

An encyclopedia intended "to bridge the gap between medicine and the law of personal injury." While making no claim to cover the entire field of medicine, the authors have included those medical topics that most frequently arise in litigation. Articles cover orthopedic, surgical, neurosurgical, psychiatric, and related topics and provide basic medical information. Each volume contains its own glossary and index, and each article includes an annotated bibliography of medical and legal references. A master index provides detailed indexing to the entire set.

2-120   **Modern Legal Systems Cyclopedia.** Edited by Kenneth Robert Redden. Buffalo: William S. Hein, 1984- . 10 vols. (in progress) bibs. illus. apps. figs. tbls.

When completed, this ten-volume set will provide an introduction to the major legal systems of the world. This encyclopedia will describe legal education, professional practice, the system of government, and the substantive and procedural law of each country. Intended as a standard reference work for members of the legal profession, it is also suitable for political scientists, historians, and public policy and foreign affairs specialists. Volume 1 covers North America. When published, other volumes will cover Western Europe, Eastern Europe, Central American and the Caribbean, Africa, South America, Asia and the Pacific Basin. Each chapter contains an annotated bibliography for additional reading and each volume will be kept up-to-date by supplements.

Formbooks and Style Manuals

2-121   **Texas Law Review Manual on Style.** 3d ed. Austin, Tex.: Texas Law Review, 1970. 50 pp.

A guide to legal style providing rules for capitalization, grammar, punctuation, and spelling. No index is included; however, the table of contents is fairly detailed.

2-122   **A Uniform System of Citation.** 13th ed. Cambridge, Mass.: Harvard Law Review Association, 1981. 237 pp. ind.

The major source for basic rules of legal citation. The first section includes general rules of citation and style, the second section includes technical rules for citing cases, statistics, and periodicals, and the third section, which is arranged by country and state, lists reporters, codes, and session laws, and gives their abbreviations. For basic rules on punctuation, capitalization, and other questions of style, the editors refer the user to the U.S. Government Printing Office *Style Manual,* and for grammar to H.W. Fowler's *Modern English Usage.*

2-123   United States. Government Printing Office. **Style Manual.** Washington, D.C.: Government Printing Office, 1984. 479 pp. ind.

A style manual intended to dictate the form and style to be used in government publications. While chiefly a GPO printer's stylebook, the manual contains chapters on style and form for court work as well as more common government publications.

2-124 Wydick, Richard C. **Plain English for Lawyers.** Durham, N.C.: Carolina Academic Press, 1979. 91 pp. ind.

Both a discussion and collection of exercises to introduce lawyers to the elements of "plain English style." Topics covered include verbose word clusters, redundant legal phrases, and adjective-adverb mania.

Guides to Legal Information

Government Publications and the Legislative Process

1-125 D'Aleo, Richard J. **Fedfind: Your Key to Finding Federal Government Information.** Springfield, Va.: ICUC Press, 1982. 278 pp. ind. ill.

This guide to information leads the user to sources of information about the organization, personnel, activities and programs of the federal government. It is organized by subject and describes and provides ordering information for approximately seven hundred publications and services. Part 1, which is devoted to the organization of the federal government, describes the major directories and biographical sources available. Part 2, which is organized by branch of government, lists basic publications available from and concerning each branch. Part 3 deals with the major publishers of government publications and services. Appendixes provide descriptions of database sources, telephone contacts for federal agencies with major statistical programs, and a list of the addresses and telephone numbers for sources of information. A helpful guide for the layman needing a place to start in obtaining information from or about the federal government.

2-126 Folsom, Gwendolyn B. **Legislative History: Research for the Interpretation of Laws.** Charlottesville, Va.: University Press of Virginia, 1972. 136 pp. ind.

An introductory manual, intended primarily for law students, which documents the legislative process and presents a step-by-step method of research in federal legislative history. Special sections treat federal tax laws, constitutional provisions, and treaties.

2-127 Goehlert, Robert. **Congress and Law-Making: Researching the Legislative Process.** Santa Barbara, Calif.: Clio Books, 1979. 168 pp. ill. tbls. figs. apps. ind.

This legal research guide is designed to help individuals trace legislation and familiarize themselves with major resources for finding information about Congress. Chapters explore the legislative process, researching Congress and legislators, and tracing legislation. Appendixes list methods for citing government publications and major depository libraries.

2-128 Morehead, Joe. **Introduction to United States Public Documents**. 3d ed. Littleton, Colo.: Libraries Unlimited, 1983. 309 pp.

A general introduction to basic public documents emanating from the federal government. This text is not an exhaustive list of titles of government publications, but a discussion of major sources in selected categories. Topics include the Government Printing Office, the depository library system, and the publications of all three branches of the government and independent agencies.

2-129 Schmeckebier, Lawrence F., and Roy B. Eastin. **Government Publications and Their Use**. 2d ed. rev. Washington, D.C.: Brookings Institution, 1969. 502 pp. ind. ill.

A classic guide to the use of government documents. Chapters cover such areas as indexes, congressional publications, federal and state laws, court decisions, and presidential papers. Although dated, it can prove helpful for historical research involving government documents. A detailed index aids in accessing information in the body of the book.

2-130 Zwirn, Jerrold. **Congressional Publications: A Research Guide to Legislation, Budgets, and Treaties**. Littleton, Colo.: Libraries Unlimited, 1983. 195 pp. inds.

This volume is a research guide to the legislative process and the enormous number of publications emanating from Congress. The first few chapters describe the legislative setting and process from the perspective of the publications resulting at each step of the way. Other chapters deal with congressional committee publications, publications resulting from the federal budget process, and publications relevant when doing research on U.S. treaties. An appendix lists Senate and House committees, the dates they were created and subsequent history, and the Superintendent of Documents classification number for the committee. A valuable source for anyone doing legislative research, and an important tool for any reference department.

Courts

2-131 Baum, Lawrence. **The Supreme Court**. 2d ed. Washington, D.C.: Congressional Quarterly, 1985. 270pp. bib. glos. ind.

This work describes the basic processes of the Supreme Court, and serves as a useful companion volume to *Congressional Quarterly's Guide to the U.S. Supreme Court*. Topics covered include the selection of justices, cases before the Court, and the decision making process. The text is followed by a glossary of legal terms, a list of court nominations, a selected bibliography, and an index of cases.

2-132 **Congressional Quarterly's Guide to the U.S. Supreme Court**. Washington, D.C.: Congressional Quarterly, 1979. 1,022 pp. illus. ind. app. glos.

The most extensive of all Congressional Quarterly's volumes on the Supreme Court, this volume discusses the origin and development of the Court, and the Court's interpretation of concepts such as due process, equal protection, and the right of political participation. The biographical section profiles past and present members of the Court, and the section on major decisions summarizes in a straightforward, simple manner major decisions from 1790 to 1979. The articles are well documented with numerous footnotes and a selected bibliography for additional reading. The appendixes include a list of the Acts of Congress held unconstitutional, Rules of the Supreme Court, and a glossary of legal terms. Both a subject and case index allow access to all references on a topic or a particular case throughout the entire volume. A comprehensive and valuable volume for students and the general public.

2-133   Greenberg, E.B. **The Layman's Guide to Legal Terminology and Documents.** 2d ed. Minneapolis: Burgess, 1978. 180 pp. glos. fms.

This guide for the layman contains charts and general descriptions for both state and federal judicial systems as well as simple definitions for a wide range of legal terms and phrases. Each of the twelve chapters deals with a specific topic, first defining relevant terms and then providing sample documents. Valuable for the layman who needs basic definitions and wants to see a sample bill or sale, subpoena for deposition, or power of attorney.

2-134   Klein, Fannie J. **Federal and State Court Systems—A Guide.** Cambridge, Mass.: Ballinger, 1977. 303 pp. apps. glos. ind.

A guide to federal and selected state courts. The text contains numerous statistics and tables on the courts and each chapter is followed by a brief bibliography.

Legal Careers

2-135   **Directory of Legal Employers.** New Orleans: National Association for Law Placement, 1979- . annual. ind.

A directory of over one thousand law firms, corporations, accounting firms, government agencies, insurance companies, banks, public interest organizations, and other legal employers. Reproducing the data supplied on questionnaires, the entries provide information on areas of specialization, salaries, benefits, and hiring policies.

2-136   Harris, Fabia, ed. **The Washington Want Ads: A Guide to Legal Careers in the Federal Government.** rev. ed. Chicago: American Bar Association, Law Student Division, 1980. 170 pp.

A guide, which provides descriptions of legal jobs found in all three branches and the multitude of independent agencies of the federal government. Included in the job description is information on the number of attorneys employed, qualifications, nature of the work, and promotion potential.

Guides to Legal Research

2-137   Bander, Edward J., and David F. Bander. **Legal Research and Education Abridgement: A Manual for Law Students, Paralegals, and Researchers.** Cambridge, Mass.: Ballinger, 1978. 214 pp. ind. bib. app.

A research guide intended to simplify legal research for the law student, paralegal, and layman. Part 1 covers basic research techniques and introduces the researcher to citation style, legal encyclopedias, dictionaries, reports, statutes, periodicals, and legal treatises. Part 2 is broken down by legal topic and includes bankruptcy, civil, consumer, family, labor, securities, and urban law. The appendix includes sample pages, a legal research checklist, and a section on how to find U.S. Statutes and U.S. Code citations.

2-138   Coco, Al. **Finding the Law: A Workbook on Legal Research for Laypersons.** Denver: Bureau of Land Management, Branch of Survey and Mapping Development, Denver Service Center, 1982. 272 pp. ind. pls. ill.

This workbook is intended primarily for boundary survey personnel and others in government service exposed to the law, but who do not have a legal background. It should, however, prove helpful to anyone required to do legal research. Emphasis is on federal law, and sources not typically found in a small- to medium-sized law library have purposely been omitted. Covering statutory law, case law, reports, and "finding tools," each section includes illustrations and exercises.

2-139   Cohen, Morris L. **Legal Research in a Nutshell.** 4th ed. St. Paul: West, 1985. 452pp. ind. apps.

Intended as a concise introduction to legal bibliography, this "Nutshell" makes no claim to being as comprehensive as Price and Bittner's *Effective Legal Research,* Jacobstein and Mersky's *Fundamentals of Legal Research,* or Cohen and Berring's *How to Find the Law.* Much bibliographic detail has been omitted, and instead the reader finds simple and concise descriptions of major legal sources and basic legal research methods. The introduction includes a basic discussion of primary and secondary materials as well as citations to other aids to legal research. Appendixes include a list of state research guides, looseleaf services, and a listing of the current status of major official state reports.

2-140   Cohen, Morris L., and Robert C. Berring. **How to Find the Law.** 8th ed. St. Paul: West, 1983. 790 pp. bib. ind. ill. apps.

A comprehensive guide to legal bibliography intended for the first year law student. Each section includes numerous footnotes and suggested readings for further research. Chapters include background information as well as discussion of the major sources accompanied by sample pages. Appendixes include a list of state guides to legal research and a list of primary legal sources for each state.

2-141   Elias, Stephen. **Legal Research: How to Find and Understand the Law.** Berkeley, Calif.: NOLO Press, 1982. 229 pp. ind. ill.

Written by a lawyer in a simple and straightforward manner, this work seeks to provide the layman with background and to enable him to conduct research into the law on almost any subject. It begins with an overview of legal research, and then proceeds with a more detailed, step-by-step discussion of various aspects of the research process.

2-142   Hodes, W. William. **Legal Research: A Self-Teaching Guide to the Law Library.** St Paul: National Institute for Trial Advocacy, 1983. 184 pp. ill.

Selected Legal Reference Sources / 69

Divided into six "tours," this guide is intended as a self-paced study guide for law students, but could be used by paralegals and legal secretaries. The "tours" cover case law, statutes, Shepard's Citators, administrative law, and legislative history. After each tour, the author includes a brief summary of the materials covered and review exercises. A teacher's manual accompanies the guide.

2-143 Jacobstein, J. Myron, and Roy M. Mersky. **Fundamentals of Legal Research.** 3d ed. Mineola, N.Y.: Foundation Press, 1985. 717pp. apps. ill. ind. bib.

A comprehensive guide to legal research, which describes the major tools in law and provides numerous illustrations. Designed as a basic text for students learning to do legal research, it discusses a wide range or sources from court reports, digests, and legislative histories to administrative law sources, Shepard's Citations, and various looseleaf services. Additional chapters cover international law, English law, and federal tax research. Appendixes include a table of legal abbreviations, a list of state guides to legal research, and a list of reporter services arranged by law school course.

2-144 Lewis, Alfred J. **Using American Law Books.** Dubuque, Iowa: Kendall/Hunt, 1983. 171 pp. tbls. ill. apps. ind.

A beginner's manual to legal research. Each discussion of the various types of legal tools includes step-by-step instructions. The author tries not to overwhelm the layman with detail, but to provide a basic framework for research. The main chapters cover cases, codes, and legal commentaries. The fourth chapter covers automated legal research and a general discussion of research strategy. Sample pages are included throughout, and each chapter contains a detailed outline.

2-145 Lloyd, David. **Finding the Law: A Guide to Legal Research.** Dobbs Ferry, N.Y.: Oceana, 1974. 119 pp. apps. bibs.

This guide should prove useful to nonlawyers and first-year law students. It is intended for use with another volume of Oceana's Legal Almanac Series by Roy M. Mersky, *Law Books for Non-Law Libraries and Laymen: A Bibliography*, Legal Almanac Series No. 44, 1969.

The text is broken down into five chapters: the legal system, case law research, statutory research, persuasive or secondary legal authority, and research in specific areas of law. A useful set of appendixes describe such matters as law libraries, legal citations, legal abbreviations, and legal almanacs.

2-146 Lowe, David, and Annette Jones Watters. **Legal Research for Educators.** Bloomington, Ind.: Phi Delta Kappa, 1984. 48 pp.

This booklet, written by two librarians, is designed to assist educators without legal training in utilizing law libraries and other libraries with legal reference materials.

2-147 Price, Miles O., Harry Bitner, and Shirley Raissi Bysiewicz. **Effective Legal Research.** Boston: Little, Brown, 1979. 4th ed. 643 pp. apps. ill. ind. bib.

A guide to major sources used in legal research. Chapters cover major law reports, legal encyclopedias, dictionaries, periodicals, and looseleaf services. The fourth edition includes new chapters on Australian, New Zealand, and South African legal materials, as well as international law and automated legal research. Appendixes include a standard form for an appellate brief, a sample memorandum, and a list of Anglo-American legal abbreviations.

2-148   Quattrochi, Joseph A. **Federal Tax Research**. New York: Harcourt Brace Jovanovich, 1982. 210 pp. ind.

A guide to the legal research process when applied to federal tax questions. Intended for the accountant as well as the lawyer, the text includes discussion of research techniques and sample exercises and discussion questions.

2-149   Rezny, Arthur A., and M. Vance Sales. **The Educator in the Law Library**. Danville, Ill.: Interstate, 1982. 3d ed. 69 pp. glos. bib.

Intended for educators and graduate students in education, this book illustrates, explains, and provides exercises on the use of major legal resources. This is a particularly good source for anyone interested in a brief introduction to materials required for conducting educational legal research.

2-150   Rombauer, Marjorie Dick. **Legal Problem Solving: Analysis, Research, and Writing**. 4th ed. St. Paul: West, 1983. 424 pp. ind. apps. ill. tbls.

This text is part of West's American Casebook Series and is intended to provide first-year law students with "a functional introduction to the analysis, research, and writing incident to research-oriented problem solving." The author has, however, written and organized the casebook so that it is also useful for the paraprofessional. Part 1 deals with interpreting and predicting the common law and construing written law. Emphasis is placed on the skills required to utilize primary and secondary authority. Part 2 describes basic legal sources and computer-assisted legal research. Of particular value is the discussion of query formulation and when to use a computer-assisted legal research system. Part 3 deals with the preparation of both written reports and oral arguments. The appendixes provide sample opinions, office memorandums, and a summary of an oral argument.

2-151   Stromme, Gary L. **Basic Legal Research Techniques**. 4th ed. rev. San Mateo, Calif.: American Law Publishing Service, 1979. 135 pp. bib. ind. apps.

A basic guide to legal research methods. Chapters cover both primary and secondary sources. The chapter on administrative law has been enlarged in the fourth edition, and an entire chapter has been devoted to various approaches to, and use of the West Key Number System. Appendices include formats for one-question and multi-question memoradums, a citation form and spacing guide, and a list of state statutory codifications.

2-152   Wren, Christopher G., and Jill Robinson Wren. **The Legal Research Manual: A Game Plan for Legal Research and Analysis**. Madison, Wis.: A-R Editions, 1983. 197 pp. ill. apps. ind. bib.

This book, which is divided into three parts, exemplifies the philosophy that a legal research guide should explain when each type of legal resource should be used rather than the kinds of research materials available. Part 1 explores a framework for understanding the law, explains citations, and demonstrates the importance of factual organization and issue identification. Part 2 explains the mechanics and details of the legal research process. Part 3, consisting of appendixes, provides information on particular resources available in legal research. Although intended primarily for law students, it should prove valuable to paralegals and legal secretaries. The primary value of this work is its theme: successful legal research is the result of an organized approach that involves breaking legal research projects into their component parts.

Handbooks and Manuals

2-153 **American Jurisprudence, Desk Book.** 2d ed. rev. Rochester, N.Y.: Lawyers Co-Operative, 1979. 848 pp. ind. tbls.

This desk book is a collection of charts, historical and legal documents, and statistics of interest to the practicing attorney. Designed as part of the publisher's Total Client-Service, the references in this volume refer the user to articles in *Am. Jur. 2d* and other units of the service. Updated by annual pocket parts, the desk book is a convenient source of information on state statutes, uniform acts, crime and prison statistics, and state government.

2-154 Arbuckle, J. Gordon, et al. **Environmental Law Handbook.** 7th ed. Rockville, Md.: Government Institutes, 1983. 507 pp. ns. ind.

Although intended for non-lawyers who are involved in administering environmental laws and regulations, environmentalists and others will find this book useful. Chapter 1 explains the fundamentals of environmental law, chapter 2 explains the National Environmental Policy Act (NAPA), and succeeding chapters analyze water, air, land use, pesticides, toxic substances, and noise pollution.

2-155 Cummings, Frank. **Capitol Hill Manual.** 2d ed. Washington, D.C.: Bureau of National Affairs, 1984. 318 pp. ind. glos. app.

A manual on legislative technique that describes Congressional rules and customs. Topics covered include an outline of the legislative process, techniques of drafting a piece of legislation, an analysis of congressional power centers, the congressional budget process, and nonlegislative matters such as the structure of a Congressman's office and his relationship with lobbyists and the Administration. The appendixes include the rules of both the Senate and the House of Representatives. This volume could prove valuable to anyone doing legislative research.

2-156 Duhl, Stuart, ed. **The Bar Examiners Handbook.** 2d ed. Chicago: National Conference of Bar Examiners, 1980. 443 pp. bib.

A useful handbook for determining each state's requirements for admission to the bar. The bulk of the text, which describes various portions of the exam and the grading system, was previously printed in *The Bar Examiner.* Also included is an annotated bibliography of law review articles on admission to the bar, a digest of

72 / Selected Legal Reference Sources

cases related to admission to practice law, and summaries of state procedures relating to admission to practice law.

2-157 **The Lawyer's Almanac: A Cornucopia of Information about Law, Lawyers, and the Profession.** New York: Law and Business, 1984. 1,022 pp. figs. tbls.

This compilation of associated facts, figures, names, and addresses covers a broad range of topics related to law and the legal profession. Divided into five major groups: 1. the Legal Profession, 2. the Judiciary, 3. government departments, 4. statutory summaries, 5. texts of selected statutes. The volume gives statistics and other information about law schools, law firms, state and federal courts, bar associations, and federal and state governments. Although the preface indicates that the information has been taken from other reference sources and not independently verified, this volume should prove valuable for any reference department.

2-158 **Lawyer's Desk Book.** 6th ed. Englewood Cliffs, N.J.: Institute for Business Planning, 1980. 650 pp. ind. tbls. fig. app.

Intended for the practitioner, this one-volume handbook may also prove useful for anyone requiring definitions of business-related legal terms. Arranged alphabetically by broad legal topic, the volume contains a detailed index and numerous references from one section to another. The appendix provides citations to state Blue Sky Laws, and a state guide to interest rates and attachments. Of particular interest to laymen are portions of the appendix that demonstrate how compounding interest builds an estate, and various interest and discount tables.

2-159 Philo, Harry M. **Lawyer's Desk Reference: Technical Sources for Conducting a Personal Injury Action.** 6th ed. Rochester, N.Y.: Lawyers Co-Operative, 1979. 2 vols. app. inds.

L.D.R. is intended primarily for lawyers, experts, and paralegals involved in the law of damages. However, as its introduction indicates, it could prove useful for safety and design specialists involved in accident and injury prevention, and for those in the insurance industry involved in evaluating the liability of their insured. Covering a wide range of topics from farm injury and railroad accident investigations to hazardous automobile design, it also has a section on safety standards and codes that describes the publications of groups responsible for writing safety codes and standards. Bibliographies refer the reader to related topics in other Lawyers Co-Operative publications.

2-160 Robinson, Joan. **An American Legal Almanac: Law in All States: Summary and Update.** Dobbs Ferry, N.Y.: Oceana, 1978. 439 pp. apps. fig. tbls.

This almanac is intended as an update for all the legal almanacs in the publisher's Legal Almanac Series. The appendix at the end of the volume relates information in the body of the almanac to specific chapters in the approximately seventy volumes of the series. Divided into four broad categories, the almanac summarizes state statutes in numerous areas such as family law, commercial law, landlord-tenant law, consumer and criminal law. While not dealing with any of the topics in depth, the volume should prove useful for ready reference questions.

2-161   Sen, Biswanath. **A Diplomat's Handbook of International Law and Practice.** 2d ed. rev. The Hague: Martinus Nijhoff, 1979. 529 pp. ind. bib. tbl.

Intended as an overview of "the law and practice with regard to some of the matters which do from time to time arise in the work of a Foreign Service Officer." Topics covered include diplomatic and consular functions, immunities, and privileges; and selected topics in international law such as asylum and extradition, treaty making, and diplomatic protection of citizens abroad. The appendixes contain extracts from both the Vienna Convention on Diplomatic Relations (1961) and the Vienna Convention on Consular Relations (1963) as well as a bibliography and a list of agreements, treaties, and conventions.

2-162   **Shepard's Acts and Cases by Popular Names: Federal and State.** 2d ed. Colorado Springs, Colo.: Shepard's, 1979. 1,373 pp.

A listing by the commonly known or popularly known names for federal and state acts and cases. Under the popular names, citations are provided to the *United States Code* and *United States Statutes at Large* or the official and unofficial reporter in which the decision in a particular case may be found. Updated periodically with cumulative supplements.

2-163   Tennenhouse, Dan J. **Attorneys Medical Deskbook.** 2d ed. Rochester, N.Y.: Lawyers Co-Operative, 1983. 2 vols. ind. figs. fms. tbls. ill.

Intended as a tool for attorneys, the legal researcher should find this two-volume work helpful in dealing with medical terms, medical records, and medical literature. While defining medical terms in a simple, straightforward manner, it also explains medical abbreviations, provides sample medical records and forms, and abstracts major texts found in most medical libraries. Also included is an "Attorney's Drug Finder" which is a comprehensive list of drugs by brand with generic and family names and information about the drug's actions and uses. Numerous cross references are provided as well as references to related topics in other Lawyers Co-Operative publications. The set is updated by cumulative supplements.

2-164   **United Nations Juridical Yearbook.** New York: United Nations, 1962- . annual.

This yearbook includes material of a legal character concerning the United Nations and related organizations. The first two chapters include legislative texts and treaty provisions dealing with the legal status of the United Nations. Chapter 3 provides an overview of the legal activities of the United Nations, and chapter 4 includes treaties concerning international law that have been concluded that year. The final portion is a bibliography of legal monographs and articles published by the U.N. during that year.

2-165   **United States Government Manual.** Washington, D.C.: Office of the Federal Register, 1946- . annual. apps. ind.

The official manual of the federal government, this basic reference source provides organizational charts, descriptions, names, and addresses for agencies, departments, boards, committees, and commissions in all branches of the government. Appendixes of particular value include a list of agencies and functions that have been abolished, transferred or changed names, commonly used abbreviations and acronyms, and agencies appearing in the *Code of Federal Regulations*. Indexing is by subject, name, and agency. Essential for any library.

2-166 **United States Supreme Court Reports, Lawyers' Edition, Second Series Desk Book.** Rochester, N.Y.: Lawyer's Co-Operative, 1978. 556 pp. inds. tbls.

A one-volume guide to the Supreme Court decisions found in *United States Supreme Court Reports, Lawyer's Edition, Second Series* and to annotations on federal subjects found in either *L Ed 2d* or *ALR Federal*. Sections of the desk book include a table of cases, Supreme Court justices as well as a table of federal laws, rules, and regulations cited and construed by the Supreme Court. The major portion of the volume is a subject index to cases and annotations. Updated by annual cumulative supplements.

2-167 Walker, David M. **The Oxford Companion to Law.** New York: Oxford University Press, 1980. 1,366 pp. bib. apps.

A one-volume compilation of information about legal institutions, courts, judges, legal systems, ideas, concepts, and doctrines. The author intended this work not only for a "reader of legal literature but readers in other disciplines and indeed any person whose work and reading in any way touches on legal matters. . . ." Entries provide concise treatments of terms, people, and concepts with occasional references to further reading. Appendixes include a list of British office holders since 1660, and a bibliographical note, which organizes additional sources by general topic.

3 SELECTED SUBJECT BIBLIOGRAPHY OF LAW-RELATED MONOGRAPHS

Comments

In this chapter we have collected an array of scholarly, explanatory, and introductory books on legal matters published within the last fifteen years. The annotations are descriptive and evaluative in nature, and out-of-print and reprinted publications have been included. Some of the works are dated, but still represent the best source.

The subject headings we have adopted are taken from a variety of sources and reflect a compromise best suited to general legal research. We have refined and blended terminology used by the Library of Congress[1] by employing terms found in resources such as H.W. Wilson's *Index to Legal Periodicals*[2] and Information Access Corporation's *Current Law Index* and *Legal Resource Index*;[3] and in legal bibliographies such as the Association of American Law Schools' *Law Books Recommended for Libraries*[4] and the American Bar Association's *Recommended Law Books.*[5] Where appropriate, we have used common terminology to permit easy and unencumbered access by the reader. Every effort was made to include as expansive a subject listing as possible in order to reflect the scope of the writings available.

We have also utilized a good number of *see* references, which refer the reader from the more specific legal terminology to a more general subject heading. It is our desire not to be overly simplistic in our approach to legal literature, but to provide researchers with easy subject access to the material, which in turn should familiarize them with the more commonly used legal terminology. We want to stress that only *see* references have been used.

While researching this chapter, we discovered a number of self-help legal publishers or distributors. The more widely known include The American Civil Liberties Union, Do-It-Yourself Legal Publishers, EXPRESS, HALT, NOLO Press, Oceana (Legal Almanacs), WANT, and West (*Nutshells*). The addresses and telephone listings of these publishers may be found in appendix B. Although West publishes *Nutshells* for use primarily by law students and lawyers, these monographs are included as self-help materials since interested individuals may find them useful for learning general legal concepts on any given number of legal subjects. Selected *Nutshells* have been annotated and may be found throughout this chapter under the appropriate subject headings. What we must conclude from our efforts is that legal literature of general interest includes a limited, but popular and marketable, range of subjects.

Finally, in addition to other sources, the following bibliographic resources were most utilized in searching for the books included in this chapter:

> *Bibliographic Guide to Law.* Boston: G.K. Hall, 1969- . Called *Law Book Guide* before 1975.
>
> *Books in Print.* New York: R.R. Bowker, 1948- . Annual publication with bimonthly issues of *Forthcoming Books.*
>
> Buckwalter, Robert L., ed. and comp. *Law Books Published.* Dobbs Ferry, N.Y.: Glanville, 1969- . Updates *Law Books in Print.*
>
> *Law Books,* 1876-1981. 4 vols. New York: R.R. Bowker, 1981.
>
> *Law Information . . .* New York: R.R. Bowker, 1982- . Annual publication continuing *Law Books,* 1876-1981. Kept up-to-date by *Bowker's Law Books and Serials Update,* a companion service issued ten times a year and called *Law Information Update* before 1984.

Notes

[1] Library of Congress, Subject Cataloging Division, *Library of Congress Subject Headings,* 9th ed., 2 vols. (Washington, D.C.: Cataloging Distribution Service, 1980). Updated by cumulative quarterly supplements with annual supplementation.

[2] *Index to Legal Periodicals* (New York: H.W. Wilson, 1908-). Published monthly, except September, with bound cumulation each year.

[3] *Current Law Index* (Belmont, Calif.: Information Access Company, 1980-). Published in eight monthly issues, three quarterly cumulations and an annual cumulation. *Legal Resource Index* is a companion microfilm service.

[4] *Law Books Recommended for Libraries,* 6 vols. Littleton, Colo.: Fred B. Rothman, 1967-). Supplements 1973-76.

[5] Sloan, Richard, ed. *Recommended Law Books* (Chicago: American Bar Association, Committee on Business Law Libraries, 1969).

Outline of Subject Headings*

Abortion and Birth Control
Accounting
Administrative Law
Admiralty
Adoption. *See* Domestic Relations
Affirmative Action. *See* Labor Law
Aged
Agency and Partnership
Air and Space Law
Alcohol. *See* Drugs
Aliens. *See* Immigration Law
Animal Law
Antitrust. *See* Trade Regulation
Arbitration. *See* Labor Law
Architecture. *See* Construction Law
Arrest. *See* Criminal Law
Associations. *See* Corporations
Atomic Energy. *See* Nuclear Energy
Attorney and Client
Authors
Automation
Automobiles. *See* Motor Vehicles

Bankruptcy
Banks and Banking
Bar Associations
Book Trade. *See* Publishers and Publishing
Business Enterprises. *See* Corporations

Cars. *See* Motor Vehicles
Child Abuse. *See* Juveniles
Children. *See* Juveniles
Cities and Counties. *See* Municipal Corporation Law
Civil Procedure
Civil Rights
Colleges and Universities. *See* Schools
Commercial Law
Community Property. *See* Domestic Relations
Comparative Law
Computers. *See* Automation; Intellectual and Industrial Property

Condominiums. *See* Property
Confidential Communications—Clergy
Conflict of Laws
Conscientious Objectors
Constitutional Law
Construction Law
Consumer Credit
Consumer Protection
Contracts
Copyright. *See* Intellectual and Industrial Property
Corporations
Corporations—Nonprofit
Corrections. *See* Prisons and Prisoners
Courts
Crime Prevention. *See* Criminal Law
Criminal Justice
Criminal Law
Criminal Procedure. *See* Criminal Law
Critically Ill
Custody. *See* Domestic Relations

Damages. *See* Torts
Defamation
Descent and Distribution. *See* Estates
Developmentally Disabled. *See* Handicapped
Discrimination. *See* Civil Rights
Displacement. *See* Eminent Domain
Dissolution. *See* Domestic Relations
Divorce. *See* Domestic Relations
Domestic Relations
Drugs

Education. *See* Schools
Elderly. *See* Aged
Elections
Eminent Domain
Employer and Employee. *See* Labor Law
Energy Law. *See* Natural Resources Law
Environmental Law
Equal Employment. *See* Labor Law

---

*This includes all subject headings following in this chapter.

78 / Selected Subject Bibliography of Law-related Monographs

Estates
Evidence
Executors and Administrators. *See* Estates

Family Law. *See* Domestic Relations
Firearms
Foreign Law. *See* Comparative Law
Freedom of (—). *See* Constitutional Law
Freedom of Information Act

Gay Rights. *See* Civil Rights
Government—Federal and State
Guns. *See* Firearms; Self-Defense

Habeas Corpus. *See* Criminal Law
Handicapped
Historic Preservation Law
Homosexuality. *See* Civil Rights
Hospitals. *See* Medicine
Hotels. *See* Innkeepers
Human Experimentation
Husband and Wife. *See* Domestic Relations

Immigration Law
Income Tax. *See* Taxation
Individual Retirement Accounts
Innkeepers
Insurance
Intellectual and Industrial Property
International Law

Journalists. *See* Authors
Judges
Judges—Biography
Judgments. *See* Civil Procedure
Jurisprudence
Juveniles

Labor Law
Labor Unions. *See* Labor Law
Land Use—Planning
Landlord and Tenant
Law
Law—Philosophy. *See* Jurisprudence
Law—Public Education

Law Firms. *See* Law Offices
Law Libraries. *See* Libraries
Law Offices
Law Practice. *See* Law Offices
Law Schools
Law Students. *See* Law Schools
Lawyers. *See* Attorney and Client
Lawyers—Biography
Lawyers—Stress
Legal Assistants
Legal Education. *See* Law Schools
Legal Ethics
Legal History
Legal Novels
Legal Reasoning. *See* Jurisprudence
Legal Research. *See chapter 2 under the heading* "Guides to Legal Research"
Legal Writing
Legislation
Lesbian Rights. *See* Civil Rights
Libel. *See* Defamation
Libraries
Litigation
Local Government. *See* Municipal Corporation Law

Marijuana. *See* Drugs
Maritime Law. *See* Admiralty
Marriage. *See* Domestic Relations
Medicine
Mental Deficiency and Retardation. *See* Handicapped
Mental Health
Military Law
Mining. *See* Natural Resources Law
Minorities. *See* Civil Rights
Minors. *See* Juveniles
Motels. *See* Innkeepers
Motor Vehicles
Municipal Corporation Law

Natural Resources Law
Naturalization. *See* Immigration Law
Negligence. *See* Torts
Notary Public
Nuclear Energy
Nurses and Nursing. *See* Medicine

Oil and Gas Law. *See* Natural Resources Law

Paralegals. *See* Legal Assistants
Parent and Child. *See* Domestic Relations
Patents. *See* Intellectual and Industrial Property
Patients. *See* Critically Ill; Handicapped; Human Experimentation; Medicine; Mental Health
Pensions. *See* Labor Law; Social Security
Personal Injury. *See* Torts
Physicians and Surgeons. *See* Medicine
Poor. *See* Civil Rights
Practice and Procedure. *See* Civil Procedure
Practice of Law. *See* Law Offices
Prenuptial Agreements. *See* Domestic Relations
Prisons and Prisoners
Privacy. *See* Civil Rights
Probate. *See* Estates
Products Liability. *See* Consumer Protection
Property
Psychology
Publishers and Publishing

Race Discrimination. *See* Civil Rights; Labor Law
Racial Minorities. *See* Civil Rights
Radio, Television, and Motion Pictures
Rape
Real Estate. *See* Property
Real Property. *See* Property
Reporters. *See* Authors
Retirement. *See* Labor Law; Social Security

Schools
Search and Seizure. *See* Criminal Law
Self-Defense
Senior Citizens. *See* Aged
Sex Discrimination
Shoplifting

Slander. *See* Defamation
Social Security
Solar Law. *See* Natural Resources Law
Sports Law
States. *See* Government—Federal and State
Students. *See* Schools
Supreme Court. *See* Courts
Suretyship. *See* Insurance

Taxation
Teachers. *See* Schools
Terminally Ill. *See* Critically Ill
Torts
Trade and Professional Corporations. *See* Corporations
Trade Regulation
Trademarks. *See* Intellectual and Industrial Property
Trusts. *See* Estates
Truth in Advertising and Lending. *See* Consumer Protection

Unemployment. *See* Labor Law
Unmarried Couples. *See* Domestic Relations
Urban Law and Planning. *See* Land Use-Planning

Veterans
Victims of Crime. *See* Criminal Law
Video. *See* Radio, Television, and Motion Pictures

Weapons. *See* Firearms; Self-Defense
Wills. *See* Estates
Witnesses
Women. *See* Abortion and Birth Control; Consumer Credit; Judges; Lawyers—Biography; Rape; Sex Discrimination; Taxation
Workers' Compensation. *See* Labor Law
Writers. *See* Authors

Zoning. *See* Land Use—Planning

Annotations

Abortion and Birth Control

3-1   Barr, Samuel J., and Dan Abelow. **A Woman's Choice.** New York: Rawson Associates, 1977. 306 pp. apps. ind.

The authors present the human and factual dimensions of the abortion controversy by relating stories of women of all ages confronting unwanted pregnancies. The authors hope that presenting the human side of the question will help contribute to a solution to this emotionally charged debate. Appendixes include an example of a model state law on quality abortion, and organizations supporting, and opposing, legal abortion.

3-2   Jaffe, Frederick S., Barbara L. Lindheim, and Phillip R. Lee. **Abortion Politics: Private Morality and Public Policy.** New York: McGraw-Hill, 1981. 216 pp. ns. ind.

The authors focus on the kind of public policy on abortion which could be adopted in a pluralistic society such as America. Chapters include a discussion of the impact of legal abortion in addition to other matters. Lawyers, legislators, theologians, feminists, and doctors—to name a few—should find this a worthwhile sourcebook on this volatile subject.

3-3   Sass, Lauren R., ed. **Abortion: Freedom of Choice and the Right to Life.** New York: Facts on File, 1978. 228 pp. bib. ind.

Developments since the U.S. Supreme Court decision in *Roe v. Wade,* 410 U.S. 113 (1973), five years earlier are explored by including editorials from the nation's newspapers. Abortion is viewed from the perspective of the Constitution, the political and legislative process, pregnancy and population control, and science and morality.

3-4   Steiner, Gilbert Y., ed. **The Abortion Dispute and the American System.** Washington, D.C.: Brookings Institution, 1983. 103 pp.

This scholarly study by the prestigious Brookings Institution will be used most by intelligent and educated laymen in politics and government. Lawyers may also find this a useful resource when they are involved in abortion legislation and litigation.

Utilizing writings and viewpoints of pro- and anti-abortionists, the editor sought an answer to the question of whether the abortion dispute would endanger governmental and political institutions that citizens depend upon. The work concludes that there is no danger to governmental institutions even with the unprecedented and unique political techniques applied by advocates on both sides.

Accounting

3-5   Causey, Denzil Y., Jr. **Duties and Liabilities of Public Accountants.** rev. ed. Homewood, Ill.: Dow Jones-Irwin, 1982. 225 pp. tbl. apps. ind.

Accountants, lawyers, and students may use this text as a sourcebook on legal responsibility and emerging patterns of civil and criminal liability. Leading cases are provided along with questions and problems so that this work may be used as a textbook in appropriate cases. Chapters include a discussion of liability, common law defenses, and malpractice insurance, to name a few.

3-6   Siegel, Stanley, and David Siegel. **Accounting and Financial Disclosure: A Guide to Basic Concepts.** St. Paul: West, 1983. 259 pp. apps. ind.

Designed for use by professionals, students, or anyone desiring an understanding of financial statements, this book may also be used as a primary or supplemental text in accounting, or as a supplemental text in courses such as corporations, taxation, finance, and business planning. Fifteen chapters explore such matters as inventories, assets, liabilities, auditing, and federal tax accounting. Appendixes provide illustrative financial statements and explain double-entry bookkeeping.

Administrative Law

3-7   Jacobini, H. B., Albert P. Melone, and Carl Kalvelage. **Research Essentials of Administrative Law.** Pacific Palisades, Calif.: Palisades, 1983. 144 pp. glos. bib. ind.

Although intended primarily for students of political science, this work should also prove most helpful to first-year law students, law students studying administrative law, attorneys, and any layperson involved in researching administrative law questions. Chapters include a summary of essential concepts of administrative law, briefing cases, research tools, major literature in the field, example citations, and a selected bibliography. The chapter on legal research ends with a series of five exercises so one may have the benefit of an actual learning experience.

Admiralty

3-8   Maraist, Frank L. **Admiralty in a Nutshell.** St. Paul: West, 1983. 390 pp. ind.

Included are chapters on jurisdiction, marine insurance, towage, salvage, maritime personal injury law, collision law, workers compensation, wrongful death, and sovereign immunity. The first chapter provides a brief, but informative, history of the law's development. Ship captains and administrators of seafaring companies— as well as lawyers and law students—may use this book as a quick reference guide to laws and customs applicable in admiralty practice.

Adoption. See Domestic Relations

Affirmative Action. See Labor Law

Aged

3-9 **Age Discrimination in Employment Act, ADEA: A Symposium Handbook for Lawyers and Personnel Practitioners.** Washington, D.C.: American Bar Association Commission on Legal Problems of the Elderly and National Council on Aging, 1983. 453 pp.

This manual was developed from a symposium held 11-12 January 1982 to educate attorneys and company personnel specialists on the myriad of legal and policy issues raised by the Age Discrimination in Employment Act (ADEA). Nearly twenty participants from industry, academia, and government presented diverse views on compliance and litigation issues. A recent paper on court decisions since the January, 1982, symposium updates the material.

This work is intended as a resource tool on the substantive and procedural requirements of ADEA, including trial tactics from both sides' perspectives and structuring company policies to avoid litigation; it provides information on current governmental attitudes about the future of ADEA. The book includes the text of ADEA and applicable regulations.

3-10 American Bar Association. **Your Rights over Age 50.** Chicago: American Bar Association Press, 1981. 41 pp. app.

The booklet covers many new rights provided by recent federal, state, and local legislation. Beginning with a prologue suggesting that filing a lawsuit takes serious consideration and consultation with a lawyer, the work proceeds—in a question and answer format—to provide information and insight into the rights of older citizens. The text is easy to understand and includes answers to common questions the elderly are confronted with every day.

3-11 Geller, Bradley. **Changes and Choices: Legal Rights of Older People.** Ann Arbor, Mich.: Br3 Press, 1982. 62 pp.

Intended for the elderly in Michigan, this straightforward question and answer book focuses on several new concepts, emphasizing Michigan and federal law. Topics covered include wills and estate planning, guardianships, conservatorships and powers of attorney, nursing home residents' rights, consumer protection, age discrimination, pensions, tax benefits, and rights of appeal. The text concludes with a list of referral services for legal and other concerns.

3-12 Sloan, Irving J., ed. **The Law and Legislation of Elderly Abuse.** Dobbs Ferry, N.Y.: Oceana, 1983. 151 pp. apps. ind.

Since exploitation, abuse, and neglect of the elderly is a developing area of concern, this work is basically a compilation of material on the subject. The book offers readers an overview of the legislative, social, and legal components of elderly abuse.

The chapters examine the nature and cause of abuse as well as surveying legislation and mandatory reporting laws for adult abuse. Extensive appendixes include the Model Adult Protective Services Act and a directory of state offices handling adult protective services.

3-13   Wishard, William R. **Rights of the Elderly and Retired: A People's Handbook.** San Francisco: Cragmont, 1978. 220 pp. app. bib. ind.

The text, written in an informal style, is intended to help the elderly and those concerned with their welfare to understand their legal rights as well as take proper action to enforce those rights. The work is not oriented towards advocacy, but merely tells the reader what legal rights are and what is the best action to take. The nineteen chapters are grouped into five parts: income, health and medical services, housing and employment difficulties, consumer protection, and miscellaneous benefits and rights.

Each chapter begins with a list of other related chapters recommended for reading before and after the chapter at hand. Examples and checklists are provided, although there are no citations or footnotes to federal and state laws. Appendixes list organizations, legal services, and offices on aging.

Agency and Partnership

3-14   Steffen, Roscoe T. **Agency-Partnership in a Nutshell.** St. Paul: West, 1980. 364 pp. app. ind.

Fundamental agency and partnership concepts are briefly outlined in eighty-eight sections with citations to relevant legal authority throughout. A table of cases, and the Uniform Partnership Act and Uniform Limited Partnership Act are also included. This is a useful guide on the law, and laypeople, law students, and attorneys will find this a fine quick-reference tool.

Air and Space Law

3-15   Rollo, V. Foster. **Aviation Law: An Introduction.** 2d ed. Lanham, Md.: Maryland Historical Press, 1982. 476 pp. ns. tbls. pls. gloss. ind.

This excellent work, drafted by a college-level teacher for use in teaching aviation law and management, explores the historical development of the field and fully describes the law's present status. It is very useful to students and administrators new to the subject as well as to individuals involved in aviation and air transport. People interested in space law will also find this book helpful in providing the background upon which space law is based.

The text is easy to understand, including chapters on federal agencies, international air law, and hijacking. A list of abbreviations precedes the text, which is followed by a selected bibliography, glossaries of aeronautical terminology and legal terminology, and a brief index. Each chapter has endnotes; references are made to laws, cases, and agency releases, among others. This is a fine starting point for the subject of aviation law.

3-16   White, Jay C. **Pilots and Aircraft Owners Legal Guide.** 3d ed. Redwood City, Calif.: Pilots, 1981. 87 pp. ind.

This work contains information on fundamental concepts common to aviation law. Eight chapters discuss general principles of aviation law, aircraft operation, individuals and organizations engaged in aviation activities, insurance, administrative matters with federal agencies, liens, and recent court decisions. The language is easy to understand and legalese is avoided where possible. A fourth edition was published in 1984.

Alcohol. *See* Drugs

Aliens. *See* Immigration Law

Animal Law

3-17   Favre, David S., and Murray Loring. **Animal Law.** Westport, Conn.: Quorum Books, 1983. 253 pp. apps. ns. ind.

Those who seek an introduction to animal law—as well as lawyers and nonlawyers involved with legal issues affecting animals—will find this helpful. Each of the twelve chapters is followed by notes to legal authority, and chapters discuss ownership, bailment, sale, and care of animals, among other matters. The last chapter explores federal wildlife statutes. A list of cases is included in one of the appendixes.

Antitrust. *See* Trade Regulation

Arbitration. *See* Labor Law

Architecture. *See* Construction Law

Arrest. *See* Criminal Law

Associations. *See* Corporations

Atomic Energy. *See* Nuclear Energy

Attorney and Client

3-18   Gillers, Stephen. **The Rights of Lawyers and Clients.** New York: Avon Books, 1979. 205 pp. ns. apps.

Beginning with the hypothesis that both attorneys and clients have affirmative rights, the author covers such matters as admission to the bar, lawyer discipline, the attorney-client relationship, attorney fees, malpractice, first amendment rights of lawyers and clients, and self-representation.

This American Civil Liberties handbook is written in a question-and-answer format. Each chapter is followed by citations to legal authority, and appendixes include state bar admission requirements and leading federal statutes authorizing an award of attorney's fees.

3-19   Hermann, Phillip J. **Do You Need a Lawyer?** Englewood Cliffs, N.J.: Prentice-Hall, 1980. 166 pp. fms. ind.

This is a "how to" book on choosing an attorney, and how to prepare to deal with, or without, such an individual. All facets of the attorney-client relationship are discussed, such as whether one can afford a lawyer, differences among lawyers, and ethical responsibilities of lawyers.

Another valuable asset of this work lies in its brief analysis of when to hire an attorney and when to act on one's own behalf. Many of the chapters provide guidelines on how to handle personal affairs such as traffic offenses, wills, and divorce without the services of an attorney. Sample forms are occasionally provided, and chapter 22 provides the names of general law lists for locating out-of-state attorneys.

3-20 Kahan, Stuart, and Robert M. Cavallo. **Do I Really Need a Lawyer?** Radnor, Pa.: Chilton, 1979. 197 pp. app. ind.

The authors, applying the premise that laws permeate every part of our lives, seek to help the reader in making an intelligent decision on his, or her, legal needs. The writers' intention is not to provide information on what to do or not to do in a given case when a legal problem arises; nor is the book an alternative to a lawyer. Rather, common legal problems are examined, and each situation is explored in terms of whether or not a lawyer is required and how a lawyer might prove useful. The first eight of the ten chapters discuss consumer protection, human rights, family matters, real property, business concerns, criminal law, negligence, and wills. The final two chapters analyze courts and their operation and the selection of a lawyer.

3-21 Marks, Burton, and Gerald Goldfarb. **Winning with Your Lawyer.** New York: McGraw-Hill, 1980. 242 pp. ind.

The purpose of this nontechnical book is to tell intelligent laypeople what they need to know about lawyers in order for them to obtain the best possible legal representation. The authors divide their work into two parts. Following a brief introduction into the history, meaning, and basis of the United States legal system, the first part analyzes the lawyer-client relationship from the time when a lawyer is hired to after the case is over. The second part provides information on basic legal areas such as personal injuries, property, taxes, and crime. The conclusion suggests seven rules for client protection, and proposes "holistic law" as an approach to the legal system; namely, becoming involved with the legal structure to do justice and not just win, and compromising where possible in order to avoid fractious lawsuits and unnecessary litigation.

3-22 Rosenthal, Douglas E. **Lawyer and Client: Who's in Charge?** New York: Russell Sage Foundation, 1974. 228 pp. ns. tbls. figs. apps. ind.

Drawing from three disciplines (political science, sociology, and social psychology) the author analyzes the lawyer-client relationship in making a personal injury claim, suggesting changes in the way lawyers and clients traditionally deal with one another. The book is theoretical in nature and may be most appropriate for lawyers, scholars, and individuals interested in improving lawyer-client interactions. The book is footnoted throughout.

3-23 Smith, Gregory White, and Steven Naifeh. **What Every Client Needs to Know about Using a Lawyer.** New York: G.P. Putnam's Sons, 1982. 240 pp. ind.

This is a timely, well-written work for any individual seeking, or considering, a lawyer. In fact, most attorneys would benefit by reading the comments and insights of the authors. As the authors say at the end of the first chapter, behind every good lawyer-client relationship is a good client; and, in turn, behind each competent attorney is a fine working relationship with the client.

The value of this work lies in its realistic and exhaustive explanation of every facet of the relationship. Chapters cover when to use and select a lawyer, negotiation of fees, calculation of fees, working with a lawyer, fee disputes, when to discharge an attorney, and disciplinary actions. There is even a fine chapter on legal malpractice and when to sue. Lawyers are not treated as the enemy, but as legal professionals with whom a client should know how to deal in every way. An excellent book, especially for public libraries.

3-24   Wehringer, Cameron K. **When and How to Choose an Attorney.** 2d ed. Dobbs Ferry, N.Y.: Oceana, 1979. 118 pp. app. ind.

This work is intended to assist individuals and organizations in not only choosing an attorney, but also what to expect and why the need for an attorney exists. Included is a chapter on what an attorney may cost for various services as well as chapters on obtaining efficient legal services and prepaid legal services.

3-25   Wolkin, Paul A., ed. **The Practical Lawyer's Manual on Lawyer-Client Relations.** Philadelphia: American Law Institute-American Bar Association Committee on Continuing Professional Education, 1983. 197 pp.

Clients of lawyers may gain insight from reading this manual even though it is geared towards lawyers and their relationship with clients. Twenty articles from past issues of *The Practical Lawyer* have been included in this book, which is divided into three sections: interviewing, informing, and billing of clients.

Authors

3-26   Gora, Joel M. **The Rights of Reporters.** New York: Avon Books, 1974. 254 pp. ns. app.

This book is somewhat dated, but is still useful for learning the basic concepts of reporters' legal rights. The text is written in the American Civil Liberties Union (ACLU) handbook question-and-answer format. Footnotes follow each of the chapters, which cover first amendment principles, protecting sources, news gathering and publishing, courts, libel and privacy, and problems involving the underground press. Appendixes include a summary of state shield laws and U.S. Department of Justice guidelines.

3-27   Likavec, Michael A., and Thomas S. Hodson. **Journalists' Handbook to Ohio Courts.** Norcross, Ga.: Harrison, 1982. 125 pp. apps. glos. ind.

Designed for working journalists, this handbook provides an outline acquainting readers with a basic understanding of the legal system. Chapter 14 provides direction on legal research beyond the scope of the work.

Although intended for use in Ohio, the book should prove useful to reporters new to legal reporting. Chapters cover the Ohio court system, the federal court system, participants and their roles in the legal system, anatomy of a typical trial, Ohio criminal and civil proceedings, administrative agencies, cameras and recorders in the courtroom, and other matters. The final chapter provides examples of Ohio reports and forms. An unusual feature is a "quick index," which preceeds the title page.

3-28   Polking, Kirk and Leonard S. Meranus, eds. **Law and the Writer.** Cincinnati: Writer's Digest Books, 1981. 258 pp. app. glos. bib. ind.

This book is designed to alert writers to major areas of concern and to help them avoid legal difficulties. The book is not a substitute for a lawyer, but should show writers when to consult an attorney while it increases their knowledge of laws related to their profession.

The text covers every major of importance such as libel, invasion of privacy, copyright laws, pornography, taxes, and social security. Useful sections at the end include a glossary of legal terms and a bibliography.

Automation

3-29   Bigelow, Robert P., and Susan Nycum. **Your Computer and the Law.** Englewood Cliffs, N.J.: Prentice-Hall, 1975. 278 pp. apps.

Although dated (it has not been republished since 1976), this work is still invaluable as an introduction to law and computers. Written for the computer manager, it points out when an attorney should be consulted. It also provides enough legal terminology and theory to enable managers to more effectively work with the lawyer. The language is straightforward and without confusing legalese.

3-30   Kutten, L. J. **Computer Buyer's Protection Guide: How to Protect Your Rights in the Computer Marketplace.** Englewood Cliffs, N.J.: Prentice-Hall, 1983. 142 pp. ind.

This ranks among the first books written on the subject of law and microcomputers. It is intended for consumers who want or need a microcomputer for their home or office, but who do not understand the legal issues and commercial pitfalls one should consider before purchasing a computer. Nine areas are explained: points to consider before purchase, general considerations about hardware and software, introduction to the law of sales, buying locally or by mail order, method of payment, what warranties really are, how to revoke or reject prior acceptance of goods, how to complain effectively, and miscellaneous hints and suggestions.

3-31   Remer, Daniel. **Legal Care for Your Software: A Step-by-Step Guide for Computer Software Writers.** Berkeley, Calif.: NOLO Press, 1982, 247 pp. fms. ill. ind.

Written primarily for the lay public, this book provides information on software law, trade secretes, copyrights, contracts, license agreements, patents, and much more. The last chapter includes tear-out contracts for use by the reader.

Automobiles.   See Motor Vehicles

Bankruptcy

3-32   Anosike, Benji O. **How to File for "Chapter 11" Bankruptcy Relief from Your Business Debts, with or without a Lawyer.** New York: Do-It-Yourself Legal, 1983. 131 pp. apps.

Written in simple, nontechnical language and intended for the average citizen, this booklet seeks to provide the steps for reorganizing one's company obligations without completely going out of business. Preliminary background information on chapter 11 is included, along with a case history and a step-by-step procedure for filing and processing the case from beginning to end. Over half of the work is comprised of appendixes illustrating a sample bankruptcy along with a glossary of terms, where to order forms, and other matters.

3-33   Kosel, Janice. **Bankruptcy: Do It Yourself.** 2d ed. Berkeley, Calif.: NOLO Press, 1982. 193 pp. apps. fms.

This guide to filing bankruptcy seeks to eliminate the confusion about such a proceeding. The work describes what bankruptcy is about, and its effects on property, debts, and creditors. It provides the do-it-yourself steps to follow if deciding to file for bankruptcy. Especially helpful is a chapter on definitions and the appendixes, which include each state's statutory exemption of property and the location of bankruptcy courts.

3-34   Milberg, Aaron S., and Henry Shain. **How to Do Your Own Bankruptcy.** New York: McGraw-Hill, 1978. 155 pp.

This volume is a simplified, large typeface, layperson's guidebook. The principal concepts and procedures of filing for bankruptcy are outlined and illustrated with typical situations and computations. The guide is intended to assist those who elect to file their bankruptcy without the benefit of legal counsel. Recent changes in federal bankruptcy laws may alter much of the content of this book.

3-35   Rogers, Harry Ellis. **The American Bankruptcy Kit.** Carmel, Calif.: Lawkits, 1981. 86 pp. fms.

Written for nonlawyers in clear and understandable language, this work provides tear-out forms and information for settling problems of indebtedness and for using the courts. It is a useful starting point for debtors seriously considering bankruptcy.

Banks and Banking

3-36   Beutel, Frederick K., and Milton R. Schroeder. **Bank Officer's Handbook of Commercial Banking Law.** 5th ed. New York: Warren, Gorham & Lamont, 1982. 590 pp. ns. tbls. ind.

Commercial bankers, dealing with normal legal problems in the ordinary course of business, will derive the primary benefit from this book, but lawyers, law students, and officers of other financial institutions may also find the work useful. Emphasis is on nontechnical language and legal treatment of problems is not exhaustive. The text is well footnoted.

The five-part, thirty-nine chapter book discusses all areas of importance including an overview of banking, commercial paper, secured transactions and bankruptcy, and special consumer relations. The text is followed by a lengthy table of cases and a detailed index.

3-37 Fischer, L. Richard. **The Law of Financial Privacy: A Compliance Guide.** New York: Warren, Gorham & Lamont, 1983. 588 pp. ns. fms. tbl. ind.

This reference guide was written to fill a need in the area of financial institutions and privacy law since a comprehensive treatment did not exist. Both compliance hints and case summaries are included. The intended audience includes executives of financial institutions and their counsel, but interested laypeople may find this guide most helpful in understanding their rights even though the text is somewhat technical and involved. Many forms, related documents, and extensive footnoting are shown.

3-38 Lovett, William A. **Banking and Financial Institutions Law in a Nutshell.** St. Paul: West, 1984. 409 pp. tbls. ind.

This book is intended for economists, bankers, business people, lawyers, and law students seeking an understanding of current developments in banking law and policy. An economic, historical, and legal analysis is presented in eight chapters on matters such as the banking market, insurance regulation, pension funds, and thrift institutions.

3-39 Mandell, Sidney. **Laws Governing Banks and Their Customers.** Dobbs Ferry, N.Y.: Oceana, 1975. 120 pp. apps. ind.

Although somewhat dated, information on the history of banking, the Federal Reserve, commercial banks, and savings and loans is included along with additional matters such as deposits, withdrawals, checks, forgeries, and loans and interests.

Bar Associations

3-40 Heinz, John P., and Edward O. Laumann. **Chicago Lawyers: The Social Structure of the Bar.** New York: Russell Sage Foundation, 1982. 470 pp. tbls. figs. apps. inds.

This book—a detailed study of the social composition of and stratification within the lawyers in the city of Chicago—should find an audience from among those in the social sciences and the interested public. In Chicago, 777 lawyers were selected at random from the city bar. Findings indicate that the Chicago bar consists of two somewhat separate, but distinct professions: one more prestigious, serving corporate clients, and the other serving individuals and small businesses. It is possible that this book could be the forerunner of further studies in other areas of the country on the social infrastructure of bar associations.

Book Trade. See Publishers and Publishing

Business Enterprises. See Corporations

Cars. *See* Motor Vehicles

Child Abuse. *See* Juveniles

Children. *See* Juveniles

Cities and Counties. *See* Municipal Corporation Law

Civil Procedure

3-41   Kane, Mary Kay. **Civil Procedure in a Nutshell.** St. Paul: West, 1979. 269 pp. tbls. ind.

The field of civil procedure is briefly examined with an emphasis on federal rules of civil procedure, which many states have adopted. Citizens interested in gaining insight into the process of litigation will benefit from this text, while lawyers and law students may use it as a reference guide in their practice and studies, respectively.

3-42   Re, Edward D. **Brief Writing and Oral Argument.** 5th ed. Dobbs Ferry, N.Y.: Oceana, 1983. 434 pp. apps. ind.

Written by a distinguished judge with academic experience and developed over a period of thirty years, this landmark work is of primary benefit to law students; it also serves as a refresher to practicing lawyers and as an aid for "jailhouse" lawyers. Material is included for drafting many briefs and memorandums with emphasis on prosecution of appeals and brief writing. Extensive appendixes include example forms for trial briefs and memorandums, office memorandums, and appellate briefs as well as Rules of the Supreme Court of the United States, Federal Rules of Appellate Procedure, and selected rules of representative state courts.

3-43   Stern, Robert L., and Eugene Gressman. **Supreme Court Practice.** 5th ed. Washington, D.C.: Bureau of National Affairs, 1978. 1,255 pp. fms. apps. ind.

This classic work is considered the bible for attorneys handling cases before the United States Supreme Court. No piece of information relevant to the court is excluded. Material includes checklists, information on day-to-day operations of the Court, and much nonlegal information helpful to lawyers as well as individuals seeking information about the Supreme Court.

There is an extensive table of cases and an appendix listing libraries with copies of Supreme Court records and briefs.

Civil Rights

3-44   Curry, Hayden, and Denis Clifford. **A Legal Guide for Gay and Lesbian Couples.** Berkeley, Calif.: NOLO Press, 1980. 288 pp. ill. fms. bib. ind.

Written in a casual style while carefully explaining legal terms, the authors—both attorneys—provide information on various legal contracts, including such matters as buying a home, child custody, guardianship, adoption, artificial insemination, joint parenting, and estate planning.

3-45 Dorsen, Norman, ed. **The Rights of Americans: What They Are—What They Should Be**. New York: Vintage Books, 1972. 679 pp. ind.

This book was written in commemoration of the fiftieth anniversary of the American Civil Liberties Union, and its contents summarize the state of citizen's rights up to 1970. Numerous authors contributed articles, which are arranged into five sections: the right to the essentials of life, such as housing and equal employment; the right to influence government or public opinion, such as voting, publishing, and associations; the right of personal autonomy, such as religion and travel; the rights against government process, including prisoners', juveniles', and mental patients' rights; and the rights of particular groups such as women, students, and aliens. Each contributor's article is followed by notes to legal and other authority.

3-46 Ginger, Ann Fagan. **The Law, the Supreme Court, and the People's Rights**. Woodbury, N.Y.: Barron's Educational Series, 1977. 716 pp. glos. bib. ind.

Landmark United States Supreme Court cases favoring individual civil rights are examined and discussed under three broad constitutional categories: freedom, justice, and equality. Minor treatment is given to those cases unfavorable to human rights. A table of cases—in addition to an extensive glossary of legal terms and lengthy bibliography—follows the text.

The continuing evolution of contsitutional law over the last seven or eight years dates this fine work, but it is a good beginning point for anyone interested in understanding the concepts involved in civil rights issues.

3-47 Hayden, Trudy. **Your Rights to Privacy**. New York: Avon Books, 1980. 190 pp. apps.

The work is divided into three parts: privacy of personal records such as school, financial, medical, employment, and social security matters; intrusion into personal thoughts such as polygraph and psychological tests; and the collection and control of government information, involving electronic surveillance and access to information. The text is arranged in question-and-answer format with notes following each chapter.

3-48 Larson, Richard E., and Laughlin McDonald. **The Rights of Racial Minorities**. New York: Avon Books, 1980. 253 pp. apps.

Topics analyzed include voting, employment, education, housing, public accommodation, and other matters. This is an American Civil Liberties Union handbook, and it is arranged in the typical question-and-answer format. Each chapter is followed by notes to legal authority, and appendixes list federal agencies and legal resources available for assisting in the enforcement of the rights of racial minorities.

3-49 Law, Sylvia. **The Rights of the Poor**. New York: Sunrise Books, 1973. 176 pp.

Even though this ACLU handbook is over ten years old, it offers a valuable starting point for legal research. Working under the assumption that individuals who are informed of their rights will exercise them, the question-and-answer text covers welfare, work requirement, general assistance, fair hearing, health services, food stamps, and free school lunches. Although dated, a chart on pages 134 to 153 lists Medicaid eligibility coverage, and the last part of the work analyses the rights of migrant workers.

3-50   Ramer, Leonard V. **Your Sexual Rights**: An Analysis of the Harmful Effects of Sexual Prohibitions. New York: Exposition Press, 1973. 126 pp. bib.

The intent of the author is to provide individuals whose lives are disrupted by their sexual beliefs with a source of information on how to deal with discrimination. Although the text is somewhat dated and most of it does not concern law, one chapter explores constitutional rights and how many sex laws violate these freedoms.

3-51   Rudenstine, David. **The Rights of Ex-Offenders**. New York: Avon Books, 1979. 238 pp. apps.

As is the case with almost every American Civil Liberties handbook, the text is written in a clear style with a question-and-answer format. Intended chiefly for laypeople, the text covers matters such as obtaining citizenship, working, voting, holding public office, and serving on a jury.

Although including many references to legal authority, tables, and organizations providing assistance, the work is somewhat dated and care must be taken to update references and legal citations. The text is a good starting point, however, for determining the rights of ex-offenders.

3-52   Stoddard, Thomas B., et al. **The Rights of Gay People**. rev. ed. New York: Bantam Books, 1983. 194 pp. apps.

Each of the ten chapters is arranged in the standard American Civil Liberties Union (ACLU) handbook question-and-answer style, and notes to legal authority follow each chapter. Areas explained include First Amendment rights of speech and association, equal employment opportunities, occupational licenses, armed forces, security clearances, immigration and naturalization, housing and public accommodation, the gay family, criminal law, and rights of transvestites and transsexuals. Appendixes include a bibliography of legal works on gay rights, criminal statutes relating to homosexual consensual acts between adults, sample antidiscrimination laws of selected jurisdictions, executive orders of two states' governors, a list of gay organizations, and ACLU state affiliates.

Colleges and Universities. See Schools

Commercial Law

3-53   Weber, Charles M., and Richard E. Speidel. **Commercial Paper in a Nutshell**. 3d ed. St. Paul: West, 1982. 404 pp. tbls. fms. ind.

Banking officials, business people, lawyers, and law students will find this is a good resource tool providing basic information on promissory notes, drafts, checks, and certificates of deposit under articles 3 and 4 of the Uniform Commercial Code

(UCC). Readers are cautioned that laws may vary from state to state, and each state's laws should be consulted in appropriate cases.

Community Property. *See* Domestic Relations

Comparative Law

3-54   Glendon, Mary Ann, Michael Wallace Gordon, and Christopher Osakwe. **Comparative Legal Traditions in a Nutshell**. St. Paul: West, 1982. 402 pp.

Three major legal systems—the Romano-Germanic (civil law), the common law, and the socialist legal system—are briefly explored. Anyone interested in gaining a broad perspective into the origins and comparative analysis of the American legal system will benefit from reading this text.

Computers. *See* Automation; Intellectual and Industrial Property

Condominiums. *See* Property

Confidential Communications—Clergy

3-55   Tiemann, William H., and John C. Bush. **The Right to Silence: Privileged Clergy Communication and the Law**. 2d ed. Nashville, Tenn.: Abingdon Press, 1983. 252 pp. ns. app. inds.

Clergy interested in understanding their relationship to the nation's courts will find this work useful and enlightening. Eighteen chapters are divided into two parts. The former explores the concept of confidentiality and churches, and the latter analyzes law and confidentiality. Notes to each chapter follow the text. An appendix lists all state statutes on privileged communication with clergy, and subject, author, and case indexes are included.

Conflict of Laws

3-56   Siegel, David D. **Conflicts in a Nutshell**. St Paul: West, 1982. 470 pp. tbl. ind.

The book is designed as a quick reference tool for lawyers and a study source for law students, but interested laypeople will find this a very helpful introduction to the subject. Basic legal doctrines are discussed on such topics as choice of law, judgments, jurisdiction, and family matters.

Conscientious Objectors

3-57   Tatum, Arlo, ed. **Handbook for Conscientious Objectors**. 12th ed. Philadelphia: Central Committee for Conscientious Objectors, 1972. 137 pp. bib.

Divided into five parts, this booklet provides all the information an individual needs to know in seeking status as a conscientious objector, or in avoiding the draft. It also discusses the resulting pitfalls. Described in detail are the Selective Service and its internal organization and structure, conscientious objection, court and prison, and conscientious objector status in the armed services.

The text is followed by a bibliography of materials on the subject. Caution is suggested here. This work is dated, and the reader should look for more current information on the law in this area, i.e., the thirteenth edition of this book was published in 1981.

Constitutional Law

3-58 Barber, Sotirios A. **On What the Constitution Means.** Baltimore: Johns Hopkins University Press, 1984. 245 pp. nts. ind.

Writing from the perspective of an informed citizen, the author considers the Constitution as a whole. The work is intended for anyone, regardless of their profession or occupation.

3-59 Kelly, Alfred A., Winfred A. Harbison, and Herman Belz. **The American Constitution: Its Origins and Development.** 6th ed. New York: W.W. Norton, 1983. 877 pp. apps. bib.

This is a readable, historical work useful as a reference tool, textbook or one-volume account of the American constitutional experience. It is lightly footnoted, containing an extensive bibliography and detailed table of cases following the text. There are thirty-three chapters, covering developments from the founding of the English colonies to the Burger Court. Appendixes include the Articles of Confederation and the Constitution.

3-60 McDonald, Forrest. **A Constitutional History of the United States.** New York: Franklin Watts, 1982. 307 pp. glos. tbl. ind.

The book is intended for undergraduate courses on U.S. constitutional history, but it is useful for all readers interested in a historical review of constitutional law. Technical detail is avoided since previous constitutional generalizations have been overturned and the author feels a short, interpretive work is necessary to explain the new material. Additionally, the author believes an easy-to-read text is more palatable for today's college students who find reading neither a favority activity nor a common skill.

The author divides the work into such matters as early issues from 1789-1807, economics and the Constitution, state and federal resolutions, the Civil War and Reconstruction, industrialization, the Constitution from 1910-1937, and the Constitution from 1937-1957. A brief, historical breakdown of earlier constitutions is provided as well as a discussion of the branches of government. Legal terms are defined in the glossary, and leading cases are cited throughout the text. Questions for discussion follow each chapter along with recommended readings.

3-61 Melone, Albert P., and Carl Kalvelage. **Primer on Constitutional Law.** Pacific Palisades, Calif.: Palisades, 1982. 116 pp. ind.

Broken down into five sections, this booklet is intended primarily for undergraduate college students taking a constitutional law course in such areas as political science and prelaw studies. Included are study aids such as how to brief a case, an introduction to legal research, legal research exercises, a glossary of legal terms, and an extensive, selected bibliography. Law students and interested individuals will find this a valuable addition to their resources for conducting legal research into constitutional law issues.

3-62   Padover, Saul K. **The Living U.S. Constitution.** 2d rev. ed., ed. Jacob W. Landynski. New York: The New American Library, 1983. 399 pp. apps. ind.

Intended primarily as a text for university and college courses on the Constitution, and as a supplementary work for courses in political and other social sciences, this book will prove valuable to anyone interested in expanding their knowledge of the origins, growth, and development of constitutional law. Included is the history of the forming of the Constitution, the text of the Constitution, and leading decisions by the United States Supreme Court. All major constitutional areas are covered such as the judicial power, commerce power, equal protection, and civil liberties. Appendixes include cited Supreme Court decisions and justices of the Supreme Court.

Construction Law

3-63   Cushman, Robert F., ed. **Avoiding Liability in Architecture, Design, and Construction: An Authoritative and Practical Guide for Design Professionals.** New York: John Wiley and Sons, 1983. 415 pp. ind.

This work offers practical guidance from legal experts for individuals or organizations designing and building technically sound structures, which not only should advance the development of the field, but which also must meet clients' specifications, satisfy requirements of local safety codes, and be completed in an economic fashion within given time limitations.

3-64   Lambert, Jeremiah D., and Lawrence White. **Handbook of Modern Construction Law.** Englewood Cliffs, N.J.: Prentice-Hall, 1982. 354 pp. app. ind.

This comprehensive guidebook is intended for building professionals, and it is a useful sourcebook for engineers, architects, contractors, subcontractors, suppliers, and attorneys confronted with any number of legal and contractual issues. Thirteen chapters are grouped into five parts, corresponding to the sequence of events involved in construction projects. The five parts include forming contracts, the substance of such contracts, everyone involved in ongoing projects, management, and dispute resolution. The text is lightly footnoted with legal and other authority.

Consumer Credit

3-65   Kaplan, Melvin J., and Phillip T. Drotning. **How to Get Your Creditors off Your Back without Losing Your Shirt.** Chicago: Contemporary Books, 1979. 205 pp. apps. ind.

Bankruptcy and alternative credit solutions are the subject of this practical book, which explores ways of avoiding creditor harassment while halting repossessions, garnishment, foreclosures, and outstanding judgments. Ways of maintaining a similar standard of living, holding onto one's possessions, and keeping a job are also examined by the authors.

3-66   **New Credit Rights for Women.** Barrington, Ill.: Consumer Credit Project, 1978. 73 pp. ill. fms. apps.

This brief, informative book is designed for women. It provides basic credit information, and how to obtain and handle credit as well as when to recognize illegal discrimination and what to do about violations of credit rights.

Consumer Protection

3-67   Fetterman, Elsie, and Margery K. Schiller. **Let the Buyer Beware: Consumer Rights and Responsibilities.** New York: Fairchild, 1976. 217 pp. apps.

Written specifically for consumers or buyers, this text explores such matters as advertising, home improvement, food, investments, and funerals. Appendixes list FTC regional offices, sample letters to creditors, FHA and VA mortgages, and federal consumer-help agencies. The language is straightforward, suggesting what to do and not to do as a consumer.

3-68   Hill, John L. **Texan's Guide to Consumer Protection.** Houston: Gulf, 1979. 211 pp. apps. ind.

This guide was written by a former Attorney General of Texas. The work covers buying goods and services, automobiles, home rental and purchase, credit, debt collection, insurance, utilities, business and investment scams, and how to obtain redress for complaints. Appendixes provide information on Texas and federal consumer agencies.

3-69   Nader, Ralph, Clarence Ditlow, and Joyce Kinnard. **The Lemon Book.** Ottawa, Ill.: Caroline House, 1980. 236 pp. apps. tbls. fms.

Drafted by Mr. Nader and his associates at The Center for Auto Safety, this brief but very well written and informative book has already found great use among dissatisfied car owners. Each chapter is followed by an appendix. Every major action to remedy the problems created by a poorly manufactured automobile is covered, including addresses of major auto company officials, what to do when every remedy fails, small claims court procedural variations, and so forth. This work is recommended for any consumer as a starting point in any dispute involving a recently purchased motor vehicle; it may also be wise for any prospective automobile owner to read this book before purchasing a car.

3-70   Ray, Larry, and Deborah Smolover, eds. **Consumer Dispute Resolution: Exploring the Alternatives.** Chicago: American Bar Association, 1983. 700 pp. app.

This book grew out of a conference held in 1982, and it is designed to educate the public and the legal profession on alternative ways of settling consumer disputes, such as mediation, arbitration, and conciliation. Ten chapters inquire into issues such as where do buyers go to complain, the most effective mechanisms for resolving disputes, and how legal, business, and government institutions can best inform consumers on the alternatives for resolving disagreements.

3-71   Striker, John M., and Andrew O. Shapiro. **Power Plays: How to Deal Like a Lawyer in Person-to-Person Confrontations and Get Your Rights.** New York: Rawson, Wade, 1979. 332 pp. apps. ind.

In plain, straightforward language the authors present information on how to assert one's legal rights under normal circumstances involving common legal problems. Extensive appendixes are included which document the writers' explanations and list comparative state laws on subjects such as vandalism, eviction laws, and other matters.

3-72   Striker, John M., and Andrew O. Shapiro. **Super Threats: How to Sound Like a Lawyer and Get Your Rights on Your Own.** New York: Rawson Associates, 1977. 324 pp. apps. ind.

The authors provide information and practical advice on how to write strong, legally valid letters to assert individual legal rights. Many topics are covered from fraud and neighborhood problems to tenancy and credit matters.

Contracts

3-73   Fried, Charles. **Contract as Promise: A Theory of Contractual Obligation.** Cambridge, Mass.: Harvard University Press, 1981. 162 pp. ns. ind.

This theoretical work received honorable mention from the American Association of Law Schools as one of the best law books published between 1980 and 1983. The book's twofold purpose is to show how a complex field is shaped by basic moral principles, and to display the underlying structure of the basic institution. Chapters explore the concepts of contracts, promise, consideration, offer and acceptance, gaps in contracts, good faith, duress and unconscionability, and the importance of being right. Notes follow the text.

3-74   Joseph, Joel D., and Jeffrey Hiller. **Legal Agreements in Plain English.** Chicago: Contemporary Books, 1982. 136 pp. apps.

Intended as a handbook, this work was written by two attorneys and includes thirty-three sample contractual forms on a good number of transactions. While seeking to simplify legal terminology and eliminate typical client confusion with legalese, the authors cover such matters as marriage, wills, the home, and borrowing money. The forms in each chapter are preceded by a brief discussion of the legal obligations that are involved. The book includes storage pockets on the inside of the front and back covers for one's contracts. Two useful appendixes cover location of state officers for filing papers and a glossary of legal terms. In the preface, the authors caution that a lawyer may be necessary, and include a chapter on this subject.

3-75   MacNeil, Ian R. **The New Social Contract: An Inquiry into Modern Contractual Relations.** New Haven, Conn.: Yale University Press, 1980. 164 pp. ind.

This work grew out of the 1979 Rosenthal Lectures at Northwestern University. It received honorable mention and recognition from the American Association of Law Schools from among all law books published between 1980 and 1983. Legal scholars should find this useful in exploring the theory of contract relations in today's world. Three chapters examine the roots of contract, the normative aspects for contracts, and analyze the ideas developed in the first two chapters in a number of problem areas.

Copyright.   See Intellectual and Industrial Property

Corporations

3-76   Barnes, James A. **A Guide to Business Law.** Homewood, Ill.: Learning Systems, 1981. 173 pp. glos. ind.

Written in a straightforward style without footnotes, this guide covers all major legal principles involving people and business transactions. The author, a practicing attorney, professor of business law, and coauthor of several leading textbooks on the subject, is able to present a concise overview of a very complex subject. This is a good starting point for the subject, but by no means should this work be utilized in lieu of sound legal advice where confusing legal issues are involved.

Preceding the typical table of contents is a brief, but useful alphabetical "Topical Outline of Course Content." The end of the text even provides examinations for each chapter along with answers for individuals inclined to test their newly-found knowledge.

3-77   Barrientos, Lawless J. **Texas Business Kit for Starting and Existing Businesses.** New York: Simon and Schuster, 1982. 90 pp. fms.

A basic guide for anyone wishing to start a business in Texas. While not providing detailed information on federal and state regulations, this kit does contain samples of both the federal and state forms one must file, along with any registration and reporting requirements.

3-78   Jacobs, Jerald A. **Association Law Handbook.** Rockville, Md.: Bureau of National Affairs, 1981. 368 pp. bibs.

Intended for those working within, or for, associations, this practical guide consists of sixty chapters on matters such as administration, activities and procedures, antitrust, and taxation. Each chapter is followed by references to additional appropriate resources: books, articles, cases, and statutory and regulatory authority.

3-79   Kintner, Earl W. **A Primer on the Law of Deceptive Practices: A Guide for Businesses.** 2d ed. New York: Macmillan, 1978. 706 pp. apps. ind.

Geared primarily to the business executive, but also useful to the general practitioner, this text covers every major area of unfair and deceptive business practices, providing legal applications to marketing practices. The author explores the historical background, and there is a discussion of deceptive trade issues. This work is intended only as an awareness tool for businessmen and it does not include many of the more esoteric areas of deceptive business practice law. However, it is a fine starting point for any business people who are interested in learning when to consult an attorney and how to avoid legal pitfalls.

3-80   Nicholas, Ted. **How to Form Your Own Corporation without a Lawyer for under $50.00**. Wilmington, Del.: Enterprise, 1972. 109 pp. fms.

The popularity of this work is reflected in its seventeen printings and a listing at the end of many companies that have indorporated using the text as a guide. Beginning with a brief history of corporations, the book provides a brief, informative analysis of all facets of incorporation, adhering to its goal of providing the simplest and lowest cost method of forming a corporation.

Every major form is included in a tear-out format, and the text in section 23 provides suggested readings, which have nothing to do with incorporating but are useful to formulating business ideas and philosophy. The most recent revised edition was published in 1983.

3-81   Ralph Nader's Conference on Excessive Corporate Legal Fees. **Cutting Legal Costs for Business: Proceedings of Ralph Nader's Conference on Excessive Corporate Legal Fees, May 18, 1981, Washington, D.C.** Washington, D.C.: Pension Rights Center, 1981. 208 pp. bib.

Sponsored by Ralph Nader, the nation's most influential consumer advocate, the conference included nine lawyers well-known throughout the country. Frank discussions took place on the excessive corporate legal fees of outside counsel. Contributors include Robert Abrams, John Zulack, Robert Reich, and Stephen Brill, among others. Executives should find the concepts and practical suggestions useful in negotiating for legal services, providing cost accounting techniques, and eliminating unnecessary legal costs.

3-82   Rice, Jerome S., and Keith Libbey. **Making the Law Work for You: A Guide for Small Businesses**. Chicago: Contemporary Books, 1980. 131 pp. glos. ind.

This book is intended to help business people with no legal background to utilize the law to serve their business needs. The most common business problems are considered and explained in nonlegal jargon. Chapters analyze such matters as negotiating loans, collection problems, buying and selling a business, warranties, contractual disputes, and more.

3-83   Scharf, Charles F. **Acquisitions, Mergers, Sales, and Takeover: A Handbook with Forms**. Englewood Cliffs, N.J.: Prentice-Hall, 1971. 332 pp. fms. ind.

Business people, lawyers, and accountants will find valuable information on business acquisitions or sales. Although dated, it is useful in providing approaches to various kinds of business transactions, and suggesting methods for avoiding problems and pitfalls.

3-84   Steingold, Fred S. **Legal Master Guide for Small Business**. Englewood Cliffs, N.J.: Prentice-Hall, 1983. 242 pp. ind.

Although admitting the continuing need for a lawyer, this work claims to help one utilize a lawyer's services more efficiently while owning or managing a small business. The book is written by a practicing attorney in Michigan, and offers guidance on all the most important legal matters such as tax breaks, warning signs indicating legal problems, and whether to incorporate.

The easy-to-read text is divided into twenty-nine chapters. Footnoting is omitted since the emphasis is on practical solutions. Each chapter is followed by helpful "points to remember."

3-85 Williams, Phillip. **How to Form Your Own Illinois Corporation before the Inc. Dries**! Oak Park, Ill.: P. Gaines, 1983. 77 pp. app.

Written specifically for Illinois individuals and businesses, this book provides information on the pros and cons of incorporation, tax matters, and employee benefits and includes a blueprint for incorporating a for-profit business. Appendixes provide example articles of incorporation, bylaws, and forms in addition to other matters. Addresses and telephone numbers of important Illinois agencies and departments follow the appendix.

Corporations—Nonprofit

3-86 Lane, Marc J. **Legal Handbook for Nonprofit Organizations**. New York: AMACOM, 1980. 294 pp.

Although this book sets forth the legal opportunities and pitfalls involved in setting up and operating a nonprofit organization, the authors still advise the use of a lawyer for handling the legal details applicable to each situation. Charitable fund raising, trusts, nonprofit corporations, and private foundations are explained. Included are examples of actual after-tax costs of donations, a guide to applicable internal revenue code sections, and a table of various required federal income tax returns.

Corrections. See Prisons and Prisoners

Courts

3-87 Choper, Jesse H. **Judicial Review and the National Political Process: A Functional Reconsideration of the Role of the Supreme Court**. Chicago: University of Chicago Press, 1980. 494 pp. ind.

The Association of American Law Schools has given an award to the author of this scholarly work, citing the book as one of the best legal publications between 1980 and 1983. The author examines the question whether the Supreme Court should adjudicate certain constitutional issues, taking into consideration the three broad provisions of the U.S. Constitution. These categories involve personal liberties, the separation of powers among the federal legislative, executive, and judicial branches, and federalism or the allocation of power between the national government and the fifty states. In addition to other findings redefining the role of the Court, the author submits that the Court should not use its authority to decide constitutional matters involving the powers of Congress and the President.

3-88 Economos, James P., and David C. Steelman. **Traffic Court Procedure and Administration.** 2d ed. Chicago: American Bar Association, 1983. 249 pp. apps. ind.

Judicial administrators, attorneys, judges, and interested citizens seeking improvement in the courts will benefit from this work, which explains developments in the last twenty years in traffic courts. This book was prepared by members of the American Bar Association Committee on the Traffic Court Program, and is divided into eight chapters, explaining trends in traffic justice, managing traffic courts, tickets and complaints, processing before appearance, courtroom procedure, posthearing disposition, and improving traffic courts. The language is technical and footnotes are scattered throughout the text.

3-89 Ely, John Hart. **Democracy and Distrust: A Theory of Judicial Review.** Cambridge, Mass.: Harvard University Press, 1980. 268 pp. ns. ind.

The author won an award from the American Association of Law Schools for one of the two best law books published between 1980 and 1983. In this work, Mr. Ely proposes a middle ground between those who believe judges should deicde constitutional issues and enforce norms clearly implied or stated in the Constitution, and those who believe that courts should go beyond the set of references and norms that cannot be discovered within the four corners of the Constitution. This scholarly book has spawned a great deal more debate and literature on the controversial question of how far courts should go in Constitutional interpretation.

3-90 **Guide to the Federal Courts: An Introduction to the Federal Courts and Their Operation. Includes Explanation of Litigation Process.** rev. ed. Washington, D.C.: WANT, 1984. 103 pp. glos. apps.

The objective of the publisher is to briefly provide the lay public with an understanding and appreciation of the federal judicial system, and how it operates. Two example cases—products liability and antitrust—are included to show how a case is litigated from beginning to end. Appendixes (which include a glossary of terms) take up half the text.

3-91 Neely, Richard. **How Courts Govern America.** New Haven, Conn.: Yale University Press, 1981. 233pp. ind.

This work addresses itself to the role of courts as political policymakers. Applying the theory that American courts have been the central institution making democracy work, the author seeks to establish principles for courts, lawyers, and the general public in deciding whether courts should intrude into other branches of government. The text is nonscholarly and lightly footnoted. Citizens interested in understanding how courts work will benefit from a reading of this book.

3-92 Neely, Richard. **Why Courts Don't Work.** New York: McGraw-Hill, 1982. 267 pp. ind.

This book is intended for a wide audience with the hope that interested citizens will provide political influence to local programs for improving the American court system. It is an analysis of civil and criminal courts in their day-to-day routines rather than a critique of courts as policymaking bodies. The author is concerned with the economics involved in the mechanics of the legal system and how it may be made more efficient. The language is nonscholarly, and the text is easy to read. There is limited use of footnotes and references to outside authority.

3-93   Warner, Ralph. **Everybody's Guide to Small Claims Court.** 2d ed. Occidental, Calif.: NOLO Press, 1978. 237 pp. ill. fms. app.

Nonlawyers are provided information on how to use this court to their best advantage. The text is clearly written and easy to understand. Twenty-four chapters examine such matters as whether one has a case, how to settle disputes, who can sue, serving papers, witnesses, and typical cases. The appendix lists small claims court rules for every state. A fifth edition was published in 1983.

3-94   Woodward, Bob, and Scott Armstrong. **The Brethren: Inside the Supreme Court.** New York: Simon and Schuster, 1979. 467 pp. pls. ind.

The authors provide fascinating insight into the workings of the nation's highest court from 1969 to 1976—the first seven years of Chief Justice Burger's tenure on the Supreme Court. Information is derived from interviews with over two hundred people, including several justices, over 170 law clerks, and former employees of the Supreme Court.

Crime Prevention. See Criminal Law

Criminal Justice

3-95   Chamelin, Neil C., Vernon B. Fox, and Paul M. Whisenand. **Introduction to Criminal Justice.** 2d ed. Englewood Cliffs, N.J.: Prentice-Hall, 1979. 514 pp. app. ill. tbls. glos. ind.

Intended primarily as a textbook for classes on criminal justice, this book is useful for anyone seeking a greater understanding of the American criminal justice system. Twenty chapters are divided into three parts, exploring the police subsystem, criminal law and the court system, and the corrections structure. The text is lightly footnoted, and inside each of the front and back covers is a diagram of the criminal justice system. Each chapter includes a summary, learning exercises, and suggested readings. Illustrations and tables are used throughout the text.

Criminal Law

3-96   Bailey, F. Lee. **How to Protect Yourself against Cops in California and Other Strange Places.** New York: Stein and Day, 1982. 90 pp. app. tbl.

This book was written by a noted trial attorney and is based upon his personal experience. It is intended for vacationers and business people traveling the fifty states and Washington, D.C., and suggests ways of avoiding the problems of undeserved charges of driving under the influence of alcohol. The appendix includes a comment on the various tests for alcohol. A table of state drunk driving laws follows the appendix.

3-97   Ballinger, Tom. **Clean Slate: A State-By-State Guide to Expunging an Arrest Record.** New York: Harmony Books, 1979. 304 pp. ind.

The guide provides information on procedures involved in sealing, annulling, and expunging arrest records. Discussed are such matters as one's legal rights, and practical advice on how to gain access to, and review of, arrest records. The latter half of the text consists of a state-by-state examination of laws and procedures.

3-98   Bard, Morton, and Dawn Sangrey. **The Crime Victim's Book.** New York: Basic Books, 1979. 223 pp. apps. bib. ind.

This work is intended for crime victims, their families and loved ones, and professionals in the field including police, lawyers, prosecutors, court officials, nurses, doctors, social workers, and counselors. It provides an understanding of the problem, ways to obtain assistance, and a practical philosophical approach. There is a chapter on how to get help, including crime victim compensation. Appendixes include crimes against people, the legal system, and access to resources. A suggested reading list follows the text.

3-99   Bassiouni, M. Cherif. **Citizen's Arrest: The Law of Arrest, Search, and Seizure for Private Citizens and Private Police.** Springfield, Ill.: Charles C. Thomas, 1977. 127 pp. app. ns. inds.

Chapters explain citizen's arrest at common law, analyze citizen's arrest in the states, discuss the changing policy of citizen's arrest, study various cases involving arrest, define liability for mistake of fact in making an arrest, explore search and seizure concepts, present a proposed model statute, and discuss the authority to detain shoplifting suspects. Appendixes list state citizen's arrest and shoplifting statutes. The text is footnoted throughout, and there are indexes to cases, states, and subject matter.

3-100   Cohen, Stanley. **A Law Enforcement Guide to United States Supreme Court Decisions.** Springfield, Ill.: Charles C. Thomas, 1972. 217 pp. ns. ind.

Directed primarily to the police officer, this somewhat dated work describes selected U.S. Supreme Court decisions in the areas of arrest, search, and seizure. The author analyzes each decision, how it impacts upon law enforcement officials, and then suggests guidelines. The text includes citations to federal and state court decisions, and has an extensive set of appendixes covering such matters as an example court order for fingerprinting and what is considered the "immediate area" of arrest.

3-101   Estrella, Manuel M., and Martin L. Frost. **The Family Guide to Crime Prevention.** New York: Beaufort Books, 1981. 253 pp. bib. ind.

Although it does not emphasize laws and what they mean, this work does propose—in simple, easy-to-understand language—how families can avoid being victims of broken laws. In this respect, its usefulness should not be underestimated. The most prevalent crimes are analyzed, and methods for avoiding victimization are suggested. Such things as consumer fraud, vehicle theft, and victim compensation, among others, are discussed.

3-102   Fellman, David. **The Defendant's Rights Today.** Madison, Wis.: University of Wisconsin Press, 1976. 446 pp. ns. tbl. ind.

The material is a bit dated, and readers should be aware of this shortcoming. Nevertheless, this work explores the fundamental constitutional rights of defendants. Ten chapters provide information on defendants' rights to notice, fair hearing, and counsel, as well as an analysis of habeas corpus, search and seizure, self-incrimination, double jeopardy, and cruel and unusual punishment. The text is lightly footnoted throughout and is followed by a table of cases.

3-103   Gammage, Alan Z., and Charles F. Hemphill. **Basic Criminal Law.** 2d ed. New York: McGraw-Hill, 1979. 344 pp. ns. tbls. ind.

Enumerating only basic concepts on substantive criminal law, this reference handbook is a practical introduction to criminal offenses and procedure. Its use is intended primarily for prospective law enforcement personnel and police officers, but interested citizens may find it worthwhile reading. The format is simple, non-theoretical, and no effort is made to discuss principles of law and their origin. Emphasis is on what the laws are rather than what they should or could be. The text is divided into two broad areas: criminal law and how it is used, and the law of crimes. The work is footnoted with references to statute and case law, and each chapter is followed by an alphabetical list of cited cases.

3-104   Henke, Shirley, and Stephanie Mann. **Alternative to Fear: A Citizen's Manual for Crime Prevention through Neighborhood Involvement.** Berkeley, Calif.: Lodestar Press, 1975. 40 pp. ill. apps.

This is a handbook designed for citizens seeking ways to reduce the threat of crime. It is based upon a successful program, and provides the details for implementing similar programs elsewhere. The text is easy-to-read and well illustrated.

3-105   Inbau, Fred E., and Marvin E. Aspen. **Criminal Law for the Layman: A Guide for Citizen and Student.** Radnor, Pa.: Chilton, 1970. 190 pp. app. glos. ind.

Although nearly fifteen years old, this book is still quite useful as a guide to basic theories and definitions in criminal law. The text is divided into four parts. The first defines crimes, the second explores the legal process from arrest to appeal, the third explains the administration of criminal law, and the final segment describes a citizen's duty as a witness and possible actions against police for misconduct. Examples are used throughout the work to clarify the meaning of legal concepts. A second edition was published in 1977 with coauthors Marvin E. Aspen and Jeremy D. Margolis.

3-106   Inbau, Fred E., Marvin E. Aspen, and James E. Spiotto. **Protective Security Law.** Boston: Butterworth, 1983. 301 pp. ns. app. ind.

This work is intended primarily for security officers, corporations, partnerships, and individually owned businesses. It provides guidelines on protecting property from theft by employees, customers, and others. It may also be used as a textbook in appropriate circumstances, such as for police training. The appendix includes statutory provisions from a number of states, and the text is well footnoted throughout. Fourteen chapters include, for example, laws on arrest, search and seizure, detention of individuals, surveillance of customers and employees, obtaining information on criminal history, courts, and preparation of a criminal case by a security officer.

3-107 Lipman, Ira A. **How to Protect Yourself from Crime: Everything You Need to Know to Guard Yourself, Your Family, Your Home, Your Possessions, and Your Business.** New York: Atheneum, 1975. 202 pp. fms.

This crime prevention handbook suggests methods of protection from acts against one's person and property. The first nine chapters provide ways of making a home safe. The next five chapters stress personal protection and property protection when one is away. The final six chapters are concerned with emergencies and other special circumstances which most of us will not have to consider. The text is followed by checklists, forms and planning aids, which are useful in implementing a self-protection plan. This fine work was reprinted in 1980 by the U.S. Government under the authority of the Office of Community Anti-Crime Programs, Law Enforcement Assistance Administration, U.S. Department of Justice.

3-108 McDonald, Hugh C. **Survival.** New York: Ballantine Books, 1982. 177 pp.

Although lacking a table of contents and index, this practical, hard-hitting book offers common sense advice on avoiding, and dealing with, situations involving violent crime. Each of the twenty sections consists of a story of a crime, a following comment or discussion on survival techniques, and how to take steps to avoid becoming a victim.

3-109 Rosengart, Oliver. **The Rights of Suspects.** New York: Avon Books, 1974. 122 pp. ns. app.

Even though the work is dated, it provides information on basic legal rights, and offers practical suggestions on dealings with police confrontations, arrest, one's rights in court, and available remedies. The text is arranged in question-and-answer format common to American Civil Liberties Union (ACLU) books. There are only scattered references to legal and other authority.

The constitutional principles on suspects' rights are continually evolving, so the reader is cautioned to look for the most current resource possible, or consult a lawyer.

3-110 U.S. Department of Justice. Law Enforcement Assistance Administration. **Crime Prevention Handbook for Senior Citizens.** Washington, D.C.: U.S.G.P.O., 1977. 53 pp. pls. ill. bib.

Four chapters briefly outline self-help methods for reducing crimes against the elderly, emphasizing such problem areas as burglary, robbery, larceny, and fraud. Photographs and illustrations enhance this easy-to-read text.

Criminal Procedure. See Criminal Law

Critically Ill

3-111 Robertson, John A. **The Rights of the Critically Ill.** rev. ed. New York: Bantam Books, 1983. 171 pp. ns. apps. fms.

This American Civil Liberties Union (ACLU) handbook describes the legal rights, duties, and responsibilities of patients, families, and providers of health care during

106 / Selected Subject Bibliography of Law-related Monographs

the time of a patient's critical illness or impending death. The text is in question-and-answer format, and legal authority is cited at the end of each chapter. Thirteen chapters cover such matters as the right to refuse treatment, the rights of critically ill children, brain death, organ transplants and autopsies, and experimentation and the critically ill. Appendixes include a summary of state laws on relevant legal issues as well as sample living will forms and organizations involved with the legal rights of the critically ill.

Custody. See Domestic Relations

Damages. See Torts

Defamation

3-112 Ashley, Paul P. **Say It Safely: Legal Limits in Publishing, Radio, and Television**. 5th ed. Seattle: University of Washington Press, 1976. 238 pp. ill. ind.

Designed as a working tool for anyone writing process copy or speaking over the airwaves, this text explains the history and meaning of libel in addition to many other legal concepts, including absolute and qualified privileges. Readers should exercise caution since the text is a bit dated.

3-113 Thomas, Ella Cooper. **The Law of Libel and Slander and Related Action**. 3d ed. Dobbs Ferry, N.Y.: Oceana, 1973. 119 pp. charts. app. ind.

Defamation law is briefly outlined and explained in eleven chapters. Included is a history of the law, elements required for a legal action, defenses, censorship, and other matters. The dated nature of this work negates the usefulness of the comparative state charts and reliance upon cited case authority.

Descent and Distribution. See Estates

Developmentally Disabled. See Handicapped

Discrimination. See Civil Rights

Displacement. See Eminent Domain

Dissolution. See Domestic Relations

Divorce. See Domestic Relations

Domestic Relations

3-114 Anosike, Benji O. **How to Draw Up Your Own Legal Separation, Property Settlement, or Cohabitation Agreement without a Lawyer**. New York: Do-It-Yourself Legal, 1982. 80 pp. fms. apps. glos. bib.

This is a basic "how to" text, utilizing the question-and-answer format in responding to reader inquiries. The manual is intended to prevent long and bitter legal actions involving property following separations and divorces. It is one of ten or more works by a publisher devoted to self-help law books for citizens.

Beginning with background concepts in contracts for people who are living together, the book provides a good discussion on legal separations and the drafting of agreements for such events. Also included is information on nonmarital cohabitation, courtship gifts and disputes, prenuptial agreements, and tax considerations. Useful appendixes provide bibliographic information as well as a glossary of legal terms and grounds for divorce or dissolution in all fifty states.

3-115   Bass, Howard L, and M. L. Rein. **Divorce or Marriage: A Legal Guide.** Englewood Cliffs, N.J.: Prentice-Hall, 1976. 209 pp. glos. ind.

Both men and women should find this a practical guide to legal issues involved when marital difficulties arise. Chapters consider matters such as the attorney-client relationship, separation, annulment, divorce, conciliation, property rights and agreements, and tax issues in divorce and separation. The text is easy to read and is followed by a glossary of legal terms.

3-116   Cassidy, Robert. **What Every Man Should Know about Divorce.** Washington, D.C.: New Republic Books, 1977. 247 pp. bib. tbl. ind.

Men undergoing the crisis of a divorce will find a wealth of information on coping with the problem. Included is a chapter on men's emotional experience during a divorce as well as chapters on children of divorce, money, courts, custody, and visitation. The text is easy to understand and is followed by a fairly long recommended reading list, a state-by-state guide to divorce laws, and a listing of divorce reform groups.

3-117   Clair, Bernard E., and Anthony R. Daniele. **Consultation with a Divorce Lawyer.** New York: Simon and Schuster, 1982. 202 pp. app. ind.

This is a very informative book written in question-and-answer format. It is arranged and indexed for quick reference, emphasizing strategy and suggestions at every stage of the divorce proceedings, including postdissolution problems. Most helpful is the listing of each state's grounds for divorce in the appendix. Included in the margins of the pages are key words and phrases indicating the contents therein. This is a practice long discontinued in book publishing, but which clearly shows the sincerity of the authors in making this work quite useful to the lay reader.

3-118   Eisler, Riane T. **Dissolution: No-Fault Divorce, Marriage, and the Future of Women.** New York: McGraw-Hill, 1977. 279 pp. nts. apps. ind.

The author, a woman lawyer, wrote this book for the layperson trying to understand how the legal system affects the relationship between family and government. The first part of this book compares old divorce laws with new no-fault provisions and describes contemporary developments as well as the mechanics of divorce. The second part analyzes marriage and divorce with an emphasis on implications for women. The last part explores alternatives to divorce and marriage, providing specific case histories to prove several points. Following the text are a divorce checklist and sample marriage contract containing practical information helpful to anyone facing either marital dissolution or marriage.

3-119   Franks, Maurice R. **Winning Custody.** Englewood Cliffs, N.J.: Prentice-Hall, 1983. 192 pp. ns. ind.

This book is intended as a "no holds barred" guide for fathers seriously seeking to gain custody of children in a divorce case. The text is realistic, exploring all facets of divorce proceedings from how to avoid the pitfalls to gaining custody. Included are chapters on finding the right lawyer, discovery proceedings, custody evaluation, and legal malpractice. Notes to legal and other authority follow each of the nineteen chapters.

3-120   Green, Robin M. **Divorce without Defeat: A Survival Handbook.** Amarillo, Tex.: Cimarron Press, 1982. 201 pp. app. fms. ind.

This is a fine book on marriage dissolution, providing an overview and general understanding of the subject. Written by a Texas attorney who represents divorce clients, the work is a discussion of choices one must make in the dirvorce process. The author appropriately points out that many decisions in divorce do not necessarily require a lawyer's advice since they may have nothing to do with law and are merely value judgments.

The first half of the text analyzes questions involving such things as whether to obtain a divorce and bargaining with one's spouse. The latter half concerns legally related matters such as choosing a lawyer, community property, taxes, child support, custody and visitation, and a trial of a contested divorce. There is an emphasis on Texas law, but this does not detract from the informative value of this book on a subject all too painful to many people.

3-121   Kastner, Carolyn R., and Lawrence R. Young, eds. **In the Best Interest of the Child: A Guide to State Support and Paternity Laws.** Denver: National Conference of State Legislatures, 1981. 148 pp. app.

This guide provides a good overview of essential state legislation on child support and paternity laws. Written on a somewhat technical level, the book is intended primarily for state officials and citizens seeking implementation of definitive laws on child support.

The chapters cover the following subjects: thirteen statutes required for a good administrative structure, child support and the judicial process, administrative procedures establishing and enforcing support, determination of paternity and support, and enforcement of support orders. Each chapter—with the exception of the concluding chapter—contains examples of different state statutes, essential components of the law being discussed, and sections analyzing variations among the states.

3-122   Katz, Sanford N. **Child Snatching: The Legal Response to the Abduction of Children.** Chicago: American Bar Association, 1981. 206 pp. ns. apps. tbls. bib. ind.

Focusing on the Uniform Child Custody Jurisdiction Act (UCCJA), the author analyzes the problem of parental kidnapping of children during, or after, divorce and separation. Even thought the text was prepared for the National Institute of Justice, U.S. Department of Justice and is a legal discourse on the problem, legislators, interested parents, and lawyers will find this book very helpful in providing information on available state remedies and possible needed changes in the laws relating to child custody.

3-123   Kiefer, Louis. **How to Win Custody**. New York: Simon and Schuster, 1982. 308 pp. apps. fms. ind.

Although written with the father in mind, this book is equally valuable to mothers. Included in its seventeen chapters are strategies and advice on seeking custody. The text is easy to understand, and appendixes include sample custody agreements and other relevant materials.

3-124   Lasnik, Robert S. **A Parent's Guide to Adoption**. New York: Sterling, 1979. 160 pp. ill. ind.

This work is aimed at parents hoping to adopt by traditional means. Caution is advised throughout with suggestions to use a lawyer in appropriate cases. Illustrations indicate the situations that can arise during legal proceedings.

3-125   Martin, Cynthia. **Beating the Adoption Game**. San Diego: Oak Tree, 1980. 304 pp. bib. ind.

Written for parents who may face rejection by an adoption agency, this book suggests newer alternatives in seeking a child, such as artificial insemination, private adoption for profit, and so forth. The text appears well thought out and researched, and it is followed by a current bibliography on the subject.

3-126   Meezan, William, Sanford Katz, and Eva Manoff Russo. **Adoptions without Agencies: A Study of Independent Adoptions**. New York: Child Welfare League of America, 1978. 237 pp. ill. tbls.

As a fine national study of legal and psychological risks in the independent adoption process, this work will find use among individuals involved in formulating public policy on adoption matters. Of particular interest is a chapter reviewing and analyzing the laws of all states relating to independent adoptions. The work is well illustrated with tables, and discusses all persons and organizations involved in this process.

3-127   Mitchelson, Marvin. **Living Together**. New York: Simon and Schuster, 1981. 220 pp. fms. ind.

Written by the attorney for the plaintiff in the landmark *Marvin v. Marvin* decision as a practical guide for unmarried cohabiting couples, this work offers realistic advice. Forms are included such as joint living and separation agreements. Well-known cases involving couples who have lived together are described in order to emphasize the author's points. The style is informal with the exception of the last chapter, which contains the text of the *Marvin* decision.

3-128 Noble, June, and William Noble. **The Custody Trap.** New York: Hawthorn Books, 1975. 163 pp. ind.

The book is dated, but it is still somewhat useful as a resource illustrating the need for custody reforms—many of which have taken place in the states. The authors explore case histories, court transcripts, and interviews to show how children are often used as weapons by hostile parents. It is a helpful text for social reformers, judges, lawyers, and interested parents and citizens.

3-129 Rogers, Harry Ellis. **The California Divorce Kit.** Carmel, Calif.: Lawkits, 1982. 240 pp. fms. apps.

Written by an attorney, this book helps eliminate confusion for individuals seeking a divorce in California. The first two chapters provide information on the subject of divorce and present problems and dangers that must be considered in such a venture.

The language is easy to understand, and very extensive appendixes provide almost everything one needs to know to handle the dissolution process.

3-130 Weitzman, Lenore J. **The Marriage Contract: Spouses, Lovers, and the Law.** New York: Free Press, 1981. 536 pp. app. ind.

Although the approach is scholarly and the primary purpose of the book is to analyze the "implicit marriage contract and the common-law tradition from which it developed," educated couples and individuals considering marriage will find the second half of the work most useful in helping to determine the nature and extent of their marital and prenuptial agreements. Although example agreements are not stressed, there is a fine analysis of the types of relationships between couples and the implications of such relationships. The result is that intelligent, serious-minded couples reading this book will be better informed in drafting the terms of any written agreement they decide upon.

3-131 Wheeler, Michael. **Divided Children: A Legal Guide for Divorcing Parents.** New York: W.W. Norton, 1980. 224 pp. ind. bib.

For those divorcing spouses wondering how to resolve custody issues, this book presents an analysis of the complex law of custody. Ten chapters cover such matters as the myth of uncontested divorce, visitation, joint custody, lawyers, and money. The text is easy to read, and offers insight on how to best handle custody matters. Following the last chapter on the need for reforms is a checklist for divorcing parents, a note on sources, and a suggested reading list.

3-132 Woody, Robert Henley. **Getting Custody: Winning the Last Battle of the Marital War.** New York: Macmillan, 1978. 178 pp. apps. bib. ind.

Written by a clinical psychologist in an understandable style, this book focuses on parents seeking custody following divorce. The first portion of this work examines the manner in which custody determinations are made. The latter portion explores twenty factors for measuring parental fitness and the use of professionals to aid parents in obtaining custody, among other matters.

3-133　Woolley, Persia. **The Custody Handbook.** New York: Summit Books, 1979. 350 pp. apps. ns. bib. ind.

This is another book intended for couples dealing with custody as a result of divorce. It is a practical, easy-to-read work with suggestions on working out custody, including the developing practice of joint custody. Chapters include ways of easing stress, reaching agreement, finding a lawyer, and coping with the court system. Appendixes list useful organizations, sample custody provisions, and a sample checklist. A reading list, providing books for both men, women, and couples, follows the appendixes and notes.

Drugs

3-134　Moller, Richard Jay. **Marijuana: Your Legal Rights.** Reading, Mass.: Addison-Wesley, 1981. 271 pp. app. ns. ind.

As one of a number of self-help law books published by NOLO Press, a subsidiary of Addison-Wesley, this work provides an informative look at individual rights involving the use and growing of marijuana. Straightforward language makes the text understandable to anyone unfamiliar with the web of criminal liability involving marijuana. Every area is included, such as arrest, entrapment, motor vehicle and airport searches, and surveillance. Especially helpful is an appendix listing marijuana crimes state by state. Footnotes are compiled at the end of the text and refer to leading case authority.

3-135　Sloan, Irving F. **Alcohol and Drug Abuse and the Law.** Dobbs Ferry, N.Y.: Oceana, 1980. 117 pp. apps. glos. ind.

This is another publication in the Legal Almanac Series intended for lay people. It explains general legal issues involving alcohol and other drug problems. Covered are such matters as liquor laws, state legislation on drug abuse, and legal aspects of involuntary and voluntary commitment. Appendixes include a glossary on drug terminology and answers to frequently asked questions on the subject.

Education.　See Schools

Elderly.　See Aged

Elections

3-136　Huckaby, Stan. **Guidelines for Federal Campaign Compliance.** 3d ed. Austin, Tex.: Guidelines for Federal Campaign Compliance, 1982. 220 pp. fms. figs. ind.

The author has published a work synthesizing all available information involving compliance with federal election campaign laws. The text is divided into two parts, one analyzing the application of the Federal Election Campaign Act, and the second establishing a method for an accounting system. This is a useful resource for political parties, campaign organizers, lawyers, and would-be politicians.

Eminent Domain

3-137　Hartman, Chester, et al. **Displacement: How to Fight It.** Berkeley, Calif.: National Law Housing Project, 1982. 225 pp. pls. ill. bibs. apps. ind.

This guidebook is written for community organizations, their advocates, and anyone being forced to move from a home. Chapters explore such areas as rental housing, resisting governmental disinvestment, displacement of homeowners, displacement due to housing rehabilitation, and much more. Each chapter is followed by a listing of additional reading and resource material.

Employer and Employee. *See* Labor Law

Energy Law. *See* Natural Resources Law

Environmental Law

3-138　Firestone, David B., and Frank C. Reed. **Environmental Law for Non-Lawyers.** Ann Arbor, Mich.: Ann Arbor Science, 1983. 282 pp. apps. ind.

The authors' intent is to pass along to laypeople an awareness of, and the reasoning behind, current environmental issues so that interested nonlawyers may assist in meaningful changes where the law is failing and avoid unnecessary resistance to laws that are successful. Nine chapters cover the field of environmental law, including pollution, land use, solid wastes, pesticides and toxic wastes, energy, population, and international environmental law. The text is also most useful to those who are unfamiliar with this area, and who are seeking a brief, informative introduction to the field.

3-139　Kersch, Mary Ellen. **How to Fight City Hall: A Guide for Citizen and Environmental Action.** Mankato, Minn.: Gabriel Books, 1980. 171 pp.

Although not strictly a descriptive law book for the lay public, this work provides interested and intelligent citizens the means by which to approach, and work within, the governmental structure of municipalities. The author explores ways to avoid breaking the law or creating fractious relations with those holding legal power to create, enforce, and change local environmental laws.

　　The first part of the text includes advice on topics such as how to become credible, and uses a lot of the author's past experiences to prove her points. The second half of the work suggests approaches to grassroots politics, including organization, maximizing potency, and approaches such as lawsuits and going to the state legislature.

3-140　Sive, Mary Robinson, ed. **Environmental Legislation: A Sourcebook.** New York: Praeger, 1976. 561 pp. bib. ind.

Citizens, lawyers, and environmentalists will be able to familiarize themselves with leading state and federal environmental laws. Even though the text is dated, it is a good starting point for a general understanding of laws such as the National Environmental Policy Act and the Clean Air and Water Acts. Various legislation is broken down by subject such as air, noise, oceans, and energy; and each subject includes a brief overview. References to U.S. and state codes are provided in this easy-to-read text.

Equal Employment. See Labor Law

Estates

2-141   Dacey, Norman F. **How to Avoid Probate–Updated!** 2d ed. New York: Crown, 1980. 596 pp. fms.

The original work, written by an attorney and published in 1966, is considered a milestone among books designed for the lay public on handling their legal affairs. Since the first edition was published, a great number of additional legal "how to" books for laymen have been written on numerous areas of law. The most interesting part of this second edition is the prologue, which outlines the difficulties the author endured from his colleagues in his efforts to make the public more aware of methods for avoiding the cost of probate.

This revised edition updates the original work, most of which consists of forms and examples for establishing a living, or *inter vivos,* trust. A living trust is one of three ways outlined in the book for avoiding probate, the two others consisting of life insurance payable to a named beneficiary and property jointly owned with right of survivorship.

3-142   Farley, John T. **You Can't Take It with You.** Palo Alto, Calif.: R. & E. Associates, 1982. 99 pp. fms.

Personal financial planning is emphasized in this book so that individuals and families, in anticipation of death, may leave their affairs in order. Six chapters examine the importance of planning, inventorying an estate, cash flow, important papers, wills, and trusts. The text is easy to read, and sample personal records and checklists are included.

3-143   Holzman, Robert S. **Estate Planning: The New Golden Opportunities.** Millburn, N.J.: Boardroom Books, 1982. 238 pp. ind.

Numerous topics are covered in this book, which is written in plain English. Subjects explained include marital deduction, gifts, tenancies, power of attorney, retained interests, buy-sell agreements, powers of an executor, and much more. Business people, families, and laypersons will benefit from this work, and they should be better prepared to plan their estates and to work with their attorneys.

3-144   Hughes, Theodore E., and David Klein. **A Family Guide to Estate Planning, Funeral Arrangements, and Settling an Estate after Death.** New York: Charles Scribner's Sons, 1983. 192 pp. tbls. fms. ind.

The purpose of this book is to relieve everyone's anxieties and assist families in dealing with bodily remains while efficiently managing the transfer of assets to survivors. A systematic course of action is provided. The first four chapters deal with matters requiring immediate attention. Chapter five suggests the course of action when death is near, and the remaining chapters explore the problems survivors must be ready to cope with and resolve. Tables and example documents aid in clarifying the authors' discussion. The text is easily understood and without footnotes.

3-145   Looney, J. W. **Estate Planning for Farmers**, 2d ed. St. Louis: Doane, 1977. 247 pp. fms. glos. ind.

The author, a lawyer and agriculturist, discusses estate planning issues from the standpoint of the independent farmer. Chapters include material on probate, taxation, co-ownership, wills, trusts, life insurance, the role of partnerships, corporation and leasing arrangements, retirement, and estate planning. There is minimal use of technical language. The text uses homespun examples to present various concepts of retirement and estate problems. A second edition was published in 1979.

3-146   Menzel, Harold H. **Write Your Own Will and Avoid Probate**. New York: Dale Books, 1978. 223 pp. fms.

The author's intent is to give laypeople the opportunity to become "at least as knowledgeable as the average lawyers," but he does warn of pitfalls. His primary purpose is to remove the mystique of probate, enabling citizens to save money. Case histories are provided along with chapters on estate planning, prenuptial agreements, and probate of an estate.

3-147   Moody, William J. **How to Probate an Estate: A Handbook for Executors and Administrators**. New York: Castle Books, 1969. 95 pp. fms. glos.

Executors and administrators should find this guide useful in performing their duties, but it is not intended as a substitute for practical legal advice. A checklist is provided at the beginning, which keys into the remainder of the text for easy reference. The most recent edition was published in 1981.

3-148   Saunders, Charles A., ed. **How to Live—and Die—with Texas Probate**. 4th ed. Houston: Gulf, 1983. 177 pp. glos. ind.

Texans will find this a useful tool for avoiding problems while achieving the maximum advantage in planning their estates. This work is not a do-it-yourself book, but it does explain almost all general legal principles. Over twenty Texas attorneys contributed to this book with the sanction and support of the State Bar of Texas. Chapters discuss community costs of probate among other matters. Each chapter ends with a brief summary of what has been explained.

Evidence

3-149   Rothstein, Paul F. **Evidence in a Nutshell: State and Federal Rules**. 2d ed. St. Paul: West, 1981. 514 pp. tbls. ind.

Designed as a study aid for law students, this book is also valuable to laypeople interested in knowing why evidence is, or is not, excluded or admitted, Lawyers can also use this work as a quick reference guide. The text includes an analysis of hearsay, privileges, admissions and confessions, and presumptions, among other matters.

3-150   Waltz, Jon R. **Introduction to Criminal Evidence.** 2d ed. Chicago: Nelson-Hall, 1983. 470 pp. ill. bib. ns. ind.

Written by a distinguished professor of law at Northwestern University, this book is intended for a wide audience, including undergraduate students, law students, law enforcement trainees, and interested laypeople. Typical legalese is avoided and common English usage is emphasized. All the important rules for submission of evidence in a criminal trial are described. Although footnotes are not used, leading cases and authority are cited throughout the text. Pictures, and a cartoon or two, are scattered throughout the book. Many examples are used throughout to clarify rules of evidence.

Executors and Administrators. See Estates

Family Law. See Domestic Relations

Firearms

3-151   Gottlieb, Alan M. **The Rights of Gun Owners.** Aurora, Ill.: Caroline House, 1981. 211 pp. ns. apps. bib.

Individuals concerned about preservation of the freedom of gun ownership should find this a good primer on legal rights and responsibilities. Each of the seven chapters consists of questions and answers to common legal questions, and chapters are followed by notes to legal authority. Over half the text consists of appendixes, listing a bibliography of books and articles, journals favoring guns, postal regulations, and much more. Although intended primarily for gun owners, the information should also prove helpful to reformers opposing guns.

Foreign Law. See Comparative Law

Freedom of (—). See Constitutional Law

Freedom of Information Act

3-152   Sherick, L. G. **How to Use the Freedom of Information Act (FOIA).** New York: Arco, 1978. 138 pp. fms. apps. ind.

The author reduces the FOIA to simple language so that the greatest number of people may understand and use the act as the need arises. Chapters explore the history of the act, how to use it, nine exemptions, industrial espionage, personal dossiers, and more. Appendixes provide information on the text of applicable laws and addresses of relevant federal agencies.

Gay Rights. See Civil Rights

Government—Federal and State

3-153   Gottron, Martha V., ed. **Regulation: Process and Politics.** Washington, D.C.: Congressional Quarterly, 1982. 184 pp. bib. ind.

This work was developed in response to President Reagan's efforts to reform the regulatory process and eliminate unnecessary, costly regulations. The publisher seeks to determine what form of regulation is most effective in addition to other issues.

The text is broken down into three areas. Beginning with matters such as a discussion of regulation and its development, the book moves on to case studies on several topics, including food, safety, and the environment; and it concludes with sketches of agencies, legislative highlights, and selected documents. Attorneys, legislators, and individuals involved in litigation or studying the regulatory functions of the federal government will find this an excellent resource in their research.

3-154   Masters, Richard, et al. **Interstate Compacts & Agencies.** Lexington, Ky.: Council of State Governments, 1983. 42 pp. inds.

Federal and state administrative officials, attorneys, and interested citizens will benefit from this update of a 1979 publication. Included is a listing of compacts arranged by subject. (Interstate compacts are formal, legal agreements establishing cooperation among states, and they are authored by the U.S. Constitution. U.S. Const. art. I, §10.) Each compact's purpose is briefly explained along with statutory references and the year of joinder with each compact. Where state agencies exist as a result of a compact, names, addresses, officers, and staffs are included along with a description of the agency.

3-155   Yudof, Mark. **When Government Speaks: Politics, Law, and Government Expression in America.** Berkeley, Calif.: University of California Press, 1983. 323 pp. bib. ind.

Mr. Yudof, a law professor at the University of Texas in Austin, was awarded the Scribes Book Award from the American Society of Writers on Legal Subjects for the outstanding law book of 1983. This scholarly book is an outgrowth of a law review article published several years earlier in *Tex. L. Rev.,* vol. 22 (1979), p. 863. The author explores the federal government's potential to induce consent of the people through its massive involvement in this country's vast communications network. A recent review states this scholarly work "belongs on the same shelf with Zechariah Chafee, Thomas Emerson, and Harry Kalven," who rank among the leading First Amendment theorists during the last fifty years. *Harv. L. Rev.,* vol. 96 (1983), p. 1745, 1757.

Guns. See Firearms; Self-Defense

Habeas Corpus. See Criminal Law

Handicapped

3-156   Amary, Issam B. **The Rights of the Mentally Retarded-Developmentally Disabled to Treatment and Education.** Springfield, Ill.: Charles C. Thomas, 1980. 196 pp. apps. bib. ind.

This work explores the broad changes that have taken place in the field of mental health, and it is a fine starting point for lawyers, professionals, administrators, and others becoming acquainted with the subject. Chapters provide a historical review as well as an examination of the rights, services, and personnel involved in the field. Appendixes include a listing of the rights of institutionalized individuals and landmark judicial decisions.

3-157   Appenzeller, Herb, Vicki M. Balker, and Terrell West. **The Right to Participate: The Law and Individuals with Handicapping Conditions in Physical Education and Sports.** Charlottesville, Va.: Michie, 1983. 405 pp. apps. ns. glos. ind.

Written for individuals with physical impairments, handicaps, or disabilities, this book reviews legislation and litigation in order to identify issues and gain insight into court decisions. Eight chapters outline the area, providing background information and examining such areas as eiligibility rules for sports participation, and injuries to participants. Each chapter is followed by a summary and footnotes. Nine appendixes include matters such as a listing of sports organizations and resource organizations. Sports educators, coaches, and school administrators will also find this work valuable as a reference tool.

3-158   Friedman, Paul R. **The Rights of Mentally Retarded Persons.** New York: Avon Books, 1976. 186 pp. ns. apps. glos. bib.

This ACLU guide first provides background information on mental retardation and then delves into problems involving classification. Subsequent chapters cover guardianship and civil commitment proceedings, rights of retarded individuals in institutions, rights in the community, rights in criminal proceedings, and right to counsel.

The text is in the ACLU question-and-answer format, each chapter is followed by "Notes" to cited authority, and appendixes include a glossary of legal and mental retardation terms, a selected bibliography, and a list of resource organizations.

3-159   Haavik, Sarah F., and Karl A. Menninger II. **Sexuality, Law, and the Developmentally Disabled Person: Legal and Clinical Aspects of Marriage, Parenthood, and Sterilization.** Baltimore: Paul H. Brooks, 1981. 191 pp. ns. app. ind.

Parents, lawyers, and professionals in the field will find this book most useful as a primary sourcebook for information. The book should also aid in the formulation of practical policies and programs when dealing with the mentally retarded in relation to sexual behavior and family status.

3-160   Herr, Stanley S. **Rights and Advocacy for Retarded People.** Lexington, Mass.: Lexington Books, 1983. 257 pp. ns. ind.

Although focusing on the role lawyers must play in asserting rights and finding remedies for retarded individuals, this work is also useful to parents, guardians, the courts, service providers, and the public as a sourcebook. The author provides information as a basis for reform, covering historical, present, and future concerns.

118 / Selected Subject Bibliography of Law-related Monographs

The language is in narrative form and easy to read. Each chapter is followed by extensive "Notes" referring to legal and other authority.

3-161   Hull, Kent. **The Rights of Physically Handicapped People.** New York: Avon Books, 1979. 253 pp. ns. apps.

This is another book in the American Civil Liberties Union Handbook series, arranged in the familiar question (in bold type)-and-answer format common to this publication. Questions involving rights to transportation, employment, and education are answered in addition to many others. Chapter 2 is especially useful in discussing basic concepts involving handicapped individuals' rights. Each chapter is followed by reference notes to legal and other citations; and the text is followed by four appendixes, including the Model White Cane law, among others.

3-162   Kindred, Michael, et al., eds. **The Mentally Retarded Citizen and the Law: President's Committee on Mental Retardation.** New York: Free Press, 1976. 738 pp. ind. tbl.

This volume is one of the principle resources in this field. It summarizes the work of the President's Conference, which convened in 1973 to inquire into the legal rights of mentally retarded citizens, and to consider practical and conceptual obstacles to full realization of those rights. Major legal papers are presented by experts in twenty-two areas of concern. Each article is followed by critical reactions by other contributing Conference participants. Part 1 deals with the personal and civil rights of mentally retarded citizens; part 2 with the rights of mentally retarded citizens within community systems; and part 3 with the institutionalization of mentally retarded citizens. Contributors include both lawyers and professionals in the mental retardation field. The lowering of communication barriers between lawyers and mental retardation professionals was a major goal of the editor. As a result, the writing is free from legal jargon and adaptable for use by nonlegal personnel.

3-163   Russell, L. Mark. **Alternatives: A Family Guide to Legal and Financial Planning for the Disabled.** Evanston, Ill.: First Publications, 1983. 194 pp. bib. glos. ind.

This book is a comprehensive source for information written specifically with the mentally disabled in mind, but with some information applicable to the physically disabled as well. Lawyers, social workers, organizations, and administrators involved in services to the handicapped may find this a useful reference guide. The author provides guidance to families caring for disabled children in such a way so as to maximize government benefits. Coverage includes wills, trusts, guardianship, tax deductions, insurance, and financial planning. Ninety-two organizations and ten governmental agencies are listed along with a glossary of terms.

Historic Preservation Law

3-164   Duerksen, Christopher F., ed. **A Handbook on Historic Perservation Law.** Washington, D.C.: Conservation Foundation, 1983. 750 pp. figs. tbls. apps. ind.

Seven chapters are included in a comprehensive handbook for lawyers and the lay public on a developing field involving law and economics. Practical legal tips on rehabilitation and reuse of old buildings are included as well as legal analysis of current applicable laws, regulations and court decisions.

Homosexuality. See Civil Rights

Hospitals. See Medicine

Hotels. See Innkeepers

Human Experimentation

3-165   Levy, Charlotte L. **The Human Body and the Law: Legal and Ethical Considerations in Human Experimentation.** 2d ed. Dobbs Ferry, N.Y.: Oceana, 1983. 150 pp. ns. bib. apps. ind.

The book is intended to acquaint readers with some of the "ethical, medical, and legal considerations" surrounding human experimentation. Beginning with a philosophical and ethical discussion as well as legal implications and control of such action, the author focuses on particular subjects: sterilization, fetal experimentation, transplants, the Uniform Anatomical Gift Act, psychological experimentation, and genetic engineering and control. Important documentary material from the U.S. government is included at the end, and important cases are cited throughout the text.

Husband and Wife. See Domestic Relations

Immigration Law

3-166   Carliner, David. **The Rights of Aliens.** New York: Avon Books, 1977. 255 pp. ns. apps.

This somewhat dated handbook is another in the series of publications by the American Civil Liberties Union. The text is in question-and-answer format and each chapter is followed by notes to legal case and statutory authority. Such matters as aliens' right to work, asylum, and military service are explained along with many other topics. Appendixes include organizations assisting aliens as well as a summary of state laws listing restrictions on alien employment.

3-167   Deutsch, Howard David. **Getting into America: The United States Visa and Immigration Handbook.** New York: Random House, 1984. 296 pp. apps. ind.

Practical solutions to immigration problems are provided in this fairly comprehensive guide, which generally avoids legal and bureaucratic jargon. Immigrants, relatives, interested employers, and immigration lawyers will find this book is a good reference source for answering many immigration questions. Appendixes include many forms in addition to the location of Immigration and Naturalization Service offices.

3-168   Jessup, Libby F. **How to Become a Citizen of the United States**, 4th ed. Dobbs Ferry, N.Y.: Oceana, 1972. 116 pp. ind.

Individuals desiring U.S. citizenship are provided information on the requirements for naturalization, eligibility of individuals in special categories, powers of the Immigration and Naturalization Service, and relevant facts about America and its system of government.

Income Tax. See Taxation

Individual Retirement Accounts

3-169   Egan, Jack. **Your Complete Guide to IRAs and Keoghs**. New York: Harper and Row, 1982. 246 pp. apps. ind.

This book is a clear guide to tax-deferred investments. Although primarily an investment guide, its secondary function is legal, providing investment alternatives as a means of avoiding taxes normally required by law. Extensive appendixes include tax schedules as well as top mutual funds and leading financial newsletters.

Innkeepers

3-170   Service, J. Gregory. **Hotel-Motel Law: A Primer on Innkeeper Liability**. Springfield, Ill.: Charles C. Thomas, 1983. 124 pp. apps.

Ten chapters briefly examine such matters as loss of guest property, food service liability, acts of employees and third parties, security personnel, injuries involving physical facilities, and more. Reader awareness is the purpose of this text, which refers to actual court cases. Management personnel, security personnel, citizens, and legal advisors should benefit from reading this work.

Insurance

3-171   Dobbyn, John F. **Insurance Law in a Nutshell**. St. Paul: West, 1981. 281 pp. ind.

Twelve chapters provide an overview of this complex field, beginning with the nature and types of insurance and concluding with insurance regulation. Also included are chapters on defenses, procedures for filling claims, waiver and estoppel, subrogation, and reinsurance.

3-172   Taylor, Irwin M. **The Law of Insurance**. 3d ed. Dobbs Ferry, N.Y.: Oceana, 1983. 156 pp. glos. tbls. apps. ind.

All major forms of insurance contracts—including the legal nature of such contracts—are discussed. Life, accident, fire, casualty, marine, and other insurance contracts are explained in understandable terms.

Principal mortality tables and life expectancy tables are included in the text, but the reader may want to look elsewhere for additional references to legal authority.

Intellectual and Industrial Property

3-173   Chickering, Robert B., and Susan Hartman. **How to Register a Copyright and Protect Your Creative Work.** New York: Charles Scribner's Sons, 1980. 216 pp. fms. apps. ind.

The first half of this work leads the reader through the copyright process; and the second half is directed to general information, answering common questions and explaining areas of special interest. Although copyright registration may be accomplished by nonlawyers, the authors caution the use of a copyright lawyer in appropriate circumstances.

3-174   Diamond, Sidney A. **Trademark Problems and How to Avoid Them.** rev. ed. Chicago: Crain Books, 1981. 276 pp. ns. ind.

Consisting mostly of a series of case histories concerning trademarks and brand name problems, this book seeks to explain how potential trademark problems may be avoided. An index of named trademarks and notes to case authority follow an easy-to-understand text. Lawyers and the lay public should benefit from a reading of this work, which includes chapters on the history and basics of trademarks, how to choose trademarks, nicknames, updating trademark designs, and much more.

3-175   Erickson, J. Gunnar, Edward R. Hearn, and Mark E. Halloran. **Musician's Guide to Copyright.** 2d ed. New York: Charles Scribner's Sons, 1983. 128 pp. app. fms. ns. ind.

Written by Bay Area Lawyers for the Arts (BALA) in the San Francisco area, and intended for songwriters, musicians, managers, and attorneys, this book seeks to provide a working knowledge of the U.S. copyright law. The authors' suggest readers should consult a music attorney where appropriate. The text is broken down into five chapters, covering copyright fundamentals, gaining copyright, length and transfer of copyright, income, and infringement. The book is followed by an appendix consisting of copyright registration forms, and extensive notes citing legal authority.

3-176   Flanagan, John R. **How to Prepare Patent Applications.** Troy, Ohio: Patent Educational Publications, 1983. 260 pp. apps.

This publication should appeal to a wide audience, including attorneys, law students, inventors, engineering firms, and members of the scientific and business communities. Actual mechanical, electrical, and chemical inventions are used as examples in this self-study course book providing information on writing patent applications. Twelve chapters include information on basic patent principles, drafting claims, preparing drawings, and so forth. Appendixes include selected provisions of the Code of Federal Regulations and patent materials.

3-177   Gasaway, Laura Nell, and Maureen Murphy. **Legal Protection for Computer Programs.** Boulder, Colo.: Cause Publications, 1980. 117 pp. ns. tbl.

This book is published by the Professional Association for Development, Use and Management of Information Systems in Higher Education. It is a basic primer on computer software and proposed forms of legal protection.

Following the introduction, the authors discuss in detail copyright, patent, trade secret protection, and unfair competition. Each chapter is followed by notes and references to principal cases, statutes, and other sources. The text is followed by an excellent comparative table listing the various forms of legal protection.

3-178 Glassman, Don. **Writers' and Artists' Rights: Basic Benefits and Protections to Authors, Artists, Composers, Sculptors, Photographers, Choreographers, and Movie-makers under the New American Copyright Law.** Washington, D.C.: Writers Press, 1978. 104 pp. pls. ill. app.

This photo-illustrated work consists of thirteen chapters divided into two parts: Authorship and Copyrights, and A New Age for Authors and Publishers. The appendix lists—among other matters—countries following the Universal and Pan American copyright conventions.

The book is easy to read, and although brief, provides practical, incisive information to common questions asked by artists and writers.

3-179 Johnston, Donald F. **Copyright Handbook**, 2d ed. New York: R.R. Bowker, 1982. 381 pp. apps. fms. ind.

The book is written by the counsel for the publisher, and it is intended for publishers and authors as well as teachers and librarians. Attorneys may also find this work useful where their work does not involve or require more detailed resources such as court decisions, treatises, or law review articles.

All aspects of copyright are discussed. Extensive appendixes include laws, regulations, forms, and texts of various guidelines developed with official sanction. A detailed table of contents provides easy access to the problems or questions arising in this area.

3-180 Pressman, David. **Patent It Yourself! How to Protect, Patent, and Market Your Inventions.** New York: McGraw-Hill, 1979. 210 pp. fms. bib. ind.

This is a practical, do-it-yourself book, providing information on how to submit patent applications. Its thirteen chapters are easy to read and understand. Practical advice is furnished throughout, and there are references to useful books, organizations, and alternative resources.

3-181 Saliwanchick, Roman. **Legal Protection for Microbiological and Genetic Engineering Inventions.** Reading, Mass.: Addison-Wesley, 1982. 256 pp. apps. fms. ns. inds.

This book is written by a lawyer with over twenty years in the patent field and extensive background in microbiology. It is specifically intended for use by scientists involved in this newly developing field.

The two major legal areas, trade secrets and patents, are covered in detail, and there are chapters devoted to legal protection outside the United States. Because of the extensive inclusion of forms and legal authority, lawyers unfamiliar with this field will find this work extremely helpful.

International Law

3-182 Kirkemo, Ronald B. **An Introduction to International Law.** Totowa, N.J.: Littlefield, Adams, 1975. 235 pp. ns. bib. ind.

Although not a definitive work, this book is intended to fill the gap in material available to undergraduate students taking world politics courses. The work provides an overview of international law, acting as a supplemental text. Even though undergraduates are the intended audience, lawyers, law students, businessmen, politicians, and interested members of the lay public will find this a useful introduction to a very important—and difficult—area of concern to all nations.

Journalists. *See* Authors

Judges

3-183 Reynolds, William L. **Judicial Process in a Nutshell.** St. Paul: West, 1980. 292 pp. tbl. ind.

This book explores the means by which judges in the United States decide cases. Although intended primarily for law students, the author expresses the hope that this work will be used by others "interested in the process."

3-184 Roberts, Marilyn McCoy, and David Rhein, eds. **Women in the Judiciary: A Symposium for Women Judges.** Williamsburg, Va.: National Center for State Courts, 1983. 102 pp. bib. apps.

This publication grew out of a conference held in Racine, Wisconsin, on 15-17 April 1982. The symposium, the first of its kind, examines personal and professional matters of sitting women judges. Presentations and discussions include topics such as sex discrimination, obstacles to judicial education, day-to-day professional experiences, and balancing one's personal life with a career. An excellent bibliography on issues involving women in the judiciary follows the text. This is a good resource for women in the legal field and interested citizens involved in women's rights issues.

3-185 Schmidhauser, John R. **Judges and Justices: The Federal Appellate Judiciary.** Boston: Little, Brown, 1979. 248 pp. tbls. ns. ind.

Designed as a textbook for courses in judicial process, or as a supplement to political science, governmental, constitutional law or history courses, this book may also be of interest to federal judges, lawyers, and the general public. The seven chapters describe the history of the federal appellate judiciary, its contemporary setting, and compare the court structure with state appellate or other national appellate court structures. Each chapter is followed by extensive notes to authority.

Judges—Biography

3-186 Coffin, Frank M. **The Ways of a Judge: Reflections on the Federal Appellate Bench.** Boston: Houghton Mifflin, 1980. 273 pp. ns. ind.

This book, a discourse on the author's life and work as a federal appellate judge on the United States Court of Appeals for the First Circuit, won honorable mention from the American Association of Law Schools as among the best law books published between 1980 and 1983. Chapters explore the appellate process, examine the working environment leading to appellate opinions, and describe the thought processes leading to decisions. The text is informative and insightful. Inside the front and back covers is an outline of the federal and state court systems.

3-187   Dunne, Gerald T. **Hugo Black and the Judicial Revolution.** New York: Simon and Schuster, 1977. 492 pp. ns. bib. ind.

The author has written about Justice Black's entire life before, and during, his years on the United States Supreme Court.

3-188   Simon, James F. **Independent Journey: The Life of William O. Douglas.** New York: Harper and Row, 1980. 502 pp. ind.

The author won the Scribes Award from the American Society of Writers on Legal Subjects for writing this biography on Justice Douglas, a libertarian who served on the United States Supreme Court for thirty-six years.

Judgments.   *See* Civil Procedure

Jurisprudence

3 189   Carter, Lief H. **Reason in Law.** Boston: Little, Brown, 1979. 258 pp. ns. ind.

Intended for nonlawyers, this work is also valuable for use in law schools, and should be read by lawyers and judges as well. Each chapter is followed by a brief summary and exploratory problems. Chapters consider matters such as elements of legal reasoning, interpreting statutes, and the common law. This is a lucid, excellent work delving into the process of legal analysis and reasoning.

3-190   Golding, Martin P. **Philosophy of Law.** Englewood Cliffs, N.J.: Prentice-Hall, 1975. 133 pp. ns. bib. ind.

Undergraduate and graduate students in philosophy, as well as law students, interested lawyers and citizens, are provided a brief introduction to legal philosphy. Chapters analyze the nature and limits of law, punishment, justice, and the settling of disputes.

3-191   Morawetz, Thomas. **The Philosophy of Law: An Introduction.** New York: Macmillan, 1980. 238 pp. ns. ind.

Legal philosophers, philosophy and law students, moralists, and interested laypersons will find this brief, introductory work informative and helpful in understanding legal philosophy. Four chapters describe the concept of law, judicial decisions, morality and legislation, and responsibility and punishment.

Juveniles

3-192   Davis, James R. **Help Me, I'm Hurt: The Child Abuse Handbook.** Dubuque, Iowa: Kendall/Hunt, 1982. 166 pp. fms. app.

Social workers, law enforcement officials, teachers, doctors, and parents will find this book informative and helpful in understanding, and dealing with, child abuse. The text includes example forms for documenting child abuse. Guidelines for recognizing and handling suspected child abuse cases are provided in addition to chapters on common medical terms, reporting laws, criminal laws, injuries common to abused children, incest, and building a community response to child abuse.

3-193   Dorman, Michael. **Under 21: A Young People's Guide to Legal Rights.** New York: Delacorte Press, 1970. 210 pp. apps. ind.

Although dated, this is an informative work and a good starting point for learning the basic concepts surrounding minors' rights. Chapters explore such issues as dress and hairstyle, employment, voting, drugs, marriage, and the draft. The text is written in a clear manner. In addition to other matters, appendixes list driving, drinking, and marriage age requirements in all the states.

3-194   Fontana, Vincent J., and Douglas J. Besharov. **The Maltreated Child: The Maltreatment Syndrome in Children: A Medical, Legal, and Social Guide,** 3d ed. Springfield, Ill.: Charles C. Thomas, 1977. 156 pp. bib. inds.

Coauthored by a doctor (Fontana) and a lawyer (Besharov), this volume is intended to be a medical-legal guide for professionals and paraprofessionals in the field of child abuse. The medical content includes material on diagnosis, social manifestations, and prevatative measures. The legal content includes material on the Model Child Protection Act and discussion of the legal responsibilities of parents, physicians, and agencies. The bibliography is extensive. There is some use of technical language in view of the intended professional audience. However, the lay public will find it readable. It is also a prime source of information about other literature and the Model Child Protection Act. A fourth edition was published in 1979.

3-195   Kalisch, Beatrice J. **Child Abuse and Neglect: An Annotated Bibliography.** Westport, Conn.: Greenwood Press, 1978. 535 pp. apps. ind.

The second in the Contemporary Problems of Childhood series, this work covers literature from the late 1800's to 1977 and includes literature from law as well as a dozen or more other fields. Nearly one hundred pages cover legal issues. Information from every type of publication is included, except foreign language materials. With over two thousand entries, this is a truly useful work for anyone involved in detailed research of this area, or initially looking for information on a specific aspect of child abuse.

3-196   Kobetz, Richard W., and Betty B. Bosarge. **Juvenile Justice Administration.** Gaithersburg, Md.: International Association of Chiefs of Police, 1973. 769 pp. tbls. apps. bib. ind.

This book is an outgrowth of conferences on delinquency prevention, which developed as a result of the report by the President's Commission on Law

126 / Selected Subject Bibliography of Law-related Monographs

Enforcement and the Administration of Justice in 1967. Components of the juvenile justice system are analyzed and recommendations are given while looking towards the twenty-first century. Juvenile justice administrators, police administrators, parents, the public, and lawyers, among others, should still benefit from this somewhat dated work that seeks to foster cooperation and system unification. Charts, or tables, are included in the text.

3-197 Loeb, Robert H., Jr., and John P. Maloney. **Your Legal Rights as a Minor.** rev. ed. New York: Franklin Watts, 1978. 154 pp. ns. tbls. bib. ind.

This is a very readable question-and-answer text with ten chapters exploring the more common issues involving minors. Subjects include driving, commercial rights, sexual rights, drugs, school matters, and the right to hold public office. Tables compare various state laws on matters involving drugs, marriage, and driving age requirements.

3-198 Sloan, Irving J. **Child Abuse: Governing Law and Legislation.** Dobbs Ferry, N.Y.: Oceana, 1983. 151 pp. bib. apps. tbl. ind.

This work provides information for recognizing child abuse and neglect in addition to other matters. Each state's laws on the definition of child abuse and the requirements for reporting the wrongs are included.

3-199 Sussman, Alan N. **The Rights of Young People: The Basic ACLU Guide to a Young Person's Rights.** New York: Avon Books, 1977. 251 pp. ns. apps. bib.

This handbook follows the typical ACLU format. Twelve chapters explore every major consideration involving the rights of minors, including matters such as employment, age of majority, access to courts, marriage, the draft, and so forth. Each chapter is followed by notes to relevant case and statutory authority. Chapter twelve lists such things as age of majority in each state, legal age for purchase of alcohol, age requirements for marriage and voting, among others. The twelfth and last appendix includes the "United Nations Declaration on the Rights of the Child."

3-200 Swiger, Elinor Porter. **The Law and You.** 3d ed. New York: Bobbs-Merrill, 1980. 150 pp. glos. ind.

This work is a brief summary of common legal problems of interest primarily to young people. The language is easy to read, and legalese is avoided. Typical inquiries involving dog bites or trespassing across a vacant lot are answered along with many other legal questions youngsters may ask.

3-201 Thomas, R. Murray, and Paul V. Murray. **Cases: A Resource Guide for Teaching about the Law.** Glenview, Ill.: Scott Foresman, 1982. 142 pp. ill.

This book is a collection of resource materials for teachers instructing students, ages eight to sixteen, about the juvenile law enforcement system and the rights of minors. Sixteen chapters are arranged in logical instructional sequence with actual cases drawn from police records, newspaper reports, and the experience of law enforcement officials. Activities, worksheets, and suggestions for discussion accompany each case story, and the text is in clear, understandable language in order to assist students in comprehending the language of the law as well as the law itself.

3-202 Vardin, Patricia A., and Ilene N. Brody, eds. **Children's Rights: Contemporary Perspectives.** New York: Teachers College Press, 1979. 182 pp.

Thirteen contributors analyze children's rights, including legal, moral, and ethical considerations, children as victims, family breakdowns, mainstreaming the handicapped, advocacy and mental health professionals, international perspectives, and reassessing educational priorities. This volume grew out of a conference held at Columbia University in 1977. Children's rights advocates, including teachers, lawyers, psychologists, and others may find this useful in their efforts to improve upon their knowledge in the field.

3-203 Wilkerson, Albert E. **The Rights of Children: Emergent Concepts in Law and Society.** Philadelphia: Temple University Press, 1973. 313 pp. ns.

This dated work is a collection of essays by various authors on major issues in child welfare. It is divded into three sections: examining the child as a person, protection of children, and decisions involving children. This book is still useful to students and professional personnel in child welfare services as well as individuals and organizations implementing social change through the courts and in the field. The text is footnoted throughout to legal authority.

Labor Law

3-204 Anderson, Howard J., and John J. Kenny. **Primer of Labor Relations.** 22d ed. Washington, D.C.: Bureau of National Affairs, 1983. 161 pp. ns. glos. ind.

Ten chapters briefly summarize labor relations law. The text is easy to read, and there are numerous references to case authority, which is listed following a very helpful glossary of labor terminology. Labor-management personnel, employers and employees, and interested citizens will find this a good introductory resource on labor law.

3-205 Anderson, Howard J., and Michael D. Levin-Epstein. **Primer of Equal Employment Opportunity.** 2d ed. Washington, D.C.: Bureau of National Affairs, 1982. 131 pp. tbl. ind.

Employers and employees, government administrators, and lawyers are given a concise, but current overview of the field of equal employment. Four parts—consisting of a total of sixteen chapters—list the many laws, regulations, and guidelines, explain the laws according to the type of applicable discrimination, analyze policy and practice issues, and discuss enforcement and administrative matters.

3-206 Coulson, Robert. **Labor Arbitration—What You Need to Know**. 2d ed. N.Y.: American Arbitration Association, 1978. 163 pp. ns. glos. bib.

Written by the president of the American Arbitration Association, this practical book is dedicated to the proposition that man's highest goal is to bring "peace and understanding to the human condition."

The text includes four chapters on the concept of a grievance, selection of an arbitrator, public sector arbitration, and preparing for a hearing. Over two-thirds of the work is devoted to the appendix, which includes material such as a glossary of terms, key court decisions, a bibliography, a classification guide, code of ethics for arbitrators, and regional directors and their offices. A third edition was published in 1981.

3-207 Ewing, David W. **Do It My Way or You're Fired: Employee Rights and the Changing Role of Management Prerogatives**. New York: John Wiley and Sons, 1983. 387 pp. ns. app. ind.

The primary purpose of this book is to aid employers in understanding emerging employee rights and how to deal constructively with these changes. Employees and others will also find this work is a useful guide to their rights when they become employed by an organization. The text is lightly footnoted and easy to read. Significant court cases since the mid-1970s are analyzed in addition to other matters.

3-208 Fisher, Roger, and William Ury. **Getting to Yes: Negotiating Agreement without Giving In**. Boston: Houghton Mifflin, 1981. 163 pp.

This work applies a method of negotiation as a way for people to deal with differences. Using a theory called "Principled Negotiation" developed by the Harvard Negotiation Project, the authors provide a means to avoid direct confrontation. Principled negotiation essentially involves deciding issues on merits rather than on the haggling process, which focuses on what each side says it will and will not do.

Everyone, including lawyers, couples, negotiators, members of Congress, and diplomats should find this method helpful in learning to solve both legal and nonlegal disputes.

3-209 **Grievance Guide**. 6th ed. Washington, D.C.: Bureau of National Affairs, 1982. 375 pp.

Written in a straightforward style by the editorial staff as a guide to grievance arbitration, this book illustrates principles applying to many bargaining situations. Employees, management, and union officials, as well as labor lawyers, will find this work most helpful in providing guidelines for such matters as vacations, poor work, union rights, disciplinary proceedings, health plans, wages and hours, and so forth. Citations are provided to *Labor Arbitration,* a BNA reporting service which is part of the *Labor Relations Reporter,* one of the oldest labor information services.

3-210 Harvey, John H., and Elizabeth M. Dickinson. **Librarians' Affirmative Action Handbook**. Metuchen, N.J.: Scarecrow Press, 1983. 305 pp. apps. ind.

This work is designed as a comprehensive handbook on affirmative action, discrimination, and equal employment opportunity in the field of librarianship in the United States. Major areas of library equal employment compliance are discussed with the exception of issues where there is little available information, such as the affirmative action need of Hispanic librarians and school media affirmative action programs.

The text consists of thirteen articles written by contributors in the field and is followed by appendixes listing library entry level required skills, an affirmative action report checklist, and a library recruitment data form.

3-211   Hill, Marvin Jr., and Anthony Sinicropi. **Evidence in Arbitration.** Washington, D.C.: Bureau of National Affairs, 1980. 201 pp. apps. ind.

Arbitrators will find this most helpful in gaining a working knowledge of the concepts and use of evidence, and in providing standards for rendering an award based upon all the facts and material considerations. Notes to legal authority and a table of cases follow the text. Appendixes include a code of ethics, and rules and acts relevant to arbitrators.

3-212   Honigsberg, Peter Jan. **The Unemployment Benefits Handbook.** Reading, Mass.: Addison-Wesley, 1981. 158 pp. fms. app. ind.

The book is intended for people in all fifty states and in U.S. possessions such as Puerto Rico and the Virgin Islands. The text points out various state differences in a very useful appendix.

Chapters explore such matters as benefits, coverage, eligibility, dealing with the bureaucracy, and appeals. The language is easy to read and legalese is avoided. Forms and factual examples of unemployment problems are scattered throughout the book.

3-213   Hood, Jack B., and Benjamin A. Hardy, Jr. **Workers' Compensation and Employee Protection Laws in a Nutshell.** St. Paul: West, 1984. 274 pp. app. ind.

Employers and employees as well as lawyers and law students are provided with an overview of worker protection and compensation laws. Specific matters such as historical background, the employer-employee relationship, and medical expenses are detailed in workers' compensation; and employee protection legislation includes an analysis of unemployment compensation, antidiscrimination laws, social security, and other major federal acts.

3-214   Levin, Noel Arnold. **Guidelines for Fiduciaries of Taft-Hartley Trusts: An ERISA Manual.** Brookfield, Wis.: International Foundation of Employee Benefit Plans, 1980. 137 pp. ind.

The Employee Retirement Income Security Act (ERISA) of 1974 is considered by many as the most significant piece of social legislation since social security, and this book provides guidelines for management and labor operating joint labor-management trusts, also known as Taft-Hartley funds. The text is lightly footnoted with legal citations, and is broken down into eight chapters. Attorneys working in this area may also find this book useful as a quick reference tool.

3-215   Loevi, Francis J., and Roger P. Kaplan. **Arbitration and the Federal Sector Advocate.** 2d ed. New York: American Arbitration Association, 1982. 80 pp. apps.

This book is intended for individuals planning to become union or management representatives in arbitration; or those with experience at the federal level who may want further insight into responsibilities imposed by a contract, including an agreement to arbitrate unresolved grievances. Chapters discuss whether to arbitrate, selection of an arbitrator, preparation, the hearing, and posthearing matters. Extensive appendixes include relevant statutes and regulations, and other information pertaining to the process of arbitration.

3-216   O'Neil, Robert. **The Rights of Government Employees.** New York: Avon Books, 1978. 176 pp. ns.

Well over 15 percent of the work force works for government, at the federal, state, or local level. This book describes these individuals and their rights, exploring such matters as qualifications for work, freedom of speech, politics and unions, private affairs of public employees, race and sex discrimination, and procedural rights. The text is in question-and-answer format common to American Civil Liberties Union books. Each chapter is followed by notes to legal authority.

3-217   Rothenberg, I. Herbert, and Steven B. Silverman. **Labor Unions: How to Avert Them, Beat Them, Out-Negotiate Them, Live With Them, Unload Them.** Elkins Park, Pa.: Management Relations, 1973. 406 pp.

Employers, trade associations and "non specialist" lawyers are the intended audience of this readable work, which explains how to avoid mistakes and miscalculations when going up against a labor union.

3-218   Shimp, Donna M., Alfred W. Blumrosen, and Stuart B. Finifter. **How to Protect Your Health at Work.** Salem, N.J.: Environmental Improvement Associates, 1976. 318 pp. tbls. fms. apps. ind.

Although the book is written with tobacco smoke as the health hazard, the same legal procedures are applicable to any unhealthy condition affecting work environments. Over three-quarters of the text consists of example pleadings and other materials. Employees, labor unions, physicians, lawyers, and health care agencies should find this handbook a useful aid in matters involving health hazards to employees.

Labor Unions. See Labor Law

Land Use—Planning

3-219   Moss, Elaine, ed. **Land Use Controls in the United States: A Handbook on the Legal Rights of Citizens.** New York: Dial Press, 1977. 362 pp. ns. ind.

Present federal and many state laws affecting control or use of land are included. Each chapter contains material on "citizen action," which suggests ways in which individuals may participate in the implementation and enforcement of the laws. Among the fourteen chapters are titles dealing with constitutional issues, various federal acts (e.g., the Coastal Zone Management Act), consumer and investor protection, the public lands of the United States, and state, regional, and local land use controls. Footnotes cite applicable laws, regulations, and case reports.

3-220   Smith, Herbert H. **The Citizen's Guide to Planning.** 2d ed. Chicago: Planners Press, 1979. 198 pp. glos. apps. bib. ind.

This revised edition is directed to all interested citizens as well as newly appointed members of planning boards. It is intended as a guidebook for those involved in urban and suburban problems, covering such matters as the relationship of zoning to planning and planning to school boards.

The text is not footnoted, but serves as an introduction to a very complex subject touching upon every populated area of the United States. A useful glossary of terms follows the text in addition to example plans for Denver, Colorado, and Albuquerque, New Mexico, which are located in the appendixes.

3-221   Smith, Herbert H. **The Citizen's Guide to Zoning.** Washington, D.C.: Planners Press, American Planning Association, 1983. 242 pp. apps. glos. bib. ind.

This work is intended as a comprehensive introduction to planning for laypeople as well as professionals in the field. Twelve chapters cover all matters of zoning from philosophy, principles, regulations, and problems to recent developments and emerging techniques. The helpful appendixes include a glossary of terms used in zoning and a brief bibliography.

Landlord and Tenant

3-222   Blumberg, Richard E., and James R. Grow. **The Rights of Tenants.** New York: Avon Books, 1978. 192 pp. ns. apps.

The text is arranged in the typical American Civil Liberties Union (ACLU) question-and-answer style with citations to legal and other authority following each chapter. Seventeen chapters are arranged in two parts. The first part explains basic rights such as evictions, housing codes and retaliatory actions, and the second half analyzes advanced reforms, including retroactive rent abatement and rent control.

3-223   Robinson, Leigh. **The Eviction Book for California.** 2d ed. Richmond, Calif.: EXPRESS, 1982. 170 pp. fms. glos. ind.

This book is intended for California landlords conducting evictions. Ten chapters include information on preventing evictions and removing problem tenants without going to court. The language is simple and easy to understand, and the text is followed by a glossary of terms and California legal forms.

3-224   Slonim, Scott. **Landlords and Tenants: Your Guide to the Law.** Chicago: American Bar Association, 1982. 48 pp. apps. glos.

132 / Selected Subject Bibliography of Law-related Monographs

This publication is intended for both landlord and tenant, and explains in question-and answer format the four fundamental concepts involved in each tenancy: leases, the premises, rent, and parting ways.

The primary intent of this pamphlet is to create an awareness of general rights and responsibilities. Readers are cautioned to consult local state laws and landlord-tenant organizations for further clarification of each state's particular requirements. Excellent appendixes explain discrimination, local conditions, and where to go for help.

3-225   Striker, John M., and Andrew O. Shapiro. **New York City Tenant Handbook: Super Tenant: Your Legal Rights and How to Use Them**, rev. ed., New York: Holt, Rinehart and Winston, 1978. 268 pp. apps. fms. ind.

Although written for the New York City tenant, this book will be of assistance elsewhere for those who desire an overview of tenant's rights and practical advice on how to pursue them. General principles on rent are presented in a concise introduction. Part 1 covers all phases of apartment living and the law, part 2 deals with rent controls and stabilization, part 3 with maintenance and repairs, and part 4 with court actions. Appendixes include tenant organizations, forms, a listing of free legal services and a directory of city agency courts.

Law

3-226   Cataldo, Bernard F., et al. **Introduction to Law and the Legal Process.** 3d ed. New York: John Wiley and Sons, 1980. 866 pp. ns. app. tbl. ind.

This is a college-level text intended for teaching law to business and liberal arts students, but it is also quite useful for any number of individuals seeking a general understanding of major legal concepts. The first eleven chapters furnish background information for understanding the law. The last eleven chapters analyze contracts and agency-areas of law fundamental to our economic and social structure. Actual cases are sometimes included at the end of each chapter, and problem exercises follow every chapter. The text is lightly footnoted and a table of edited cases follows the appendix.

3-227   Coughlin, George Gordon. **Your Introduction to Law**, 4th ed. New York: Barnes and Noble, 1982. 358 pp. glos. ind.

More than twenty areas of law are briefly explored in a very readable book intended for citizens interested in learning about legal concepts. Both procedural and substantive areas of law are covered, including court procedure, contracts, defamation, wills, criminal law, business and commercial matters, and personal and social matters. An excellent glossary of legal terms and a brief index follow an unfootnoted text. Individuals seeking expansion of their knowledge by references to sources elsewhere will need to look for other, more involved and detailed resources.

3-228   Farnsworth, E. Alan. **An Introduction to the Legal System of the United States.** 2d ed. Dobbs Ferry, N.Y.: Oceana, 1983. 172 pp. bib. ns. app. ind.

Anyone interested in understanding and learning about the American legal system will benefit from this work. Rather than exhaustive, it is illustrative, and the legal structure of the United States is described in general terms. The two parts of the book are divided into twelve chapters, discussing historical background, legal education, the legal profession, the judicial structure, case law, legislation, statutes, secondary legal authority, classification, procedures, and public and private law. The text is lightly footnoted and the end of each chapter provides a suggested reading list. The appendix includes two example cases and how case and statutory law are intrepreted.

3-229 Fincher, E. B. **The American Legal System.** New York: Franklin Watts, 1980. 65 pp. pls. glos. bib. ind.

Written by a student and teacher of history and political science, this book is best suited for juveniles up to the high school level. The text is essentially an introductory statement on the concept of law and the legal system, relating the experience of two teenagers in trouble with the law. One is tried as a juvenile, and the other is tried as an adult. A somewhat dated diagram of the state and federal court systems is found on page forty-one.

3-230 Fisher, Bruce D. **Introduction to the Legal System.** 2d ed. St. Paul: West, 1977. 846 pp. glos. ind.

This book was designed for undergraduate business and graduate nonlaw college courses. Beginning with a description of the theory and concept of law, the text analyzes civil and criminal lawsuits, legal reasoning, substantive law, the nature of property, white collar crimes, and torts. The remainder of the book considers contracts, labor relations, partnerships and corporate legal theories, and practice and regulation. Questions and comments are scattered throughout the work. The book is arranged in a format very similar to typical law student textbooks, and the general reader may find this somewhat intimidating.

3-231 Friedman, Lawrence M. **American Law.** New York: W. W. Norton, 1985. 362 pp. ns. ind.

The author is a fellow of the American Academy of Arts and Sciences, and Professor of Law at Stanford Law School. In an understandable manner, the writer provides insight into the complex system which makes up American law. Fifteen chapters explore matters such as what constitutes a legal system, the courts, statues, crimes and punishments, the legal profession, and so forth. An interesting, informative "Documents" section following the last chapter briefly describes some of the most prominent sources discussed in the text, and examples of constitutions, legislation, administrative regulations, and case law are included.

3-232 Furcalo, Foster. **Law for You.** Washington, D.C.: Acropolis Books, 1975. 192 pp. glos. ill. ind.

Written by a former governor and congressman, and intended for the average individual desiring a general knowledge of the law without a lawyer's expertise, this work concerns itself with daily problems faced by citizens. The language is simple and clear, the text is not footnoted, and humorous cartoons are scattered throughout.

The author covers a myriad of legal concepts, including sources and attributes of our legal system, constitutional guarantees, criminal matters, briefing cases, contracts, personal injury, wills, divorce, and women's rights, among others. The glossary is useful, but very brief, including only selected legal terms. The strong suit of this book is its simple explanation of legal concepts. A subsequent edition was published in 1977 as *Law for the Layman*.

3-233　　Gilmore, Grant. **The Ages of American Law.** New Haven, Conn.: Yale University Press, 1977. 154 pp. ind.

Although of fairly recent origin, this brief, but well-written book is already considered by some as a classic in American legal literature. The text is based upon the Storrs Lectures given in 1974 at Yale Law School. The author briefly summarizes 150 years of American law from 1800 to about 1950.

3-234　　Harnett, Bertram. **Law, Lawyers, and Laymen: Making Sense of the American Legal System.** New York: Harcourt Brace Jovanovich, 1984. 324 pp. bib. ind.

Citizens, judges, lawyers, law students, and those considering law school are provided with a clear approach to the American legal system and how it really operates. Written by a judge, the book's eleven chapters yield an enlightening analysis of such matters as lawyers, legal ethics, paying for a case, on becoming a client, selecting judges, and much more.

3-235　　Helm, Alice K., ed. **The Family Legal Advisor: A Clear, Reliable and Up-to-date Guide to Your Rights and Remedies under the Law.** New York: Greystone Press, 1978. 480 pp. glos. ind.

The primary purpose of the twenty-six chapters that make up this book is to provide an understanding of the general rules governing the law touching the daily lives of the average family. The text is very easy to read, and written in a style intended to entertain as well as instruct. Numerous example cases are provided on subjects such as children, wills, property rights, names, and criminal law. There are no footnotes or references to authority, so individuals interested in expanding their research will have to consult alternative resources. A dictionary of common legal terms, and a general index follow the body of the work.

3-236　　Henszey, Benjamin N., Barry Lee Myers, and Reed T. Phalan. **Introduction to Basic Legal Principles.** 3d ed. Dubuque, Iowa: Kendall/Hunt, 1982. 720 pp. ns. ind.

This book is intended primarily for undergraduate college courses in law and business, but it is also useful as a legal resource guide for anyone interested in understanding law as an integral part of our free enterprise system and learning basic legal concepts. Major areas of law influencing business, from personal injury to agency, commercial matters, and gifts and inheritance are discussed. Problems follow

Selected Subject Bibliography of Law-related Monographs / 135

each chapter, and example cases are included throughout the book. The text is lightly footnoted to legal authority.

3-237   Last, Jack, Douglas B. Oliver, and Betsy B. McKenney. **Everyday Law Made Simple.** rev. ed. Garden City, N.Y.: Doubleday, 1978. 172 pp. figs. tbls. glos. ind.

Basic legal principles are surveyed in an uncomplicated manner with twenty-five chapters briefly enumerating rights on everyday concerns such as contracts, sales, checks, agency, employment, partnerships, corporations, property, mortgages, landlord and tenant, estates, domestic relations, criminal law and much more. An excellent glossary of legal terms follows the text.

3-238   Mermin, Samuel. **Law and the Legal System: An Introduction.** 2d ed. Boston: Little, Brown, 1982. 462 pp. apps. ns. ind.

This book was written to meet the varied demands of college students considering law school, prelaw advisors in universities, lawyer parents desiring their college-aged children to be exposed to the concept of legal studies, educated citizens interested in the legal system, and first-year law students.

The writer begins by providing a general view of the legal system. Then, starting with an illustrative case, the author describes the impact of precedent, and statutory and constitutional authority upon the outcome. A postscript analyzes the future of the legal profession, and the text ends with tips on the mechanics of law study and a description of the Bill of Rights protection in criminal cases. There are over 240 footnotes throughout the work citing legal authority.

3-239   **Reader's Digest Family Legal Guide: A Complete Encyclopedia of Law for the Layman.** Pleasantville, N.Y.: Reader's Digest Association, 1981. 1,268 pp. tbls. ind.

The text is arranged in alphabetical order similar to a dictionary or encyclopedic format. Although it is not a substitute for a lawyer, it offers a basic outline of the law for a multitude of legal situations. Example case histories appear throughout, and highlights or summaries of long articles are included along with many cross-references. This informative, voluminous, and extensive work also includes special articles on topics such as dealing with one's lawyer, landord, and so forth; and it includes thirty-four charts or tables on major areas of state laws.

3-240   Sabin, Arthur J. **All about Suing and Being Sued.** Mountain View, Calif.: Anderson World, 1981. 91 pp. ill. apps. fms. glos. ind.

This brief work is intended to eliminate the ignorance surrounding litigation and what being sued, or suing, means. It does not tell one how to sue or be sued, but rather provides an understanding of the legal process so parties to a lawsuit may act rationally and efficiently.

The author, an attorney and law professor, briefly explains such matters as the American legal system, choosing an attorney, settlements, and evidence. A glossary of legal terms is followed by a number of sample legal documents.

3-241 Sarshik, Steven, and Walter Szykitka. **Without a Lawyer.** New York: New American Library, 1980. 212 pp. fms. tbls. glos. ind.

People who want to handle their own legal problems without a lawyer will find this book useful in areas such as contracts, leases, corporations, consumer credit, divorce, and bankruptcy. The text is in everyday language with examples and actual case histories interspersed throughout. The authors caution on the evolving nature of law and using a lawyer in certain situations.

3-242 Shain, Henry. **Legal First Aid: Your Complete Basic Guide to the Law (in Understandable Language).** New York: Funk and Wagnalls, 1975. 366 pp. tbls. glos. ind.

Designed to provide citizens with a good background on the laws governing everyday life, the author emphasizes California law; but he is quick to point out that the laws of the states "are so similar . . . this book is useful everywhere in America." Thirty-three chapters are arranged under five parts: origin and structure of law, criminal and civil lawsuits, the family, injury claims, and consumer protection.

Legalese is avoided and nontechnical terms are used. Examples are used throughout to explain legal concepts and a glossary of legal terms follows the text along with the U.S. Constitution. Comparative tables, or charts, list the laws of the state in appropriate cases.

3-243 Steingold, Fred S. **The Practical Guide to Michigan Law.** Ann Arbor, Mich.: University of Michigan Press, 1983. 283 pp. fms. glos.

The title explains the purpose of this work, which is to inform interested Michigan residents about law and the legal system. Twelve chapters cover familiar legal areas most encountered by individuals such as hiring a lawyer, criminal matters, divorce, consumer protection, wills and estates, business problems, landlord-tenant issues, purchasing a home, personal injuries, and using small claims court.

Legal citations and footnoting are eschewed by the author, a Michigan attorney. Instead, the emphasis is on practical approaches to solving legal problems and questions. The first two chapters are especially useful, explaining how the legal system functions, and what goes on in a lawsuit.

3-244 Very, Donald L. **The Legal Guide for the Family.** Garden City, N.Y.: Doubleday, 1982. 435 pp. ind.

The book is not a definitive statement of any one area of the law, but offers an overall view of the legal system with an emphasis on those areas of law most individuals will come into contact with during their lives. The work begins with a discussion of what law is all about, and provides insight into the relationship of attorney and client, including how to find a lawyer.

Covered are homeowner problems such as purchasing a home, zoning, condemnation, and leases; family matters such as life insurance, divorce and marriage, pensions, social security, wills and estates, and death; economic problems such as unemployment, business organizations, consumer protection, copyright and patents; and special problems such as defamation, personal injury actions, and juvenile matters.

The language is easy to understand and legalese is avoided. The text is not footnoted, nor are citations to legal authority given. The result is a book families will find useful as a starting point for understanding their legal rights and responsibilities.

3-245 Walton, Ralph, and Charles Turner. **Texas Law in Layman's Language.** 3d ed. Houston: Gulf, 1983. 250 pp. ind.

Divided into two parts, this work attempts to provide a concise, understandable resource for Texas citizens on those laws affecting their daily lives. Only general legal principles are discussed in each part. The first part covers civil law, including family law, wills and estates, land and personal property, and damage suits. The second half explores criminal law subjects such as the Texas Penal Code, state regulatory agencies, and the Code of Criminal Procedure.

3-246 Warner, Ralph, et al., eds. **The People's Law Review.** Menlo Park, Calif.: NOLO Press, 1980. 359 pp. ill. fms.

The text is divided into six parts. Although it is not a "how-to-do-it" book, it is a useful guide for laypeople desiring an expanded awareness of the law, and for those who feel competent to represent themselves in appropriate circumstances. The editors freely admit to a bias against the legal profession, but advise following a lawyer's advice in certain cases. Common areas of legal concern are explained in easily understood terms. Part 5 lists numerous self-help groups and contacts, and Part 6 is a catalog of approximately seventy pages of self-help law books, a number of which are included in this chapter.

3-247 Weinerman, Chester S. **Practical Law: A Layperson's Handbook.** Englewood Cliffs, N.J.: Prentice-Hall, 1978. 254 pp.

This book explains laypeople's rights in a nonlegal fashion. Emphasis is on common civil matters, but one chapter is devoted to criminal law. Typical problems are analyzed such as wills, insurance, contracts, and so forth. The last chapter offers suggestions on choosing an attorney.

3-248 **You and the Law.** 2d rev. ed. Pleasantville, N.Y.: Reader's Digest Association, 1977. 863 pp. tbls. glos. ind.

This work—divided into fourteen chapters and 651 consecutively numbered legal topical sections—is intended to inform laypeople about general legal principles so they may know when to utilize a lawyer's services as well as become a better informed client. The topical sections are cross-referenced to related legal topics. The glossary defines over 1,000 legal terms. Tables and charts, summarizing some of the more important laws of the fifty states, are scattered throughout the work. A third revised edition was published in early 1984.

3-249 Zepke, Brent E. **Law for Non-Lawyers.** Totowa, N.J.: Littlefield, Adams, 1983. 292 pp. tbls. glos. ind.

An attorney has written a basic guide to legal principles on subjects with which everyone should be familiar. Thirty-four chapters are arranged into nine sections exploring such matters as financial transactions, real estate, business and family relationships, criminal law, and estate planning. The work is useful as a quick reference guide as well as for general knowledge.

Law—Philosophy. See Jurisprudence

Law—Public Education

3-250   Peck, Robert S., and Charles J. White, eds. **Understanding the Law: A Handbook on Educating the Public.** Chicago: American Bar Association, 1983. 232 pp.

Bar Associations, lawyers, judges, educators, politicians, law enforcement officials, and the business community, among others, are presented with models and methods for helping communities gain a better understanding of the American legal and judicial system. This is an excellent resource for implementing programs to expand public awareness through bar activities, court programs, media efforts, and so forth. Numerous writers have contributed articles on the many ways to develop the public's knowledge of the law.

Law Firms. See Law Offices

Law Libraries. See Libraries

Law Offices

3-251   Gillers, Stephen. **I'd Rather Do It Myself: How to Set Up Your Own Law Firm.** New York: Law Journal Press, 1977. 189 pp. apps.

Law students thinking about setting up their own firm or attorneys in the first or second year of practice will find useful information in this brief and well-written book. Eight chapters outline such matters as operating procedures, client relations, and the form of practice (e.g., partnership, solo practice, or professional corporation). Appendixes include a sample retainer letter, an example partnership agreement, and information relating to incorporation.

3-252   Hoffman, Paul. **Lions of the Eighties: The Inside Story of the Powerhouse Law Firms.** Garden City, N.Y.: Doubleday, 1982. 370 pp. ns. ind.

Written by a layman for laypeople, this book is also of interest to lawyers and law students. It is a survey of New York City's leading law firms written in an easy-to-read, informal style. This book really updates what has happened since *Lions in the Street* was written a decade earlier by the same author.

3-253   Munneke, Gary A., ed. **Your New Lawyer: The Legal, Employer's Complete Guide to Recruitment, Development, and Management.** Chicago: American Bar Association, Section of Economics of Law Practice, 1983. 290 pp. apps. bib. ind.

The hiring of quality young lawyers is a serious business, and this manual represents many years of cumulative experience and knowledge obtained from law firms all over the country. The advice and experience in every chapter is geared to all types of legal employer. The book is divided into three major parts. The first involves the recruitment process, including hiring nonlawyers as an alternative, locating legal talent, using law school placement services, interviewing, training attorneys to interview, and so on. The second part considers programs for developing new attorneys for maximum utilization of their talents and abilities to the needs of the law firm. And finally, the last section on management considers matters such as the law office environment, compensation, legal and labor relations, and so forth. Appendixes contain numerous forms.

Although intended primarily for law firms and legal employers, law students, attorneys, paralegals, and anyone seriously interested in working for a law firm will benefit from reading this work.

3-254 Singer, Gerald M. **How to Go Directly into Solo Law Practice without Missing a Meal.** Rochester, N.Y.: Lawyer's Co-operative, 1976. 604 pp.

Law students seriously considering their own law practice will benefit from this nuts-and-bolts work pointing out the pitfalls involved in establishing a solo practice. Sixteen parts—broken down into over eighty chapters—explain many areas, including contingent fees, office management, and relationships between the attorney and clients and judges. This book is also valuable to prelaw students and the lay public since it provides valuable insight into how a beginning solo practice should operate.

3-255 Stewart, James B. **The Partners: Inside America's Most Powerful Law Firms.** New York: Simon and Schuster, 1983. 395 pp. apps. ind.

Using some of the more significant legal events in recent years as examples, the author—who spent over two years researching the material for this book—provides insight into the workings of this country's most prestigious and leading law firms. Although only about three thousand of America's half million or so lawyers practice in these elite law firms, their impact is considerable considering their representation of leading banks, financial institutions, and corporations. Appendixes list leading corporate law firms and clients in addition to other matters.

Law Practice. See Law Offices

Law Schools

3-256 Canada, Ralph, Charles Cheatham, and Tony Licata. **Surviving the First Year of Law School.** Dover, Mass.: Lord, 1978. 160 pp. app.

Written by Harvard law students for students entering, or seriously considering, law school, this book offers realistic advice based upon firsthand experience. Practical suggestions are given on class preparation, study habits, and preparing for exams in addition to numerous other helpful insights. The appendix briefly explains the federal system, litigation, court structure, law and equity, and common law.

3-257 Davis, J. P. **How to Make It through Law School.** New York: Conch Magazine, 1982. 111 pp. app.

Minority and disadvantaged first-year law students, or such individuals considering law school, are the intended audience for this brief but informative, work. Ten chapters describe the law school experience, including how to study, take examinations, and remain motivated. Appendixes include a brief glossary of legal terms, a prelaw reading list, a sample complaint and answer, and a sample law school exam.

3-258   Delaney, John. **How to Brief a Case: An Introduction to Legal Reasoning.** New York: John Delaney, 1983. 133 pp. app.

Intended for law students and those people seriously thinking about law school, this enlightening text may also lend insight to law professors and other instructors teaching introduction to law courses. Chapters examine common questions asked about law in the first year of study, and present a six-step approach to briefing cases.

3-259   Gillers, Stephen, ed. **Looking at Law School: A Student Guide from the Society of American Law Teachers.** New York: Taplinger, 1977. 234 pp. app.

Members of the legal profession have written a book for anyone considering a law school education and a legal career. This work is divided into three parts, the first describing the law school experience, the next exploring the first year of law school, and the last considering career issues. An appendix lists both accredited and unaccredited American law schools.

3-260   Goldfarb, Sally F. **Inside the Law Schools: A Guide by Students, for Students.** rev. 3d ed. New York: E. P. Dutton, 1983. 336 pp.

Divided into six chapters, this insightful work is intended for those seeking a law school. The first five chapters cover such questions as whether law school is right for "you," choosing the right school, getting in, paying for a legal education, and how to use the book. The last, and longest, chapter briefly describes individual law schools. More than the usual information is provided, including critical comments about campus life, the local community, faculty strengths, and law school reputations on the job market.

3-261   Roth, George J. **Slaying the Law School Dragon.** New York: Dodd, Mead, 1980. 184 pp. glos.

This is another book for individuals considering law school. Twenty-five chapters explore the nature of legal education, and how to study, act, prepare for class, and take examinations. Four chapters briefly describe major first-year courses: contracts, torts, crimes, and property. There are even chapters on what kinds of law to go into, and how to gain clients and pick a place to practice. A selected list of law review readings is also included.

3-262   Turow, Scott. **One L.** New York: G. P. Putnam's Sons, 1977. 300 pp.

This book is considered a leading work on the subject of a first-year law student's personal experience in law school. It is written in a narrative style, describing events in a manner very similar to a diary from the initial shock of entering Harvard Law School in the fall to taking exams in the spring. It is an enlightening work for first-year students and anyone considering law school.

3-263　Vanderbilt, Arthur T. **Law School: Briefing for a Legal Education.** New York: Penguin Books, 1981. 186 pp. ind.

This work was first published in 1979 under the hardcover title *An Introduction to the Study of Law*. It is intended for individuals seriously considering law school, offering advice on prelegal education and the skills and abilities required for legal study, practical information on classroom procedure and methods of study, and an an analysis of legal work from the perspective of courtroom practice. It is an informative, no-frills text, providing a view into the law school experience and courtroom advocacy.

Law Students. See Law Schools

Lawyers. See Attorney and Client

Lawyers—Biography

3-264　Belli, Melvin M. **The Belli Files: Reflections on the Wayward Law.** Englewood Cliffs, N.J.: Prentice-Hall, 1983. 269 pp. ind.

Written by one of America's more flamboyant lawyers—known as the "King of Torts" for his impact on personal injury law—with more than fifty years of active legal practice, this book provides an insight into the love-hate relationship clients have with lawyers, and describes the history and practice of law today. Belli also has entertaining and informative comments upon the legal system and the people who have been involved in its development. The author concludes that in spite of the absurd and illogical appearance of our laws, they only reflect the social structure that created them.

3-265　Jaworski, Leon, and Mickey Herskowitz. **Confession and Avoidance: A Memoir.** Garden City, N.Y.: Anchor Press/Doubleday, 1979. 325 pp. ind.

The author, who was a nationally prominent and well-respected attorney, recounts highlights of his career in a very readable style. Included is his experience during the war crimes trials in Nuremberg and his tenure as Special Prosecutor during the Watergate proceedings, in which he gained public acclaim.

3-266　Kinoy, Arthur. **Rights on Trial: The Odyssey of a People's Lawyer.** Cambridge, Mass.: Harvard University Press, 1983. 340 pp. ill. ind.

Professor Kinoy has been involved in major legal events—from the Rosenbergs to the Chicago Seven trial—during the last three decades. This autobiographical account of his career as a human rights advocate, liberal, practicing attorney, and scholar is fascinating reading recounting how a lawyer for the people has worked for individual human rights.

3-267　Schwartz, Helene E. **Lawyering.** New York: Farrar, Straus and Giroux, 1976. 308 pp.

Written by a woman lawyer, this interesting work covers her first decade of practice involving major litigation. The writer has represented William F. Buckley, Jr., and members of the Chicago Seven, among others; her work also explores the experiences of a woman in a traditionally male-dominated profession. It is a helpful, easy-to-read text for women seriously considering law as a career and looking for insight into the experiences women might go through as an attorney.

3-268   Spence, Gerry, and Anthony Polk. **Gerry Spence: Gunning for Justice**. Garden City, New York: Doubleday, 1982. 470 pp.

This autobiographical work by one of the nation's leading trial lawyers offers an inside view into his maverick lifestyle and his trial experiences. The text is easy to read and full of stories and experiences about the Wyoming attorney. Individuals considering law as a career, or nonlawyers interested in lawyers, should enjoy this book.

Lawyers—Stress

3-269   Barber, David. **Surviving Your Role as a Lawyer: A Program to Reduce Stress and Increase Productivity**. Gardena, Calif.: Law Distributors, 1983. 379 pp. bib.

All lawyers, law students, judges, and prospective law students should benefit from this work, which proposes a major concept called "relaxed attention" as a means of reducing stress and increasing efficiency. In addition to describing stress and its problems, the author outlines a stress management program. References to other readings are cited as well as numerous ways of alleviating stress.

Legal Assistants

3-270   Brunner, Thomas W., Julie P. Hamre, and Joan F. McCaffrey. **The Legal Assistant's Handbook**. Washington, D.C.: Bureau of National Affairs, 1982. 218 pp. app. glos. ind.

This work was written as a practical guide for paraprofessionals, and lawyers and administrators working with these individuals. A description of the legal system is provided along with the legal assistant's role in discovery and trial proceedings, legal research tools, proper citation rules for legal documents, ethical considerations, and administering a legal assistant's program.

3-271   Cunningham, William E. **The Paralegal and the Lawyer's Library**. Colorado Springs, Colo.: Shepard's/McGraw-Hill, 1973. 64 pp.

This booklet—republished in 1978 and 1980—was designed to provide paralegals with information on lawyers' law libraries, an understanding of common legal terms, and knowledge about major legal publications. Although the text is dated, the information provides a starting point for knowledge on legal resources and research. This should prove useful to anyone interested in gaining an understanding of legal resources in law libraries.

3-272   Deming, Richard. **The Paralegal**. New York: Elsevier/Nelson Books, 1980. 142 pp. ind.

The book was written for individuals considering a paralegal or legal assistant career. No attempt is made to sell this developing area in the legal field. The text merely seeks to provide sufficient information to allow interested people to make an informed choice.

The eight chapters include information on what paralegals do, where such jobs may be found, training, the schools, jobs and wages, and paralegal associations.

3-273   Larbalestrier, Deborah E. **Paralegal Practice and Procedure: A Practical Guide for the Legal Assistant.** Englewood Cliffs, N.J.: Prentice-Hall, 1977. 446 pp. tbls. apps. ind.

This work contains all information normally required for routine work in the paralegal field, but in another sense it is also useful to anyone seeking a greater understanding of how the law works in practice. It includes many charts, tables, graphs, and numerous examples in its twenty-one chapters, which are divided into three parts. Part 1 includes duties and procedures legal assistants should understand; part 2 explores the practice and procedure used in litigation; and part 3 explains the details involved in assisting attorneys with legal practice in such areas as probate, personal injury, contracts, and criminal matters.

Legal Education. See Law Schools

Legal Ethics

3-274   Aronson, Robert H., and Donald T. Weckstein. **Professional Responsibility in a Nutshell.** St. Paul: West, 1980. 399 pp. tbl. ind.

Twenty-one chapters arranged in four parts briefly analyze matters of legal and judicial ethics. The four sections examine the structure and supervision of the legal profession, the duty to make legal services available, the attorney-client relationship, and functions and responsibilities of lawyers. A table of authorities is also included. Interested citizens should find this very helpful in understanding the ethical responsibilities of the legal profession.

3-275   Lieberman, Jethro Koller. **Crisis at the Bar: Lawyers' Unethical Ethics and What to Do about It.** New York: W. W. Norton, 1978. 247 pp. ns. ind.

The author is a lawyer whose thesis is that the legal profession damages its own public image by adhering to an unethical and unworkable code of ethics. The text analyzes various conflicts in the code of ethics, abuses, and problems arising between lawyers and their clients or between lawyers and society in general. The issues of group practice, advertising, minimum fees, and contingency fees are also dealt with at length. The book concludes with twelve proposals for reform. This is a book of individual analysis and opinion. However, it contains many useful insights regarding the relationship between lawyers and clients and the ethical problems and abuses which arise in various circumstances.

3-276   Luban, David, ed. **The Good Lawyer: Lawyers' Roles and Lawyers' Ethics.** Totowa, N.J.: Rowman and Allanheld, 1984. 366 pp. ns. ind.

Lawyers, law students, philosophers, and individuals interested in legal morality should find this book—volume 7 in the Maryland Studies in Public Philosophy—useful as a resource guide to controversial legal ethics issues facing society today. Contributors include lawyers, philosophers, and legal scholars discussing such issues as confidentiality, the adversary system, clinical legal education, and the development of moral character.

Legal History

3-277 Lieberman, Jethro K. **Milestones! 200 Years of American Law: Milestones in Our Legal History**. St. Paul: West, 1976. 422 pp. pls. ns. ind.

Published during the U.S. bicentennial and the one hundredth birthday of West Publishing Company as a law book publisher, this book explores leading events in the development of American law. These events were selected on the basis of tear-out ballots submitted by readers of the *American Bar Association Journal*. The text is easy to read, and anyone using this work will be able to better understand leading events in America's legal history.

3-278 Speiser, Stuart M. **Lawsuit**. New York: Horizon Press, 1980. 617 pp. ns. ind.

A nationally known and respected lawyer has written a book which anyone interested in law, government, consumer protection, sociology, or business will find interesting and informative. Landmark cases are described as well as the history and current development of tort, or personal injury law. Chapters on product liability and government liability and the effects of U.S. personal injury law on the world are included. The final chapter is an interview, consisting of answers to questions asked by journalists, lawyers, and students who read the manuscript. Notes to major cases, books, and articles follow the text.

3-279 Stevens, Robert. **Law School: Legal Education in America from the 1850s to the 1980's**. Chapel Hill, N.C.: University of North Carolina Press, 1983. 334 pp. bib. ind.

Legal historians, lawyers, law professors and students, and interested members of the general public will learn about the history, current standing, and influence of America's law schools. All law libraries and academic libraries may want to include this in their collections. Although it is a scholarly work, the language is clear and easy to understand. Extensive notes follow each chapter, and a detailed bibliography follows the text.

Legal Novels

3-280 Kretschman, Karen L., and Judith Helburn. **Legal Novels: An Annotated Bibliography**. Austin, Tex.: Tarlton Law Library, University of Texas School of Law, 1979. 31 pp.

This bibliographic work updates a list of leading legal novels published by John Henry Wigmore, a former dean and professor at Northwestern. The focus of this updated listing is from 1940 to 1979. Anyone interested in leading legal novels should benefit from consulting this work.

3-281   Osborn, John J. **The Paper Chase**. Boston: Houghton Mifflin, 1971. 181 pp.

This is an imaginative novel written by a Harvard Law School graduate while a student in law school. It is a story about a law student's interaction with a contracts professor, Mr. Kingsfield, and how the student falls in love with the professor's daughter. This work spawned a movie and a television series of the same name. Lawyers, law students, and lay readers will appreciate the prototypical law professor whose authoritative teaching style could be compared to a professor or two in nearly every law school.

Legal Reasoning. See Jurisprudence

Legal Research. See chapter 2 under the heading "Guides to Legal Research"

Legal Writing

3-282   Block, Gertrude. **Effective Legal Writing: A Style Book for Law Students and Lawyers,** 2d ed. Mineola, N.Y.: Foundation Press, 1983. 212 pp. app. ind.

The author points out the usefulness of this book not only to law students, legal writing instructors, and lawyers, but also to individuals planning to enter law school. The emphasis is not on complete grammar or substantive legal doctrines, but on case analysis and organization as well as techniques basic to any effective legal writing. A very useful appendix provides questions and answers based upon principles enumerated in each chapter. Citizens representing themselves in legal matters will benefit from reading this book.

3-283   Goldfarb, Ronald L., and James C. Raymond. **Clear Understanding: A Guide to Legal Writing**. New York: Random House, 1982. 172 pp. ind.

Applying the premise that the language of law should be easy to understand, the authors provide a concise approach for achieving clarity and precision in legal writing. Judges, attorneys, law students, and interested laypeople will benefit from a reading of this work. Rules of punctuation and grammar are provided along with tips on organizing legal forms, briefs, opinions, and memorandums. The book ends with the "Ten Commandments of Legal Writing," beginning with, "Write like a Human Being!"

Legislation

3-284   Lammers, Nancy, ed. **Powers of Congress**. 2d ed. Washington, D.C.: Congressional Quarterly, 1982. 380 pp. bib. ind.

Beginning with an overview, this expanded text explores congressional powers in all major areas such as budget, foreign affairs, confirmations, impeachment, and electing the president. Footnotes follow each chapter. Individuals beginning research on the subject should find this a most useful tool.

3-285 Pelton, Robert W. **Loony Laws ... You Didn't Know You Were Breaking.** New York: Walker, 1981. 151 pp.

Divided into nineteen chapters, this lighthearted look at unusual laws pokes fun at foibles and follies in enacted legislation. Covered are such diverse subject areas as sports and gambling, pets, guns, food and drink, and police and fire fighter legislation. The irony of many of these laws from numerous states is that some are still on the books although the more outrageous provisions are seldom enforced.

The work serves more as a source of humor rather than a "how to" text, and readers may even find similar laws in their state of residence!

Lesbian Rights. See Civil Rights

Libel. See Defamation

Libraries

3-286 Bosmajian, Haig, comp. **Censorship, Libraries, and the Law.** New York: Neal-Schuman, 1983. 217 pp. ind.

This work should prove most useful to library officials and administrators, and attorneys representing libraries. The approach is fairly scholarly, dividing the book into two parts: "School Library Censorship Cases" and "United States Supreme Court Decisions Relied On by the Lower Courts in Library Censorship Cases."

Both parts reprint major legal decisions. The thirteen-page introduction provides a good overview of the problem. This book is a good starting point for anyone seeking leading case authority in this area.

3-287 Matthews, Elizabeth W. **Access Points to the Law Library: Card Catalog Interpretation.** Buffalo: William S. Hein, 1982. 66 pp. bib. ind.

Intended primarily for library assistants and student assistants in law firms and law school libraries, this work will also prove very useful to any number of individuals seeking to understand how to gain access to the resources of a law library through the card catalog. Although brief, the text is clear and easy to understand. Six chapters include discussions on the catalog as an index, reporters, statutes, documents, continuing publications, and alternative media such as microform and audiovisual materials.

Litigation

3-288 Lieberman, Jethro K. **The Litigious Society.** New York: Basic Books, 1981. 212 pp. ns. inds.

The work was written specifically for the general reader. It is an inquiry into the issue of whether America is becoming an overly litigious society. The primary study of the book is an analysis of the right of redress, the exercise of such right, and the consequences of exercising this right. Notes follow the text and the indexes include a table of cases.

3-289   Manville, Daniel E. **Prisoners' Self-Help Litigation Manual**. 2d ed. Dobbs Ferry, N.Y.: Oceana, 1983. 684 pp. app. fms. tbl. ns. ind.

This book was written by a former inmate. It is intended for use by prisoners, but it is also a useful reference tool for correctional administrators and attorneys specializing in corrections law and prisoners' rights. This voluminous work includes a comprehensive table of contents, a detailed index, table of cases, and is extensively footnoted to legal authority. Chapters cover every major area of concern such as legal research and writing, the legal system, litigation, parole, and postconviction remedies. Appendixes include forms, a federal court directory, information on habeas corpus and detainers, and the minimum holdings a prison law library collection should include.

3-290   Striker, John M., and Andrew O. Shapiro. **How You Can Sue without Hiring a Lawyer: A Guide to Winning in Small Claims Court**. New York: Simon and Schuster, 1981. 269 pp.

The authors recount many instances of real court cases in an effort to assist readers in standing up for their legal rights in appropriate circumstances. In each controversy, the authors include the elements of the case and show how to prove one's position. The first part of the book outlines what steps to take in preparing for a case, such as whether to hire an attorney or negotiate a settlement, and so forth.

Local Government. See Municipal Corporation Law

Marijuana. See Drugs

Maritime Law. See Admiralty

Marriage. See Domestic Relations

Medicine

3-291   Annas, George J. **The Rights of Hospital Patients**. New York: Sunrise Books/E. P. Dutton, 1975. 246 pp. ns. apps. ind.

This is another guidebook sponsored by the American Civil Liberties Union, and it is arranged in the standard question-and-answer format with each chapter followed by references to legal and other authority. Appendixes include references to medical terms, abbreviations, and literature as well as a list of organizations supporting patients' legal rights. Chapters cover every major topic on patients' rights from the emergency ward, informed consent, and hospital records to children, the terminally ill, and payment of bills.

3-292   Annas, George J., Leonard H. Glantz, and Barbara F. Katz. **The Rights of Doctors, Nurses, and Allied Health Professionals: A Health Primer**. New York: Avon Books, 1981. 382 pp. ns. apps. glos. ind.

This ACLU question-and-answer guide is a valuable resource to individuals, administrators, and organizations involved in health care and administration. Citations to authority follow each of the fifteen chapters, which are arranged under three headings. The first part involves the right to practice (e.g., licensing), the second section explores the provider-patient relationship, and the last portion explains liability and income issues. Appendixes include a glossary of legal terms and a very brief outline on how to use a law library in addition to other information.

3-293 Burt, Robert A. **Taking Care of Strangers: The Rule of Law in Doctor-Patient Relations.** New York: Free Press, 1979. 200 pp. app. ns. ind.

This is a fairly scholarly work that is still easy to read. The writer's purpose is to suggest that current laws on the physician-client relationship need reforming—especially those relating to the patients' right to die—so that both doctors and patients will be protected. Doctors, lawyers, medical administrators and other interested individuals should find this a useful, informative work on an area involved in some controversy.

3-294 Christoffel, Tom. **Health and the Law.** New York: Free Press, 1982. 450 pp. bib. ns. ind.

This book is intended for the health professional. It is divided into three parts: the first defines the essentials of health law and general law in relation to administrative agencies and rules. The second part explores legal issues such as hospital regulations, certification of health professionals, food and drug laws, the elimination of health hazards, etc. The author concludes by reviewing legal conditions surrounding consent to treatment, medical records, malpractice, abortion, children, and so forth.

Each chapter is followed by extensive endnotes, and a brief appendix describes how to use a law library. The result is a book combining the usefulness of a primer with that of a reference guide. Attorneys requiring legal information on an issue in the field may find this text quite helpful since the author, a Harvard Law School graduate, refers to numerous case and statutory authorities.

3-295 Fineborg, Keith S., et al. **Obstetrics/Gynecology and the Law.** Ann Arbor, Mich.: Health Administration Press, 1984. 616 pp. ns. tbls. apps. glos. bib. inds.

Hospital administrators, medical-legal educators and students, lawyers with medical-legal practices, obstetricians, and gynecologists will find this book an excellent reference and resource guide on legal issues relevant to their practice and study. Actual case histories are used to emphasize and clarify important areas, and each chapter is followed by notes to legal authority. The book is not intended as a substitute for legal counsel, and it is written with the idea that well-informed physicians will choose courses of action consistent with their own and society's best interests.

3-296 Fiscina, Salvatore Francis. **Medical Law for the Attending Physician: A Case-Oriented Analysis.** Carbondale, Ill.: Southern Illinois University Press, 1982. 496 pp. tbl. glos. ind.

Case studies are used to assist physicians in determining legally acceptable principles of professional conduct in their medical practice, including such matters as diagnosis, consent, treatment, and patient records.

3-297 Flaster, Donald J. **Malpractice: A Guide to the Legal Rights of Patients and Doctors.** New York: Charles Scribner's Sons, 1983. 212 pp. apps. ind.

The writer, a doctor and lawyer, analyzes the relationship between the physician and patient from both sides. Both medical personnel and laypeople will benefit from this easy-to-read book. Appendixes include a sample informed-consent form, a sample medical bill, and statutes of limitation by state. The value of this work lies in the advice to both physicians and patients so that each may protect the other's interests and reduce the chances of medical malpractice claims.

3-298 James A. Everette, ed. **Legal Medicine, with Special Reference to Diagnostic Imaging.** Baltimore: Urban and Schwarzenberg, 1980. 403 pp. ind.

The text is intended for practicing physicians and attorneys concerned with their medical-legal activities. Basic concepts are emphasized in an attempt to promote understanding of law and medicine and their relationship to one another. Diagnostic imaging, or radiography, is emphasized in the latter half of the book.

Over twenty articles from various contributors—many of whom have both medical and law degrees—are included on such subjects as evidence law, medical corporations, malpractice insurance, and Federal health policies affecting medical imaging.

3-299 Langsley, Donald G., ed. **Legal Aspects of Certification and Accreditation.** Evanston, Ill.: American Board of Medical Specialties, 1983. 308 pp. app. ind.

This book consists of thirteen edited and expanded papers originally presented at a conference of the same name, which took place in Chicago 15-16 April 1983. Doctors, lawyers, and especially interested laypersons should expand their awareness of the interaction of law and medicine in seeking to provide citizens with their right to health in our society.

3-300 Mancini, Marguerite R., and Alice T. Gale. **Emergency Care and the Law.** Rockville, Md.: Aspen Systems, 1981. 255 pp. ns. tbl. glos. ind.

Written primarily for health care professionals and administrators providing hospital emergency room services, this book serves as a general legal guide for avoiding the pitfalls of unnecessary malpractice litigation. Ten chapters are divided into five parts: the concept of law and emergency room law, admission and transfer of patients, death and discharge, laws and regulations, and administrative questions. Legal terms, and a table of cases, which are cited throughout the work, follow the text.

3-301 Miller, Robert D. **Problems in Hospital Law.** 4th ed. Rockville, Md.: Aspen Systems, 1983. 379 pp. ns. inds.

Doctors, medical lawyers, health care administrators, professionals, and technical services staff will benefit from this work which begins with an overview of American law. Chapters explore regulation and accreditation, taxation, civil liability, confidentiality, matters involving death, and so forth. An index to cases follows the text.

3-302   Pozgar, George D. **Legal Aspects of Health Care Administration.** Germantown, Md.: Aspen Systems, 1979. 247 pp. ns. tbl. glos.

The author seeks a partnership between law and medicine by producing a work helping administrators, doctors, and nurses to better identify and avoid practices or actions likely to result in legal liability. A broad overview of the legal system and the pitfalls which exist is presented. All major areas are discussed, such as personal injury, hospital and personnel liability, consent of patients, abortion, autopsy and donation, sterilization and artificial insemination, labor relations, insurance, and so forth. A table of cases, referring to a number of leading cases cited throughout the work, follows the text.

3-303   Quimby, Charles W. **Law for the Medical Practitioner.** Washington, D.C.: AUPHA Press, 1979. 187 pp. ns. tbl. ind.

The author, holding both medical and law degrees, has written a brief "primer" for physicians in order to assist them in identifying potential legal conflicts and seeking advice of an attorney in appropriate cases. The book is divided into nine chapters dealing with major issues such as consent, confidentiality, malpractice, hospitals and physicians, and the administrative process.

The text is easy to understand and is only lightly footnoted. Several leading cases are cited and listed in an alphabetical table following the text.

3-304   Richards, Edward P., III, and Katherine C. Rathbun. **Medical Risk Management.** Rockville, Md.: Aspen Systems, 1983. 311 pp. bib. ind.

This work is coauthored by a doctor and a lawyer. The central theme of this work is that if emotional and legal needs of patients are met, overall quality of medical care will improve, thereby reducing the possibility of litigation. Emphasis is placed upon a preventive legal approach to everyday situations that create legal risks in health care delivery. Practical experience is combined with scholarly work in medical law to identify those events with a high probability of litigation.

Each chapter is followed by references to further research on the subject. Covered are such matters as the concept of preventive law, quality control and assurance, legal liability in teaching, and patients' rights. Administrators, lawyers, and doctors involved in medicine will find this a good reference source on potential legal liability.

Mental Deficiency and Retardation. See Handicapped

Mental Health

3-305   Beis, Edward B. **Mental Health and the Law.** Rockville, Md.: Aspen Systems, 1983. 380 pp. apps.

Mental health care professionals and institutions should find this book valuable as a desk top reference guide for answering legal issues in mental health care practice. The text is organized into five sections consisting of a total of fifteen chapters. These sections explain the current status of mental health law, define the various concepts of liability, examine legal responsibilities in outpatient settings, focus on legal considerations in inpatient settings, and provide insight into the role of expert witnesses—such as psychiatrists, psychologists and psychiatric nurses—in court. State by state differences are noted throughout the book, and nine appendixes include relevant sections of state statutes, consent and information rights, and other matters.

3-306   Cohen, Ronald Jay, and William E. Mariano. **Legal Guidebook in Mental Health.** New York: Free Press, 1982. 492 pp. bib. ind.

This book is written by a psychologist and lawyer, respectively, and is intended primarily for those involved in medicine, psychology, social work, and nursing. However, the content of the text includes much relevant information for professionals such as lawyers and administrators involved in mental health.

Although the work is not intended as a substitute for a lawyer, it does provide a compendium of case and statutory law, and other legally related material important to mental health professionals. Many legal concepts are discussed, such as the legal and ethical basis for law and regulations, malpractice and causes of action, and such matters as breach of contract, privacy, and defamation. This work should prove invaluable to anyone involved in the field of mental health.

Military Law

3-307   Shanor, Charles A., and Timothy P. Terrell. **Military Law in a Nutshell.** St. Paul: West, 1980. 378 pp. ind.

Service members, veterans, law students, future military lawyers, and interested citizens will benefit from this book, which generally outlines the law. Ten chapters consider matters such as civilian control of the military, first amendment rights of military personnel, the military criminal justice system, personal injury claims, and labor-management relations.

Mining. See Natural Resources Law

Minorities. See Civil Rights

Minors. See Juveniles

Motels. See Inkeepers

Motor Vehicles

3-308   Mickens, Kenneth L. **Odometer Law.** Boston: National Consumer Law Center, 1982. 63 pp. tbl. apps.

This guide is one of a practice series of ten or more on various areas of consumer law. Designed primarily as a practice guide and reference work for attorneys representing clients in odometer tampering cases, this manual may also be used by automobile dealers and interested consumers in order to better their communication with their attorneys. There is a table of cases at the front. Chapters include an overview of odometer law, prohibited conduct, liability, suggestions, and procedural issues. Appendixes include case summaries, legislative history, a model complaint, sample deposition questions, and other useful information.

152 / Selected Subject Bibliography of Law-related Monographs

3-309   Woodroof, M. G., III, and Alphonse M. Squillante. **Automobile Liability and the Changing Law**. Dobbs Ferry, N.Y.: Oceana, 1972. 124 pp. ind.

Automobile insurance development, its trends and proposed reforms, and a discussion of model legislation are explored. This dated text is not so much a discourse on law as it is an explanation of the trend towards automobile insurance reforms.

Municipal Corporation Law

3-310   McCarthy, David J. **Local Government Law in a Nutshell**. 2d ed. St. Paul: West, 1983. 404 pp. ind.

Although intended primarily for law students, this book is also useful to attorneys as a reference guide, and to informed citizens and local government officials interested in understanding legal principles affecting their governmental institutions. Six chapters briefly outline the source of power, organizational problems, litigation, the use of land, revenue, and much more.

3-311   Matthews, Byron S. **Local Government: How to Get into It. How to Administer It Effectively**. Chicago: Nelson-Hall, 1970. 256 pp. pls. figs. ind.

Elected and appointed government officials, members of administrative boards, civic groups, and interested citizens are provided a general working handbook on county and municipal government operations, legal matters, and administrative concerns.

3-312   Vogt, John A., and Lisa A. Cole, eds. **A Guide to Municipal Leasing**. Chicago: Municipal Finance Officers Association, 1983. 239 pp. apps. glos. bib.

This volume was written in order to clarify leasing practices and make leases a more useful tool in the public financier's practice. The nine chapters include discussions on the concept of leasing, various kinds of contracts, methods of cost calculations, and five case studies. Appendixes include a glossary, and interest factors for compounding and discounting. The bibliography is annotated.

Natural Resources Law

3-313   Lowe, John S. **Oil & Gas Law in a Nutshell**. St. Paul: West, 1983. 443 pp. tbl. figs. glos. app. ind.

Basic oil and gas concepts are explained along with a discussion of the legal rules governing development of privately owned mineral rights. Lawyers, law students, executives of oil and gas companies, entrepreneurs, and interested citizens should find this a good, quick reference source on the subject.

3-314   Maley, Terri S. **Handbook of Mineral Law**. 3d rev. ed. Boise, Idaho: Mineral Land, 1983. 711 pp. ns. glos. ind.

Written by an expert in the field, this practical reference work is intended for government resource managers, land managers, geologists, engineers, and lawyers involved in acquiring and managing mineral resources. Every major topic is covered from location and discovery rights to patents and contests.

The text includes references to a great deal of case and statutory authority, and a glossary of important terms used in mining law precedes the index. The value of this work lies in its wide use in the mineral industry as well as in numerous mining and law school courses.

3-315 Minan, John H., and William H. Lawrence, eds. **Legal Aspects of Solar Energy.** Lexington, Mass.: Lexington Books, 1981. 231 pp. ns. ills.

Interested citizens are provided a book on legal issues of solar energy. It seeks to facilitate development of solar energy by analyzing basic legal barriers hindering growth. The first chapter outlines essential technical principles, and subsequent chapters explore such issues as tax incentives, common law doctrines, product standards, and warranties as well as other matters. The text is somewhat technical, but it is easy to understand; each chapter is followed by references to legal and other authority.

3-316 Thomas, William A., Alan S. Miller, and Richard L. Robbins. **Overcoming Legal Uncertainties about Use of Solar Energy Systems.** Chicago: American Bar Association, 1978. 80 pp. ns.

Although not a primer on the theory or use of solar energy systems, this book provides a view of legal issues, and suggests statutes for resolving legal uncertainties. Legislators, solar energy advocates, and federal, state, and local government officials will find this helpful in developing statutes suitable to the laws of the particular jurisdictions.

Naturalization. See Immigration Law

Negligence. See Torts

Notary Public

3-317 **The California Notary Law Primer.** Woodland Hills, Calif.: National Notary Association, 1978. 119 pp. glos. app.

This is a brief analysis and explanation of notary law in California, and it is intended for both future and current notaries in that state.

3-318 Rothman, Raymond C. **Notary Public: Practices and Glossary.** Woodland Hills, Calif.: National Notary Association, 1978. 192 pp. fms. glos. apps. ind.

Intended for notaries as a guide on proper practices and procedure, this clearly written, nontechnical book covers all areas of notary practice from taking acknowledgments to procedures involving absentee ballots. A glossary of terms follows the text, and is followed by six appendixes furnishing, for example, rules of practice, state officers who appoint notaries, and sample forms. Questions, which may be used for testing the reader's newly found knowledge, follow each chapter.

3-319　　**The Texas Notary Law Primer.** Woodland Hills, Calif.: National Notary Association, 1982. 90 pp. app.

Prepared by the editors of *The National Notary Magazine,* the booklet seeks to acquaint laypeople with notary practices and the important aspects of Texas notary law. The complete text of the Texas Notary law is also included.

Nuclear Energy

3-320　　Laitner, Skip. **Citizen's Guide to Nuclear Power.** Washington, D.C.: Center for the Study of Responsive Law, 1975. 67 pp. apps.

This manual is a resource guide for citizens opposing nuclear energy power plants. Included are chapters on action strategies and research skills. Appendixes and text include references to groups, working materials, and citizen action stories. Cartoons are included not so much for the sake of humor, but to emphasize the seriousness of the issue in the mind of the author.

3-321　　Wood, William C. **Nuclear Safety: Risks and Regulation.** Washington, D.C.: American Enterprise Institute for Public Policy Research, 1983. 89 pp. ns.

Interested citizens, federal energy administrative officials, congressmen, and environmentalists will find this recent publication most helpful in seeking improvements in the Nuclear Regulatory Commission's (NRC) operations. The author recommends reorganization of the NRC—among other matters—and he concludes the country may have to choose its mix of energy resources by default if the current state of indecision on cost-effective safety measures and risks to society continues.

Nurses and Nursing. See Medicine

Oil and Gas Law. See Natural Resources Law

Paralegals. See Legal Assistants

Parent and Child. See Domestic Relations

Patents. See Intellectual and Industrial Property

Patients. See Critically Ill; Handicapped; Human Experimentation; Medicine; Mental Health

Pensions. See Labor Law; Social Security

Personal Injury. See Torts

Physicians and Surgeons. See Medicine

Poor. See Civil Rights

Practice and Procedure. See Civil Procedure

Practice of Law. See Law Offices

Prenuptial Agreements. See Domestic Relations

Prisons and Prisoners

3-322 American Correctional Association. **Providing Legal Services for Prisoners: A Tool for Correctional Administrators**, rev. and expanded ed., College Park, Md.: American Correctional Association, 1982. 96 pp. bib.

This revised and expanded edition, first published in 1972 under another title, has the cooperation and permission of the American Association of Law Libraries, Special Interest Section on Law Library Service to Institutional Residents. It is especially useful to interested citizens, administrators, legislators, and attorneys dealing with the problem of inmate access to the courts. The work is divided into four parts. The first provides the legal framework for legal services. Parts 2 and 3 suggest recommended general and state collections, respectively; and part 4 lists law libraries furnishing legal services to prisoners.

3-323 Rudovsky, David, Alvin J. Bronstein, and Edward I. Koren. **The Rights of Prisoners**. rev. ed. New York: Bantam Books, 1983. 145 pp. ns. apps.

This is another handbook in the American Civil Liberties Union (ACLU) continuing series. It is a guide, offering information on such matters as due process, access to courts, prison censorship, political rights, medical care, parole, and remedies. Appendixes include a listing of prisoners' rights organizations and a brief, selected bibliography. The text is in question-and-answer format with notes to cited legal authority at the end of each chapter.

Privacy. See Civil Rights

Probate. See Estates

Products Liability. See Consumer Protection

Property

3-324 Blagden, Nellie, and Edith Paul Marshall. **The Complete Condo and Co-op Information Book**. Boston: Houghton Mifflin, 1983. 258 pp. ind.

Laypeople intending to purchase cooperative or condominium housing may use this guide, which answers common questions and explains typical problems. Chapters cover such matters as mortgage financing, purchasing, and vacation housing.

3-325 Bove, Alexander A., Jr. **Joint Property: Everything You Must Know to Save Time, Trouble, and Money on Your Jointly Owned Property**. New York: Simon and Schuster, 1982. 232 pp. glos. ind.

Although this book is designed for use in every state, the author cautions readers to check the laws of their state in each particular situation. Joint property is a confusing area and the author provides information on every major form of coownership, exploring tenancy in common, joint tenancy, and tenancy by the entirety, to name a few. Problems in joint tenancy such as those involving divorce, trusts, and creditors' rights are also analyzed in language easy to understand.

3-326 Gadow, Sandy. **All about Escrow, or How to Buy the Brooklyn Bridge and Have the Last Laugh.** Richmond, Calif.: EXPRESS, 1982. 183 pp. ill. fms. glos. ind.

This is a practical working tool for any prospective buyer of real estate. The writer takes the mystery out of escrow by clearly explaining all matters such as title searches, title insurance, financing, and closing escrow. Although this confusing subject is dealt with in a serious manner, levity is maintained by the inclusion of Dave Patton's humorous illustrations.

Buyers' and sellers' checklists are included following chapter 10, and a useful glossary of escrow terms—defined in everyday language—is included at the end of the text.

3-327 Henszey, Benjamin N., and Ronald M. Friedman. **Real Estate Law.** 2d ed. New York: John Wiley and Sons, 1984. 383 pp. glos. ind.

This work is structured to meet a variety of educational needs, including use as a basic textbook in undergraduate courses on real estate, and by professionals in the field. Anyone interested in furthering their understanding of real property will find this easy to understand since a purely academic approach is avoided and legal principles are explained by simple examples. Each of the fourteen chapters includes a summary, questions for discussion, and problem cases. All topics in the area of real estate law are covered, from interests in land to financing.

3-328 Milligan, W. D., and Arthur G. Bowman. **Real Estate Law.** Englewood Cliffs, N.J.: Prentice-Hall, 1984. 465 pp. glos. ind.

The text is intended for anyone interested in real estate law, although attorneys and real estate brokers may find this work most useful in their practice. Fifteen chapters cover the field, including such areas as agency, licensees' rights and obligations, closings, types of ownership, security interests, tax matters, adjoining land problems, and the landlord-tenant relationship. This is a general work, providing an overview of real estate law, and it does not provide information about each state's particular laws. Readers should consult the laws of the state in which such a transaction takes place in order to fully comply with that state's requirements.

Psychology

3-329 Bartol, Curt R. **Psychology and American Law.** Belmont, Calif.: Wadsworth, 1983. 373 pp. ns. tbl. inds.

The book is intended primarily as a textbook for undergraduate behavioral science students with limited knowledge of our legal system. However, the text is also a useful reference guide for psychologists, lawyers, and others having an interest in the area. Twelve chapters cover such matters as criminal law, civil and mental health law, the psychology of the jury, the psychology of lawyering, and the psychology of incarceration, punishment and treatment. A list of cases, lengthy references to authority, and author and title indexes follow the text.

Publishers and Publishing

3-330   Duboff, Leonard D. **Book Publishers' Legal Guide.** Seattle: Butterworth, 1984. 359 pp. apps. ns. ind.

The author, a law professor at Northwestern School of Law at Lewis and Clark College in Portland, Oregon, has written a book intended for anyone connected with publishing. Writers, publishers, and attorneys will find seventeen helpful chapters on matters such as the history of publishing, the structure of business organizations, accounting, and new technology. Remaining chapters analyze areas such as contracts, copyright, censorship, privacy, unfair trade practices, and antitrust. Nine appendixes include relevant forms commonly used in the publishing business.

Race Discrimination. *See* Civil Rights; Labor Law

Racial Minorities. *See* Civil Rights

Radio, Television, and Motion Pictures

3-331   De Grazia, Edward, and Roger K. Newman. **Banned Films: Movies, Censors, and the First Amendment.** New York: R.R. Bowker, 1982. 455 pp. pls. app. glos. tbls. bib. ind.

Anyone interested in understanding the history and legal record of movie censorship in the United States up to 1982 will find this informative reading. The first part of the book summarizes the social, political, religious, and legal reasons why moving pictures were brought under censorship. The second part of the book describes 122 individual accounts of American and foreign films banned in the United States. Central to the theme of this book is the role the United States Supreme Court has played since 1952 in granting First Amendment freedoms to moving pictures. The appendix includes a listing of acronyms and abbreviations, abbreviations of court cases, and a glossary of legal terms. The listing of cases is alphabetically arranged into tables by case name and by film title.

3-332   Miller, Ellen J. **Video: A Guide for Lawyers.** Santa Monica, Calif.: Law-Arts, 1983. 133 pp. bib. glos. ind.

Although written for lawyers and legal educators unfamiliar with video recording, this book is valuable to any number of individuals, including business people and those interested in knowing how the legal profession and modern video technology interface.

Chapters explaining how video works—and the uses of video for legal purposes—are supplemented by listings of audio-visual manufacturers, video dealers, and a glossary of video terminology.

Rape

3-333 Bode, Janet. **Fighting Back: How to Cope with the Medical, Emotional, and Legal Consequences of Rape.** New York: Macmillan, 1978. 279 pp. apps. ns. bib. ind.

Written by a rape victim, this book is a compilation of research and information gathered over a period of several years. It is a practical, realistic approach to the problem in simple, understandable language. Appendixes include a summary of state rape laws and examples of two leading state rape statutes. Notes are at the end of the text along with a brief bibliography.

3-334 Bode, Janet. **Rape: Preventing It; Coping with the Legal, Medical, and Emotional Aftermath.** New York: Franklin Watts, 1979. 103 pp. app. bib. ind.

This is another work on rape by Ms. Bode, and the title best explains the nature of its contents. Antirape organizations are listed in the appendix with a brief listing of bibliographic resources. Chapters 5 and 6 provide suggestions on how to deal with the legal system after rape occurs.

Real Estate. See Property

Real Property. See Property

Reporters. See Authors

Retirement. See Labor Law; Social Security

Schools

3-335 Bolmeier, Edward Claude. **Legality of Student Disciplinary Practices.** Charlottesville, Va.: Michie, 1976. 194 pp. bib. tbls. ind.

The author, an educator, views student discipline as the predominant legal issue confronting the public schools. Chapters examine the nature and scope of student misconduct and available disciplinary practices, the *in loco parentis* doctrine, due process and school discipline, the administration of corporal punishment, exclusionary and suspension practices, and unorthodox discipline practices. The latter heading includes material on such measures as exclusion from graduation exercises, grade reduction, humiliation before classmates, and deprivation of privileges for married students, and secret societies. The text depends heavily on quotations from court cases and other sources. Comparatively little original analysis is presented.

3-336 Budoff, Milton, and Alan Orenstein. **Due Process in Special Education: On Going to a Hearing.** Cambridge, Mass.: Wave Press, 1982. 368 pp.

Designed for parents and school administrators, this useful work provides five sections of information relating experiences of parents who have appealed, and the views of administrators and hearings officers. It concludes by evaluating and

and providing suggestions for due process reforms as well as indicating tips for school administrators and parents on the hearing process.

3-337 Fischer, Louis, and David Schimmel. **The Rights of Students and Teachers: Resolving Conflicts in the School Community.** New York: Harper and Row, 1982. 447 pp. apps. ind.

This is a very informative and helpful work intended for students and teachers alike. It is also useful to lawyers and administrators because of its citations to court cases. Each chapter is well footnoted. The language avoids legal jargon common to law books. Especially useful is an appendix defining legal terms used in court cases.

This work is really a revised edition, combining two previous works, *Civil Rights of Teachers* and *Civil Rights of Students.* All areas are covered such as unauthorized searches, race and sex discrimination, and freedom of association.

3-338 Frels, Kelly, and Timothy T. Cooper. **A Documentation System for Teacher Improvement or Termination.** Topeka, Kans.: National Organization on Legal Problems of Education, 1982. 19 pp. app.

This brief booklet does not review the procedural requirements necessary for termination. Rather, it provides practical advice on systematically documenting the evaluation process, and materials which should be presented at a hearing in support of a recommendation for termination. Appendixes include sample memorandums. Teachers, principals, interested attorneys, and educational administrators should find this publication a worthwhile reference guide.

3-339 Garber, Lee Orville, and Floyd G. Delon. **The Law and the Teacher in Missouri: A Handbook for Teachers, Administrators, and School Board Members,** 2d ed. Danville, Ill.: Interstate, 1977. 156 pp. bib.

The authors strive to "convey [a] basic understanding of education as a function of government and of the legal rights, duties, and obligations of teachers in Missouri." It is not a comprehensive text on "school law" but rather a guide to the more important legal principles relating to schools and school districts. Chapters include treatment of the structure of education in Missouri and its relationship to government, the legal status of teachers, certificates, contractual status, professional status, tenure, and retirement. There are also chapters devoted to the tort liability of school districts and employees, and to collective negotiations for teachers. A final chapter discusses ethics for the teaching profession. A third edition was published in 1982.

3-340 Goldberg, Steven S. **Special Education Law: A Guide for Parents, Advocates, and Educators.** New York: Plenum Press, 1982. 229 pp. ns. apps. ind.

As a volume in the Critical Topics in Law and Society series, this excellent work begins with the historical legal basis for special education, and then proceeds to discuss and describe major laws and regulations as well as placement and due process hearings. It concludes with developing issues in the field. Appendixes cover major laws and regulations. Most helpful is a listing of legal organizations and their addresses. As indicated by the title, this book is useful to all parties. It is well footnoted, citing leading authorities and cases.

3-341   Hollander, Patricia. **Legal Handbook for Educators**. Boulder, Colo.: Westview Press, 1978. 287 pp. apps. tbl.

Even though it is intended for an audience at all levels of education, this volume will be of greatest interest to educational administrators at the college and university level. The author, a lawyer, seeks to alert "educators to areas of legal concern, informing them of possible legal remedies, and making recommendations to assist in preventing litigation." Practical "do's and don'ts" are used along with illustrative cases. The text begins with a discussion of legal concepts affecting education from a historical perspective. Succeeding chapters deal with due process, recruitment, admissions, financial obligations of students, disciplinary treatment of students, faculty, and administrators, funding, and facilities.

3-342   Knight, Richard S. **Students' Rights: Issues in Constitutional Freedoms**. Boston: Houghton Mifflin, 1974. 122 pp. pls. ill. ns. bib. ind.

Although dated and somewhat oriented towards a sociological view of students' rights, this easy-to-read book provides the underlying concepts and issues invoved in students' rights. The text is lightly footnoted, and there are pictures and cartoons throughout the work. Chapters cover dress codes and personal appearance, freedom of expression, privacy, and discipline and due process.

3-343   LaMorte, Michael W., Harold W. Gentry, and D. Parker Young. **Students' Legal Rights and Responsibilities**. Cincinnati, Ohio: W.H. Anderson, 1971. 241 pp. bib. tbl. ind.

Addressing itself only to case law dealing with public secondary schools, this book has particular value for students, parents, public school officials, board members, and college and university professors and administrators. Commentaries in each chapter provide insight, and leading cases are edited for easy reading. Chapters cover dress codes, freedom of expression, rights of married students, secret organizations, searches, and due process. A table of cases is at the end of the text, and each chapter ends with selected, reported cases and articles of interest.

3-344   Laudicina, Robert, and Joseph L. Traumutola. **A Legal Perspective for Student Personnel Administrators**. Springfield, Ill.: Charles C. Thomas, 1974. 140 pp. ind.

Reductions in the age of majority from twenty-one to eighteen years in many states has brought changes in the relationship between colleges and students. This book was written as a guide for student personnel administrators faced for the first time with "adult" students. It is written from both the legal and educational perspective. Chapter 2 reviews traditional relationships; chapter 3 examines students' civic and campus responsibilities; chapter 4 discusses drug abuse problems; chapter 5 explores the rights of students and provides model university and campus policies; chapter 6 covers administrative decision-making; and chapter 7 notes various student-related issues. Although some of the content is now dated, this book is recommended for administrators and students at the university level.

3-345   Levine, Alan. **The Rights of Students.** New York: E.P. Dutton, 1973. 160 pp. app. bib.

The text is in question-and-answer format. Although this American Civil Liberties Union handbook is over ten years old, it is still very good in providing the reader with enough information to understand the legal concepts concerning students' rights. Among the topics covered are First Amendment freedoms, due process, corporal punishment, marriage, pregnancy, parenthood, and school records. A selected bibliography, and a list of resource information centers is included. A revised edition was published in 1977 with coauthor Eve Cary.

3-346   McCarthy, Martha M., and Paul T. Diegnan. **What Legally Constitutes an Adequate Public Education: A Review of Constitutional, Legislative, and Judicial Mandates.** Bloomington, Ind.: Phi Delta Kappa Educational Foundation, 1982. 127 pp. ns. apps.

Teachers, administrators, and interested citizens will benefit from a reading of this book, analyzing the legal basis for the right to an adequate education, what constitues an adequate education, and standards for measuring an adequate education. Legislative, judicial, and administrative concepts are explored in this study. Notes to legal authority follow each of the chapters. Appendixes include selected cases on educational adequacy and all state constitutional provisions on the legislative duty to provide elementary and secondary education.

3-347   Rubin, David. **The Rights of Teachers.** New York: Avon Books, 1971. 176 pp. ns. bib.

Although dated, this American Civil Liberties Union handbook provides a good introduction to teachers' rights, including the following topics: freedom to teach, freedom of religion, freedom of speech and association outside the classroom, freedom in private life, freedom in mode of dress or grooming, and freedom from arbitrary or discriminatory action by school officials. The text concludes with a discussion of procedural rights provided by the Constitution.

The book is written in question-and-answer format and each chapter is followed by notes to legal and other authority. A revised edition was published in early 1984.

3-348   Schimmel, David, and Louis Fischer. **The Civil Rights of Students.** New York: Harper and Row, 1975. 348 pp. ns. apps. bib.

This is a comprehensive work, and although nearly ten years old, it is still valuable as a reference work or starting point for research on students' rights. Educators, administrators, and students will find such matters as freedom of speech, press, association, and religion included as well as an analysis of segregation problems, sex discrimination, and due process. Appendixes include a listing of leadingc cases, sample dress and grooming codes and a brief bibliography. The print is small; each chapter is followed by notes to legal authority, but there is no index to legal cases or key words.

3-349   Shrybman, James A. **Due Process in Special Education.** Rockville, Md.: Aspen Systems, 1982. 512 pp. glos. ind.

This guidebook was written for parents, school system personnel, administrators, hearing officers, lawyers, and advocates of free, appropriate public education for handicapped children. Its seven parts are broken down into twenty-nine chapters. They include information on legal sources, the special education process, rights and duties of participants, procedural due process, effective hearing procedures, hearing decisions, and miscellaneous concerns. The glossary of terms is based upon federal laws and regulations, and policy statements issued by the Office of Special Education, U.S. Department of Education.

3-350   Stelzer, Leigh, and Joanna Banthin. **Teachers Have Rights, Too: What Educators Should Know about School Law.** Boulder, Colo.: Social Science Education Consortium, 1980. 164 pp. ns.

The eight chapters of this book are written from the perspective of the classroom teacher, but include relevant information of concern to school administrators, board members, attorneys, parents, and students. Major areas of importance are covered such as tenure, discipline, negligence, and lifestyle choices. The emphasis of this work necessarily excluded much information on student expulsions; and First Amendment rights, school integration, and contract law are not dealt with. Furthermore, unionization, and emerging legislative issues such as teacher accountability and competency are not included since they deal with a special field and developing fields, respectively.

The bulk of this work was developed in a four-year study conducted by the American Bar Association with the support of the Ford Foundation. Extensive footnotes follow each chapter.

3-351   Weeks, Kent M. **Legal Deskbook for Administrators of Independent Colleges and Universities.** Notre Dame, Ind.: Center for Constitutional Studies, Notre Dame Law School, 1982. 356 pp. bib. ns. apps.

Intended for college administrators and legal counsel of independent colleges and universities, this book in looseleaf style is intended for use as a problem solving tool as well as for preventive application of the law. Each chapter explores specific problems and each is preceded by a detailed table of contents. An annotated list of bibliographic resources and case citations at the end of each chapter provide for further research.

The deskbook is set out in a simple, understandable format. Although the work is informative, individual state requirements are not detailed, and administrators must examine these in order to accurately assess their legal positions.

Search and Seizure.   See Criminal Law

Self-Defense

3-352   Baum, Frederick S., and Joan Baum. **Law of Self-Defense.** Dobbs Ferry, N.Y.: Oceana, 1970. 123 pp. ns. apps. ind.

The historical background and the essential differences between legal self-defense and its popular concept is explained. A chapter is also included on vigilante and paramilitary groups. Notes follow each chapter and appendix 2 includes selected cases in each major subdivision of self-defense.

3-353   Cruit, Ronald L. **Intruder in Your Home.** New York: Stein and Day, 1983. 277 pp. bib. ind.

The book is a guide to self-defense of one's home with a firearm, including a summary of all fifty state laws and the law of the District of Columbia. The author details the problem of intruders and the dangers of keeping a gun. He considers ways to improve security of doors, windows, and how to use burglar alarms. He also discusses handguns and shotguns and how to buy, fire, and safely use them. A useful chapter on how to confront an intruder is also included.

Senior Citizens. See Aged

Sex Discrimination

3-354   Alexander, Shana. **Shana Alexander's State-by-State Guide to Women's Legal Rights.** Los Angeles: Wollstonecraft, 1975. 224 pp. ill. glos.

Eleven chapters explore common legal matters such as domestic relations, rape, employment, criminal acts, and so forth. The text is very easy to read, and each major topic has a state-by-state analysis. No footnotes or citations are included. The book is intended merely as a guide for women, providing information which will assist them in better handling their everyday affairs.

3-355   Bird, Caroline. **Everything a Woman Needs to Know to Get Paid What She's Worth.** New York: David McKay, 1973. 304 pp. ind.

Written over a decade ago, this work is still helpful as a reference or starting point on the subject. The book is written in a question-and-answer format. Several chapters near the end discuss affirmative action programs, legal remedies, and union grievance procedures. A useful but dated "Resource Section" following the text provides information relative to women's rights such as documenting discrimination, asserting rights, and legal advice and counseling. An updated revision was published in 1981 with coauthors Helen Mandelbaum and Marjorie Godfrey.

3-356   Clark, Elissa. **Stopping Sexual Harassment: A Handbook.** Detroit: Labor Education and Research Project, 1981. 57 pp. app.

This informative pamphlet, published by an organization created to educate and provide communication among union activists, outlines sexual harassment and how women can combat it. The language is simple and easy to understand. Six chapters provide both an individual and organizational approach to the problem. The fourth chapter provides an outline of legal remedies. Included in the appendix is a list of organizations throughout the country providing assistance for this kind of problem.

3-357   Feldman, Sylvia. **The Rights of Women.** Rochelle Park, N.J.: Hayden, 1974. 136 pp. apps. ind.

This book is part of a series of books written to present social issues to the public. Although there is more emphasis on women's rights in the social context, the book analyzes federal legislation and the Equal Rights Amendment. The text is easy to read, and appendixes include selected readings, films, and other matters.

3-358   Hemphill, Anita M., and Charles F. Hemphill, Jr. **Womanlaw; A Guide to Legal Matters Vital to Women.** Englewood Cliffs, N.J.: Prentice-Hall, 1981. 241 pp. ns. glos. ind.

The book addresses itself to all women, regardless of status. It is intended as a handbook and guide for those legal issues and problems most affecting women. The work is not comprehensive, but does cover major legal questions. The authors state the book is not a substitute for a lawyer, but does provide a bridge of information between a woman and her attorney by informing the reader of basic legal principles.

The format and language are nonlegal, but occasionally legal citations are thrown in. Topics include marriage, domicile, battered women, abortion and birth control, property rights, credit, and so forth. An excellent glossary of common legal terms follows the text.

3-359   Kanowitz, Leo. **Women and the Law: The Unfinished Revolution.** Albuquerque, N. Mex.: University of New Mexico Press, 1970. 312 pp. apps. ns. inds.

The surge of interest over the past fifteen years in women's rights has produced many books. This volume was among the first to examine the legal status of women. Although subsequent developments have greatly altered the scene, much of the content remains pertinent. The most useful chapters discuss the laws relating to single and married women and the constitutional aspects of sex-based discrimination.

3-360   Lynch, Jane Shay, and Sara Lyn Smith. **The Women's Guide to Legal Rights.** Chicago: Contemporary Books, 1979. 125 pp. ind.

This book is written in question (in italics)-and-answer format. It is divided into four chapters, exploring home and family matters, employment, the marketplace, and crimes against women. Each subject is broken down into various subheadings under which the questions appear. The text is easy to read and understand.

3-361   Pomroy, Martha. **What Every Woman Needs to Know about the Law.** Garden City, N.Y.: Doubleday, 1980. 416 pp. bib. ind.

Eight subject areas are explored: family, employment, housing, money, one's self, governmental dealings, consumer problems, crime and punishment, and advocacy. There are twenty-four chapters arranged under each of these subjects with a "rule" given for every major legal problem or issue. The text is easy to read, and legalese is avoided.

3-362   Price, Barbara Raffle, and Natalie J. Sokoloff, eds. and comps. **The Criminal Justice System and Women**. New York: Clark Boardman, 1982. 490 pp. ns.

Twenty-six articles—written by experts in the field—examine traditional theories and recent research on women offenders, female crime victims, and women who work in a male-dominated system. The book concludes with an analysis of possible steps towards changing the system and creating social changes. Each of the articles is followed by notes, references, or both. This work provides information for anyone representing female defendants, individuals dealing with women in the juvenile justice system, those involved with or helping female victims of crime, and administrators in the criminal justice system.

3-363   Ross, Susan Deller, and Ann Barcher. **The Rights of Women**. rev. ed. New York: Bantam Books, 1983. 406 pp. ns. apps.

Arranged in the well-known American Civil Liberties Union (ACLU) question-and-answer format, this ACLU guide is broken down into ten chapters. The authors explain the legal concepts involving constitutional rights, employment discrimination, education, mass media, criminal law, divorce, name changes, sex discrimination, miscellaneous problems, and the legal system. Appendixes consist of five charts: one on several women's organizations, and the others summarize state laws on employment and housing discrimination, changing one's name, and laws on domestic violence. Citations to legal authority follow each chapter.

Shoplifting

3-364   Sklar, Stanley L. **Shoplifting: What You Need to Know about the Law**. New York: Fairchild, 1982. 229 pp. ns. fm. app. ind.

This book is intended to assist store owners, managers, security guards, and other employees in taking the right steps to reduce shoplifting, increase sales, and prevent litigation over improper procedures against customers. The subject of employee thefts is not dicussed. Attorneys and law and business students should also find this work helpful. Readers will find this work most useful in determining how far retailers can go in protecting property rights while respecting customers' rights.

The whole shoplifting problem, from its impact on prices to criminal actions, is discussed in detail. A useful form for reporting a shoplifting incident is provided along with suggested insurance coverage. Footnotes to legal and other citations follow the text, and a helpful listing of each state's shoplifting laws is included.

Slander. See Defamation

Social Security

3-365   Ball, Robert M. **Social Security Today and Tomorrow**. New York: Columbia University Press, 1978. 528 pp. ns. tbls. figs. apps. bib. ind.

This book is easy to read and has been written in response to many questions asked of the author over many years. Beginning with an explanation of social insurance concepts, the author considers every major issue (e.g., the disabled), including what jobs are covered; and he concludes with methods for financing the system and a program for the future.

3-366   Munnell, Alicia H. **The Future of Social Security.** Washington, D.C.: Brookings Institution, 1977. 190 pp. ns. tbls. figs. apps. ind.

The author, admitting social security enjoys broad public support and is in no danger of collapse, concludes there are problems with financial stability and the various inequities in the structure. Options for reform and improvement are suggested. Legislators, government officials, and concerned citizens should benefit from this book. Although recent action by Congress has avoided financial problems for the immediate future, this work retains its value as a resource guide for long-term improvements in the system.

3-367   Schottland, Charles I. **The Social Security Program in the United States.** 2d ed. New York: Appleton-Century-Crofts, Educational Division, Meredith Corporation, 1970. 210 pp. tbls. ns. ind.

Nineteen chapters explore the history and growth of social security for those who are interested in obtaining a brief overview of the program and its development up to 1970.

Solar Law. See Natural Resource Law

Sports Law

3-368   Appenzeller, Herb. **Physical Education and the Law.** Charlottesville, Va.: Michie, 1978. 185 pp. apps. tbl. bib. ind.

Intended for teachers of physical education, this work describes all aspects of physical education law. Included are discussions of negligence of teachers, administrators, and school districts, administrative issues, athletic equipment and facilities, and independent activities. Each section of every chapter is followed by a brief summary.

The work is followed by a table of cases, and there are appendixes including a survey of state laws on immunity and contracting. Bibliographical references are included.

3-369   Appenzeller, Herb, and Thomas Appenzeller. **Sports and the Courts.** Charlottesville, Va.: Michie, 1980. 423 pp. ns. glos. tbl. app. ind.

This book is the final volume in a series of four books on physical education and sports. The work is intended for administrators, coaches, and athletes, but it is also useful to attorneys because of its extensive references to case authority. The authors cover a wide range of legal issues such as discrimination and injuries, officials and spectators, and sports facilities.

Extensive appendixes include such matters as Title IX interpretation and coaches' status in the United States. The text is followed by a glossary of legal terms and an alphabetically arranged table of cases.

3-370   Grieve, Andrew. **The Legal Aspects of Athletics.** New York: A.S. Barnes, 1969. 183 pp. ns. bib.

Written by an assistant professor of physical education, this dated but informative work provides an insight into amateur sports before the 1970s. The perspective is that of one in the field of physical education, covering such topics as equipment and facilities, legal aspects of spectator injuries, and insurance. Legal citations and appendixes are provided.

3-371   Nygaard, Gary, and Thomas H. Boone. **Law for Physical Educators and Coaches.** Salt Lake City: Brighton, 1981. 150 pp. glos. ns. tbl. bib. ind. apps.

The book is intended for educators at all levels of instruction, and it provides operational guidelines as well as an overview of sports injury litigation. Five chapters briefly discuss legal concepts in sports and physical activities, teacher and student rights, safe environments, supervision, and miscellaneous problems such as insurance, product liability, and unsupervised use of facilities. Notes at the end of each chapter refer to legal and other authority. Appendixes covering major court cases on women in sports, a table of cases, and a selected bibliography precede a fine index.

The language is clear and all major areas of concern are covered. Chapter 1 includes a narrative description of common legal words and phrases (for those unaccustomed to legal jargon) as well as a glossary of legal terms.

3-372   Ruxin, Robert H. **An Athlete's Guide to Agents.** Bloomington, Ind.: Indiana University Press, 1983. 163 pp. glos. fms. apps. bib.

This timely work, based upon a paper written in the author's law school days at Harvard, is endorsed by the Collegiate Commissioners Association (CCA) as a tool for assisting student-athletes in preparing themselves for the business of becoming professional athletes.

Written in question-and-answer format, it covers all aspects of the player-agent relationship. Included in the appendixes are, among other things, sample contracts, salary information, and a directory of league offices and player associations. This is an excellent resource for young athletes and their families seeking insight on how to protect their interests from incompetent and unscrupulous agents.

3-373   Sloan, Phillip Samuel. **The Athlete and the Law.** Dobbs Ferry, N.Y.: Oceana, 1983. 152 pp. ns. fms. apps. ind.

Beginning with a discussion and legal analysis of the status of amateur athletes, the author proceeds to explore professional athletes and the taxation of such individuals. The last chapter focuses on professional sports, explaining major areas of interest. The text is followed by the 1980 Major League baseball and basketball agreements and the 1982 National Football League agreement. Typical player contracts are also included. Leading cases are occasionally cited in the text.

3-374   Sobel, Lionel S. **Professional Sports and the Law.** New York: Law-Arts, 1977. 839 pp. ns. fms. bib. ind.

As the first major legal work on sports law, the book's primary focus is upon problems faced by the practicing attorney. All significant areas of professional sports law are examined from antitrust problems to tax questions. The text is very good, including forms, appendixes of Federal statutes and regulations, and a bibliography of sports-related materials. Interested athletes, agents, and citizens may find the book helpful. A 1981 supplement has been published.

3-375 Waicukauski, Ronald J., ed. **Law and Amateur Sports**. Bloomington, Ind.: Indiana University Press, 1982. 298 pp. bib. ind.

This work is a collection of essays developed from a national conference in 1981 sponsored by the Center for Law and Sports at Indiana University. Many facts of law and amateur sports are discussed, and the work concludes with a thirty-page bibliography on sports law. The text is helpful to coaches, athletic administrators, parents of student athletes, and lawyers and law professors.

3-376 Weistart, John C., and Cym H. Lowell. **The Law of Sports**. Charlottesville, Va.: Michie/Bobbs Merrill, 1979. 1,154pp. ns. ind.

This treatise is one of two classic works (the other is by Sobel, *Professional Sports and the Law,* see 3-374) on the subject of sports law. Covering both amateur and professional sports, it is the most recent, comprehensive work published; and it is oriented towards athletes, administrators, and coaches as well as attorneys. Coverage is extensive and in detail.

States. See Government—Federal and State

Students. See Schools

Supreme Court. See Courts

Suretyship. See Insurance

Taxation

3-377 Anderson, B. Ray. **How to Save 50% or More on Your Income Tax— Legally**. New York: Macmillan, 1982. 322 pp.

The author emphasizes tax planning, stressing the need to plan ahead instead of trying to save money when the time to pay taxes arrives. The text begins with an introduction analyzing the impact of the Economic Recovery Tax Act of 1981 (ERTA) and the Tax Equity and Fiscal Responsibility Act of 1982 (TEFRA).

The book covers a wide range of tax subjects, which are divided into three major divisions: why taxes will continue to increase, keys to successful tax avoidance, and ways of effectively saving money. The language is easy to read and the author keeps the subject interesting without becoming unduly technical.

The work concludes by suggesting resources for helping to save on taxes such as a home-study course, selected books, and a newsletter service.

3-378 Blaustein, Randy Bruce. **How to Do Business with the IRS; The Complete Guide for Tax Professionals**. Englewood Cliffs, N.J.: Prentice-Hall, 1982. 342 pp. fms. apps. ind.

Intended primarily for the tax practitioner representing clients before the IRS, this book provides answers to procedural and practical questions. However, taxpayers and tax professionals representing themselves should also find this work illuminating and helpful since the author has a background as an attorney and former IRS agent.

The text is well indexed, and chapter and subchapter headings provide easy access. Sample letters are included throughout, and answers to common problems encountered with the IRS are provided. This is a very useful, practical work packed full of information.

3-379   Dickson, David T. **Tax Shelters for the Not-So-Rich**. Chicago: Contemporary Books, 1980. 182 pp. tbls. figs. apps. ind.

There are nine tax loopholes outlined in this book, which was written for the average taxpayer seeking ways of eliminating taxes. The author provides examples, tables, and figures to explain how taxes may be avoided. Various annuities and tax-qualified retirement plans are compared and analyzed in the appendixes. However, the author does not analyze the cash surrender value of life insurance policies as a tax loophole: since the policies are owned by the insurance companies, they do not collect interest; and upon the death of the insured, only the face amount of the life insurance contract is paid. The nine tax loopholes explored by the author may all be owned by individuals, and they can increase in value due to interest or earnings.

3-380   **Fear of Filing: A Beginner's Handbook on Record Keeping and Federal Taxes for Performers, Visual Artists and Writers**. rev. ed. New York: Volunteer Lawyers for the Arts, 1982. 56 pp.

This booklet is not comprehensive. It is only designed as an aid to enable individuals in the named fields to better understand and organize their tax materials for the person or organization preparing tax forms. The reasoning is that if one is more organized, the tax preparer will have an easier time, and preparing the tax return will be less costly. The text is divided into seven sections, including, for instance, an income chart, credits against taxes, and an example factual pattern with completed forms. Annual updated forms and information may be obtained from the publisher at the beginning of each calendar year.

3-381   Fierro, Robert Daniel. **Tax Shelters in Plain English**. New York: McGraw-Hill, 1978. 72 pp.

This is an understandable book with fifteen chapters arranged into six parts explaining such topics as real estate, energy (oil), farming, equipment leasing, and miscellaneous ways of sheltering one's income. A 1983 revised edition has been published as *Tax Shelters in Plain English: New Tax Strengths for the 1980s.*

3-382   Holzman, Robert S. **Holzman's New Guide to the Accumulated Earning Tax**. Englewood Cliffs, N.J.: Prentice-Hall, 1982. 289 pp. ns. apps. fms. tbl. ind.

Corporate directors, executives, accountants, attorneys, and professional advisors will find this most helpful in avoiding an unnecessary tax imposed upon earnings

170 / Selected Subject Bibliography of Law-related Monographs

that have been hoarded or unnecessarily accumulated instead of being distributed to shareholders of the corporation. Twelve chapters explore such matters as the dangers of an accumulated earnings tax (including personal liability), how it works, reasons for legitimate retention of earnings, and matters to avoid. The text is filled with citations to case and statutory authority. Appendixes include citations and abbreviations, forms, guidelines, and a table of cases.

3-383   Holzman, Robert S. **A Survival Kit for Taxpayers: Staying on Good Terms with the I.R.S.** New York: Macmillan, 1979. 149 pp. ind.

This book outlines what taxpayers must know and do in order to ensure that relations with the IRS run smoothly, especially in those cases where an audit takes place. The language is easy to understand, and chapters include an explanation of fines and penalties, tax traps, and ten ways to be a good taxpayer. A revised edition was published in 1981.

3-384   McDaniel, Paul R., and Hugh J. Ault. **Introduction to United States International Taxation.** Boston: Kluwer, 1981. 209 pp. ind.

Intended primarily for tax practitioners, law professors, and students, this work will also find use with accountants, multinational corporate executives, and other business individuals interested in knowing about, or dealing with, their multinational tax accountability.

The text is not for those inexperienced in international business taxation. It is somewhat technical, dealing with jurisdiction, taxation of foreign corporations and nonresident aliens, foreign income sources for U.S. citizens, and income tax treaties, to name a few.

3-385   McNulty, John K. **Federal Income Taxation of Individuals in a Nutshell.** 3d ed. St. Paul: West, 1983. 487 pp. tbls. ns. ind.

Ninety-nine sections are arranged under nine chapters, offering an introduction to, and overview of, the subject. Income is explained in addition to what may be deducted, and so forth. Tables include revenue rulings, revenue code sections, treasury regulations, and cases.

3-386   Sprouse, Mary L. **Taxable You: Every Woman's Guide to Taxes.** New York: Penguin Books, 1984. 349 pp. fms. ind.

This book is intended for any woman who wants to file her own tax return, whether single, married, divorced, or widowed. The text is in clear, easily understood language and is broken down into eleven chapters. Included are the twelve basic principles for understanding tax laws, chapters on married women, working mothers, tax consequences of divorce, and much more. Examples, forms and "tax tips" are included throughout the text. Although slanted towards women, anyone interested in learning the basics about taxes will find this worthwhile reading.

3-387   Steiner, Barry R., and David W. Kennedy. **Perfectly Legal: 300 Foolproof Methods for Paying Less Taxes**, 1983 ed. New York: John Wiley and Sons, 1983. 230 pp. fms. app.

This second edition of a "highly popular book" seeks to help taxpayers save on taxes. Brevity, clarity, and accuracy are the methods by which the authors present their material to the reader, but the authros do caution readers to consult a specialist before making any final decisions.

Areas explored include charitable giving, income averaging, investments, medical bills, insurance trusts, and small businesses. Readers should be cautioned that a 1984 edition does exist, and that this may be published on a regular basis in the future.

3-388   Talbott, John. **A Practical Tax Guide for the Horse Owner.** Worthington, Ohio: Publishing Horizons, 1982. 72 pp. tbls. fms.

Balancing theory and practice, and intended as a learning tool, this book presents basic tax concepts so that an individual engaged in the horse business may be able to understand most tax problems relating to the horse trade. Professional accounting assistance is suggested for esoteric areas such as farming syndicates, accrual methods of accounting, and partnerships with over ten partners, among others. The five chapters are loaded with examples, tables and forms on deducting losses, recordkeeping, depreciation and investment tax credit, gains and losses on sales and exchange of horses, death of horses due to disease and casualty, and other matters.

3-389   Wade, Jack Warren, Jr. **When You Owe the IRS.** New York: Macmillan, 1983. 246 pp. fms. ind.

This is one of those works to address the problem of dealing with the Internal Revenue Service from the standpoint of the average taxpayer. It is an excellent resource for individuals owing the IRS and wanting to know what to do. Scattered throughout the book are "SURVIVAL RULES", suggesting ways to work with the IRS, how to save money on interest and late payments, and how to avoid seizure.

Teachers. See Schools

Terminally Ill. See Critically Ill

Torts

3-390   Miller, Vernon X. **What Some People Ought to Know about Personal Injury Law.** New York: Vantage Press, 1978. 198 pp. ind.

Professionals and laypeople interested in a clear, simply written explanation of personal injury law should benefit from this work, which is written by an emeritus law professor and former dean.

3-391   Schuck, Peter H. **Suing Government: Citizen Remedies for Official Wrongs.** New Haven, Conn.: Yale University Press, 1983. 262 pp. apps. ns. ind.

Although rather scholarly, this work is very useful in focusing upon civil remedies under public tort (personal injury) law, and how such remedies affect an important subset of officials. The author argues that the existing system of personal injury remedies needs reconstruction with a broader concept of governmental liability more in tune with private law principles. Governmental leaders, lawmakers, and attorneys will find this useful in redefining federal tort liability concepts.

Trade and Professional Corporations. See Corporations

Trade Regulation

3-392 Rockefeller, Edwin S. **Antitrust Counseling for the 1980s.** Rockville, Md.: Bureau of National Affairs, 1983. 268 pp. ns. apps. tbl. ind.

Business advisors, executives, and attorneys should find this work a useful guide for conducting business and avoiding antitrust litigation. Chapters explore such matters as acting alone, relations with competitors and customers, discrimination, patent licensing, mergers, enforcement, and compliance programs. Important acts are included in the appendixes, and leading cases are easily located by reference to the table of cases following the text.

Trademarks. See Intellectual and Industrial Property

Trusts. See Estates

Truth in Advertising and Lending. See Consumer Protection

Unemployment. See Labor Law

Unmarried Couples. See Domestic Relations

Urban Law and Planning. See Land Use—Planning

Veterans

3-393 Addlestone, David F., Susan Hewman, and Frederic Gross. **The Rights of Veterans.** New York: Avon Books, 1978. 269 pp. ns. apps.

This American Civil Liberties Union Handbook presents a fine analysis of U.S. Armed Forces veterans' rights. In typical question-and-answer format, the text examines nearly the entire range of issues involving veterans. An oversight seems to exist in this work since no discussion exists on federal programs providing education and home loan assistance. The appendixes list counseling groups and assistance centers among other matters. Notes to legal authority follow each chapter.

Victims of Crime. See Criminal Law

Video. See Radio, Television, and Motion Pictures

Weapons. *See* Firearms; Self-Defense

Wills. *See* Estates

Witnesses

3-394   Tierney, Kevin. **How to Be a Witness**. Dobbs Ferry, N.Y.: Oceana, 1971. 108 pp. apps. ind.

This booklet explains the process one goes through as a witness in a legal action. Chapters include a discussion of the subpoena, witnesses' financial rights, and an explanation of such matters as behavior, honesty, reputation, privileges, immunity, cross-examination, and so forth.

Women. *See* Abortion and Birth Control; Consumer Credit; Judges; Lawyers—Biography; Rape; Sex Discrimination; Taxation

Workers' Compensation. *See* Labor Law

Writers. *See* Authors

Zoning. *See* Land Use—Planning

APPENDIXES

APPENDIX A
OUTLINE OF THE UNITED STATES COURT SYSTEM*

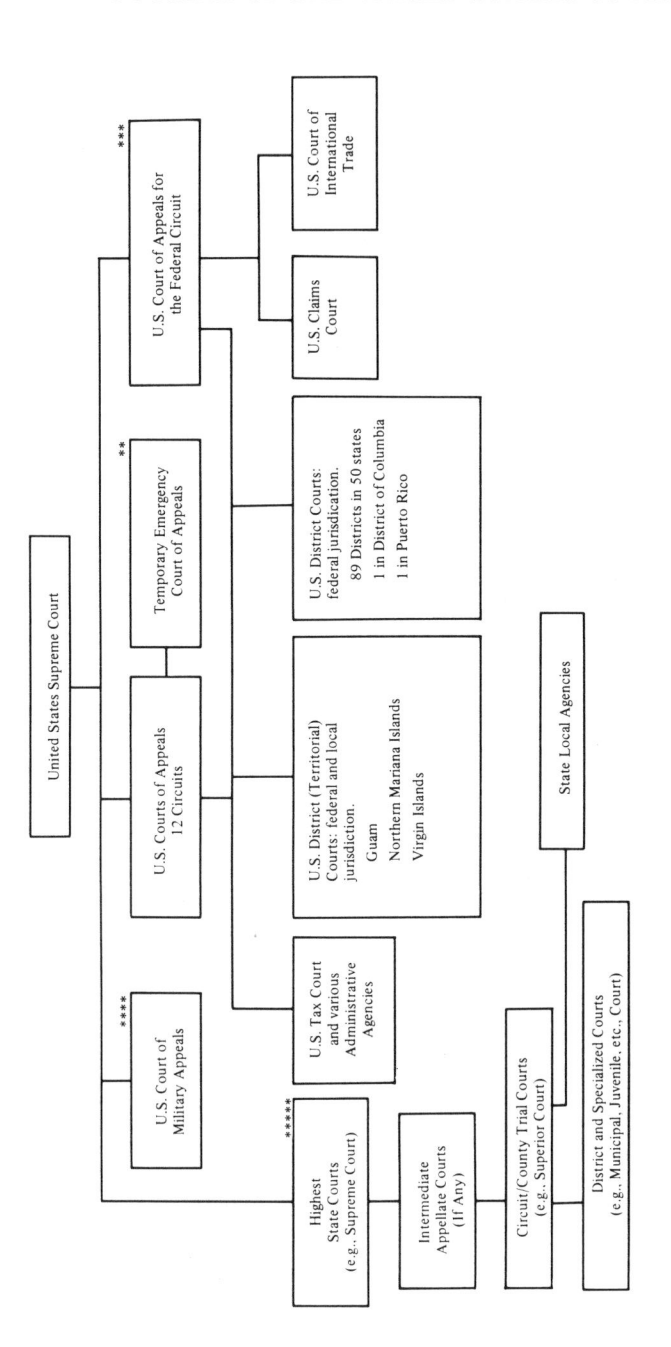

```
                              United States Supreme Court
                                        |
    ┌───────────────────┬───────────────┼───────────────────────┐
    |                   |               |                       |
 U.S. Court of     U.S. Courts of  Temporary Emergency   U.S. Court of Appeals for
 Military Appeals  Appeals         Court of Appeals**    the Federal Circuit***
 ****              12 Circuits
                        |                                       |
            ┌───────────┼──────────────┐                ┌───────┴────────┐
            |           |              |                |                |
     U.S. Tax Court  U.S. District  U.S. District   U.S. Claims     U.S. Court of
     and various    (Territorial)   Courts:         Court           International
     Administrative Courts: federal federal                         Trade
     Agencies       and local       jurisdiction.
                    jurisdiction.   89 Districts in 50 states
                    Guam            1 in District of Columbia
                    Northern Mariana 1 in Puerto Rico
                    Islands
                    Virgin Islands

 Highest
 State Courts
 (e.g., Supreme Court)
 *****
    |
 Intermediate
 Appellate Courts
 (If Any)
    |
 Circuit/County Trial Courts      State Local Agencies
 (e.g., Superior Court)
    |
 District and Specialized Courts
 (e.g., Municipal, Juvenile, etc., Court)
```

*Information taken from *The United States Government Manual, 1983/84*, Washington, D.C.: Office of the Federal Register; *United States Code Congressional and Administrative News*, St. Paul: West; *United States Code Annotated*, St. Paul: West; and Coffin, Frank M. *The Ways of a Judge: Reflections from the Federal Appellate Bench*, Boston: Houghton Mifflin, 1980.

**Exclusive jurisdiction of all appeals from U.S. District Courts in cases and controversies involving economic stabilization laws.

***Exclusive jurisdiction of U.S. District and Territorial Courts, and administrative agency decisions in certain cases.

****Appellate tribunal for criminal matters and court-martial convictions in all branches of the armed services.

*****Direct appeal where U.S. laws held unconstitutional. United States Supreme Court also has discretion to grant requests for certiorari.

177

APPENDIX B
SELECTED LIST OF LAW BOOK PUBLISHERS*

Academic Press, Inc.
111 Fifth Ave.
New York, NY 10003
(212) 741-6800

ALI–ABA Committee on Continuing
    Professional Education
4025 Chestnut St.
Philadelphia, PA 19104
(215) 243-1600

American Arbitration Association
140 West 51st St.
New York, NY 10020
(202) 484-4000

American Association of Law Libraries
53 W. Jackson Blvd.
Chicago, IL 60604
(312) 939-4764

American Bar Association
Publication Planning and Marketing
1155 East 50th St.
Chicago, IL 60637
(312) 947-4000

American Civil Liberties Union
132 W. 43rd St.
New York, NY 10036
(212) 944-9800

American Enterprise Institute
1150 - 17th St., N.W.
Washington, DC 20036
(202) 862-5800

American Judicature Society
200 West Monroe St.
Suite 1606
Chicago, IL 60606
(312) 558-6900

American Planning Association
1313 E. 60th St.
Chicago, IL 60637

American Society of Law and
    Medicine
765 Commonwealth Ave., 16th Floor
Boston, MA 02215
(617) 262-4990

Anderson Publishing Co.
646 Main St.
Cincinnati, OH 45201
(513) 421-4142

Arno Press, Inc.
3 Park Ave.
New York, NY 10016
(212) 725-2050

Aspen Systems Corporation
1600 Research Blvd.
Rockville, MD 20850
(301) 251-5000

The Association of Trial Lawyers of
    America
1050 31st St., N.W.
Washington, DC 20007
(202) 965-3500

---

*This list includes major law book publishers, self-help law book publishers, and those publishers who frequently publish legal materials.

180 / Selected List of Law Book Publishers

Matthew Bender & Co., Inc.
235 East 45th St.
New York, NY 10017
(800) 833-9844

Clark Boardman Company Ltd.
435 Hudson St.
New York, NY 10014
(212) 929-7500
(800) 221-9428

Bureau of National Affairs
Distribution and Customer Service Ctr.
9401 Decoverly Hall Rd.
Rockville, MD 20850
(301) 258-1033

Butterworth Legal Publishers
11004 Metric Blvd.
Austin, TX 78758
(512) 835-7921

California Continuing Education of the Bar
2300 Shattuck Ave.
Berkeley, CA 94704
(415) 642-6546

Callaghan & Co.
3201 Old Glenview Rd.
Wilmette, IL 60091
(312) 256-7000

Cambridge University Press
510 North Ave.
New Rochelle, NY 10801
(914) 235-0300
(800) 431-1580

The Center for Urban Policy Research
P.O. Box 489
Piscataway, NJ 08854
(201) 932-3101

Chancery Publishers
102 West Pennsylvania Ave.
Baltimore, MD 21204
(301) 821-5143

Columbia University Press
136 S. Broadway
Irvington-on-Hudson, NY 10533
(914) 591-9111

Commerce Clearing House, Inc.
4025 West Peterson Ave.
Chicago, IL 60646
(312) 583-8500

Congressional Information Service, Inc.
4520 East-West Highway
Bethesda, MD 20814
(301) 654-1550

Congressional Quarterly, Inc.
1414 - 22nd St., N.W.
Washington, DC 20037
(202) 296-6800

Conservation Foundation
Publications Department
1717 Massachusetts Ave., N.W.
Washington, DC 20036
(202) 797-4300

The Consumer Bankers Association
1300 North 17th St., Suite 1200
Arlington, VA 22209
(703) 276-1750

Cornell University Press
124 Roberts Place
P.O. Box 250
Ithaca, NY 14850
(607) 257-7000

Council of State Governments
P.O. Box 11910
Iron Works Pike
Lexington, KY 40578
(606) 252-2291

Do-It-Yourself Legal Publishers
150 Fifth Ave.
New York, NY 10011
(212) 242-2840

Elsevier-North Holland
52 Vanderbilt Ave.
New York, NY 10164
(212) 867-9040

Enterprise Publishing, Inc.
725 Market St.
Wilmington, DE 19801
(302) 654-0110

Environmental Law Institute
1346 Connecticut Ave., N.W.
Washington, DC 20036
(202) 452-9600

Equity Publishing Corp.
Main St.
Orford, NH 03777
(603) 353-4351

EXPRESS
P.O. Box 1373
Richmond, CA 94802
(415) 236-5496

Federal Bar Association
1815 H St., N.W.
Suite 420
Washington, DC 20006
(202) 638-0252

Federal Programs Advisory Service
2120 L St., N.W.
Suite 210
Washington, DC 20037
(202) 872-1766

Federal Publications, Inc.
1120 20th St., N.W.
Washington, DC 20036
(202) 337-7000

Foundation Press, Inc.
170 Old Country Rd.
Mineola, NY 11561
(516) 248-5580

Gale Research Co.
Book Tower
Detroit, MI 48226
(313) 961-2242

Greenwood Press
88 Post Road West
P.O. Box 5007
Westport, CT 06881
(203) 226-3571

HALT
Suite 319
201 Massachusetts Ave., N.E.
Washington, DC 20002
(202) 546-4268

The Harrison Co.
3110 Crossing Park
Norcross, GA 30071
(404) 447-9150

Harvard University Press
79 Garden St.
Cambridge, MA 02138
(607) 228-2800

Health Administration Press
1021 East Huron
The University of Michigan
Ann Arbor, MI 48109
(313) 764-1380

D. C. Heath and Co.
2700 North Richardt Ave.
Indianapolis, IN 46219
(800) 428-8071

William S. Hein & Co., Inc.
1285 Main St.
Buffalo, NY 14209
(716) 882-2600

Hoover Institution Press
Stanford University
Stanford, CA 94305
(415) 497-3373

182 / Selected List of Law Book Publishers

Inform Press
4150 St. Clair
Studio City, CA 91604

Infosources Publishing
118 West 79th St.
New York, NY 10024
(212) 595-3161

The Institute of Continuing Legal
  Education - ICLE
Hutchins Hall
Ann Arbor, MI 48109
(313) 764-0533

International Foundation of Employee
  Benefit Plans
18700 Bluemound Rd.
P.O. Box 69
Brookfield, WI 53005
(414) 786-6700

Kluwer Boston, Inc.
190 Old Derby St.
Hingham, MA 02043
(617) 749-5262

Law and Business
Harcourt Brace Jovanovich, Inc.
757 Third Ave.
New York, NY 10017
(212) 888-2652

Law Journal Seminars-Press
111 Eighth Ave.
New York, NY 10011
(212) 741-8300

The Lawyer's Co-Operative Publishing
  Co. and Bancroft-Whitney Co.
Aqueduct Building
Rochester, NY 14694
(716) 546-5530

Lawyer's Register
5325 Naiman Parkway
Solon, OH 44139
(216) 248-0135

The Legal Classics Library
(Div. of Gryphon Editions, Ltd.)
P.O. Box 76108
Birmingham, AL 35253
(205) 879-8380

Little, Brown and Co.
Law Division
34 Beacon St.
Boston, MA 02106
(617) 227-0730

Macmillan Publishing Co.
Front and Brown Sts.
Riverside, NJ 08370
(212) 935-2000

Mason Publishing Co.
366 Wacouta St.
St. Paul, MN 55101
(612) 227-4200

McGraw-Hill Book Co.
13955 Manchester Rd.
Manchester, MO 63011
(314) 227-1600

Michie/Bobbs-Merrill
P.O. Box 7587
Charlottesville, VA 22906
(804) 295-6171

The MIT Press
28 Carlton St.
Cambridge, MA 02142
(617) 253-5642

National Institute for Trial Advocacy
Legal Education Center
40 N. Milton, Suite 106
St. Paul, MN 55104
(612) 292-9333

National Law Publishing Corp.
99 Painters Mill Rd.
Owings Mills, MD 21117
(301) 363-6400

Selected List of Law Book Publishers / 183

New York State Bar Association
One Elk St.
Albany, NY 12207
(518) 463-3200

Martinus Nijhoff
190 Old Derby St.
Hingham, MA 02043
(617) 749-5262 (Kluwer Boston)

NOLO Press
950 Parker St.
Berkeley, CA 94710
(415) 549-1976

North Carolina Bar Foundation
P.O. Box 12806
Raleigh, NC 27605
(919) 828-0561
(800) 662-7407

Oceana Publications
75 Main St.
Dobbs Ferry, NY 10522
(914) 693-5944

Oxford University Press
16-00 Pollitt Drive
Fair Lawn, NJ 07410
(201) 796-8000

Panel Publishers
14 Plaza Rd.
Greenvale, NY 11548
(516) 484-0006

Practising Law Institute
810 Seventh Ave.
New York, NY 10019
(212) 765-5700

Praeger Publishers
383 Madison Ave.
New York, NY 10017
(212) 750-1330

Prentice-Hall, Inc.
Information Services Division
Englewood Cliffs, NJ 07632
(201) 368-4402

Rand Corporation
Publications Department
1700 Main St.
Santa Monica, CA 90406
(213) 393-0411

Research Institute of America
589 Fifth Ave.
New York, NY 10017
(212) 755-8900

Fred B. Rothman and Co.
10368 West Centennial Rd.
Littleton, CO 80127
(303) 979-5657

Rutgers University Press
P.O. Box 4869
Hampden Station
Baltimore, MD 21211
(301) 338-7791

Sage Publications, Inc.
275 South Beverly Hills Dr.
Beverly Hills, CA 90212
(213) 274-8003

Scholarly Resources Inc.
104 Greenhill Ave.
Wilmington, DE 19805
(302) 654-7713

Shepard's/McGraw-Hill
P.O. 1235
Colorado Springs, CO 80901
(303) 475-7230

Allen Smith Co.
1435 North Meridian St.
Indianapolis, IN 46202
(317) 634-4098

Selected List of Law Book Publishers

Stanford University Press
Stanford, CA 94305
(415) 497-9434

University of California Press
2223 Fulton St.
Berkeley, CA 94720
(415) 642-4562

University of Chicago Press
5801 Ellis Ave.
Chicago, IL 60637
(312) 753-3344

University Microfilms
300 N. Zeeb Rd.
Ann Arbor, MI 48106
(313) 761-4700

University of North Carolina Press
P.O. Box 2288
Chapel Hill, NC 27514
(919) 966-3561

University Press of America
4720 Boston Way
Lanham, MD 20706
(301) 459-3366

University Press of Virginia
Box 3608
University Station
Charlottesville, VA 22903
(804) 924-3468

University Publications of America, Inc.
44 North Market St.
Frederick, MD 21701
(301) 694-0100

W. E. Upjohn Institute for Employment Research
300 South Westnedge Ave.
Kalamazoo, MI 49007
(616) 343-5541

WANT Publishing Co.
1511 K. St., N.W.
Washington, DC 20005
(202) 783-1887

Warren, Gorham & Lamont, Inc.
210 South St.
Boston, MA 02111
(617) 423-2020

West Publishing Co.
50 W. Kellogg Blvd.
P.O. Box 3526
St. Paul, MN 55165
(612) 228-2500

John Wiley & Sons, Inc.
605 Third Ave.
New York, NY 10158
(212) 850-6000

The H.W. Wilson Co.
950 University Ave.
Bronx, NY 10452
(212) 588-8400

Yale University Press
92 A Yale Station
New Haven, CT 06520
(203) 432-4969

APPENDIX C
SELECTED LIST OF MAJOR LEGAL RESEARCH TEXTS

Brigham Young University Law Library. *Legal Research Manual for Law Students.* Provo, Utah: Brigham Young University Law Library, 1985.

Bromberg, Alan R. *Research Methods/Legal Writing Manual.* Dallas: Southern Methodist University School of Law, 1976.

Cohen, Morris L. *Legal Research in a Nutshell.* 4th ed. St. Paul: West, 1985.

Cohen Morris L., and Robert C. Berring. *How to Find the Law.* 8th ed. St. Paul: West, 1983.

Jacobstein, J. Myron, and Roy M. Mersky. *Fundamentals of Legal Research.* 3d ed. Mineola, N.Y.: Foundation Press, 1985.

Lloyd, David. *Finding the Law.* Dobbs Ferry, N.Y.: Oceana, 1974.

Price, Miles Oscar, Harry Bitner, and Shirley Raissi Bysiewicz. *Effective Legal Research,* 4th ed. Boston: Little, Brown, 1979.

Reams, Bernard D., Jr., ed. *Reader in Law Librarianship.* Englewood, Colo.: Information Handling Services, 1976.

Rombauer, Marjorie. *Legal Problem Solving.* 4th ed. St. Paul: West, 1983.

Schmeckebier, Lawrence F., and Roy B. Eastin. *Government Publications and Their Use.* 2d rev. ed. Washington, D.C.: Brookings Institution, 1969.

Statsky, William P. *Legal Research, Writing, and Analysis.* 3d ed. St. Paul: West, 1985.

*State Guides**

California   Granberg, Ron. *California Legal Research.* 2d ed. Monterey, Calif.: R. S. Publications, 1979.

              Henke, Dan F. *California Law Guide.* 2d ed. Los Angeles: Parker & Son, 1976.

Florida   Brown, Richard L. *Guide to Florida Legal Research.* Tallahassee, Fla.: Florida Bar, Continuing Legal Education, 1980.

---

*There are only a few such guides available since formally published texts for conducting legal research do not exist for most states.

Georgia	Chanin, Leah. *Reference Guide to Georgia Legal History and Legal Research.* Charlottesville, Va.: Michie, 1980.
Illinois	Jacobs, Roger F., et al. *Illinois Legal Research Sourcebook.* Springfield, Ill.: Illinois Institute for Continuing Legal Education, 1977.
Louisiana	Chiang, Win-Shin S. *Louisiana Legal Research.* Austin, Tex.: Butterworth Legal Publishers, 1985.
North Carolina	Kavass, Igor, and Bruce Christensen. *Guide to North Carolina Legal Research.* Buffalo: William S. Hein, 1973.
South Carolina	Mills, Robin, and Jon Schultz. *South Carolina Legal Research Handbook.* Buffalo: William S. Hein, 1976.
Tennessee	Laska, Lewis. *Tennessee Legal Research Handbook.* Buffalo: William S. Hein, 1977.
Texas	Boner, Marian. *A Reference Guide to Texas Law and Legal History: Sources and Documentation.* Austin, Tex.: University of Texas Press, 1976.
Wisconsin	Danner, Richard. *Legal Research in Wisconsin.* Madison, Wis.: University of Wisconsin Ext., Law Dept., 1980.

APPENDIX D
SELECTED LIST OF ONLINE DATABASE FILES AND VENDORS

AUTO-CITE
Lawyers Co-operative Publishing Company
Aqueduct Building
Rochester, NY 14694
Phone: (800) 828-6373

Bibliographic Retrieval Services (BRS)
702 Corporation Park
Scotia, NY 12302
Phone: (518) 372-5011

Dialog Information Services, Inc.
Lockheed Corporation
3460 Hillview Ave.
Palo Alto, CA 94304
Phone: (415) 858-2700

Electronic Legislative Search System (ELSS)
Commerce Clearing House
4025 W. Peterson Ave.
Chicago, IL 60646
Phone: (312) 583-8500

FLIGHT (Federal Legal Information Through Electronics)*
Denver, CO 80279
Phone: (303) 370-7531

JURIS (Justice Retrieval And Inquiry System)*
Department of Justice
10th and Constitution Ave., N.W.
Washington, DC 20530
(202) 633-5658

LEGIS (Legal Information and Status System)
Office of Legislative Information
House Office Building, Annex #2
3rd and D Streets, S.W., #696
Washington, DC 20515
Phone: (202) 225-1772

Legi-Slate
Legi-Slate, Inc.
444 North Capitol Street, N.W.
Washington, DC 20001
Phone: (202) 737-1888

LEXIS/NEXIS
Mead Data Central
9333 Springbora Pike
Miamisburg, OH 45457
Phone: (513) 865-6800

PHINet FedTax Database Service
Prentice-Hall Information Network
Prentice-Hall, Inc.
292 Madison Avenue
New York, NY 10017
Phone: (212) 685-2121

SDC Search Service
System Development Corp.
2500 Colorado Ave.
Santa Monica, CA 90406
Phone: (213) 453-6194

WESTLAW
West Publishing Co.
Box 43779
50 W. Kellogg Blvd.
St. Paul, MN 55164
Phone: (800) 328-9352

---

*Database available to Federal Offices

AUTHOR INDEX

Abelow, Dan, 3-1
Addlestone, David F., 3-393
Alexander, Shana, 3-354
Amary, Issam B., 3-156
American Bar Association, 3-10
American Correctional Association, 3-322
Anderson, B. Ray, 3-377
Anderson, Howard J., 3-204, 3-205
Anderson, Ralph J. B., 2-77
Annas, George J., 3-291, 3-292
Anosike, Benji O., 3-32, 3-114
Appenzeller, Herb, 3-157, 3-368, 3-369
Appenzeller, Thomas, 3-369
Arbuckle, J. Gordon, 2-154
Armstrong, Scott, 3-94
Aronson, Robert H., 3-274
Ashley, Paul P., 3-112
Aspen, Marvin E., 3-105, 3-106
Ault, Hugh J., 3-384

Bailey, F. Lee, 3-96
Balker, Vicki M., 3-157
Ball, Robert M., 3-365
Ballentine, James A., 2-63
Ballinger, Tom, 3-97
Bander, David F., 2-137
Bander, Edward J., 2-137
Banthin, Joanna, 3-350
Barber, David, 3-269
Barber, Sotirios A., 3-58
Barcher, Ann, 3-363
Bard, Morton, 3-98
Barnes, Catherine A., 2-42
Barnes, James A., 3-76
Barr, Samuel J., 3-1
Barrientos, Lawless J., 3-77
Bartol, Curt R., 3-329
Bass, Howard L., 3-115
Bassiouni, M. Cherif, 3-99
Baum, Frederick S., 3-352
Baum, Joan, 3-352
Baum, Lawrence, 2-131

Beis, Edward B., 3-305
Belli, Melvin M., 3-264
Belz, Herman, 3-59
Berring, Robert C., 2-31, 2-140
Beseler, Dora Hedwig von, 2-78
Besharov, Douglas J., 3-194
Besterman, Theodore, 2-23
Beutel, Frederick K., 3-36
Bieber, Doris M., 2-73, 2-74
Bigelow, Robert P., 3-29
Bird, Caroline, 3-355
Bitner, Harry, 2-147
Black, Henry C., 2-64
Blagden, Nellie, 3-324
Blandford, Linda A., 2-16
Blaustein, Randy Bruce, 3-378
Block, Gertrude, 3-282
Blumberg, Richard E., 3-222
Blumrosen, Alfred W., 3-218
Boast, Carol, 2-33
Bode, Janet, 3-333, 3-334
Bolmeier, Edward Claude, 3-335
Boone, Thomas H., 3-371
Bosarge, Betty B., 3-196
Bosmajian, Haig, 3-286
Bove, Alexander A., Jr., 3-325
Bowman, Arthur G., 3-328
Brody, Ilene N., 3-202
Bronstein, Alvin J., 3-323
Browne, Cynthia E., 2-20
Brunner, Thomas W., 3-270
Bryson, William H., 2-75
Buckwalter, Robert L., 2-36
Budoff, Milton, 3-336
Burt, Robert A., 3-293
Burton, William C., 2-94
Bush, John C., 3-55
Bysiewicz, Shirley Raissi, 2-147

Canada, Ralph, 3-256
Carliner, David, 3-166
Carter, Lief H., 3-189

Author Index

Cartwright, John M., 2-84
Cassidy, Robert, 3-116
Cataldo, Bernard F., 3-226
Causey, Denzil Y., Jr., 3-5
Cavallo, Robert M., 3-20
Chamelin, Neil C., 3-95
Chapman, Mary R., 2-17
Chase, Harold, 2-43
Cheatham, Charles, 3-256
Chickering, Robert B., 3-173
Choper, Jesse H., 3-87
Christoffel, Tom, 3-294
Clair, Bernard E., 3-117
Clark, Elissa, 3-356
Clifford, Denis, 3-44
Coco, Al, 2-138
Coffin, Frank M., 3-186
Cohen, Morris L., 2-139, 2-140
Cohen, Ronald Jay, 3-306
Cohen, Stanley, 3-100
Cole, Lisa A., 3-312
Columbia University Law Library, 2-28
Cooper, Timothy T., 3-338
Coughlin, George Gordon, 3-227
Coulson, Robert, 3-206
Cruit, Ronald L, 3-353
Cummings, Frank, 2-155
Cunningham, William E., 3-271
Curry, Hayden, 3-44
Cushman, Robert F., 3-63

Dacey, Norman F., 3-141
D'Aleo, Richard J., 2-125
Daniele, Anthony R., 3-117
Davis, J. P., 3-257
Davis, James R., 3-192
De Grazia, Edward, 3-331
Delaney, John, 3-258
Delon, Floyd G., 3-339
Deming, Richard, 3-272
Deutsch, Howard David, 3-167
Diamond, Sidney A., 3-174
Dickinson, Elizabeth M., 3-210
Dickson, David T., 3-379
Diegnan, Paul T., 3-346
Ditlow, Clarence, 3-69
Dobbyn, John F., 3-171
Doimi di Delupis, Ingrid, 2-24
Dorman, Michael, 3-193
Dorsen, Norman, 3-45
Drotning, Phillip T., 3-65
Duboff, Leonard D., 3-330
Duerksen, Christopher F., 3-164
Duhl, Stuart, 2-156
Dunne, Gerald T., 3-187

Eastin, Roy B., 2-129
Economos, James P., 3-88
Egan, Jack, 3-169
Egbert, Lawrence D., 2-79
Eisler, Riane T., 3-118
Elias, Stephen, 2-141
Ely, John Hart, 3-89
Erickson, J. Gunnar, 3-175
Estrella, Manuel M., 3-101
Evans, Patricia R., 2-16
Ewing, David W., 3-207

Farley, John T., 3-142
Farnsworth, E. Alan, 3-228
Favre, David S., 3-17
Feldman, Sylvia, 3-357
Fellman, David, 3-102
Fetterman, Elsie, 3-67
Fierro, Robert Daniel, 3-381
Fincher, E. B., 3-229
Fineborg, Keith S., 3-295
Finifter, Stuart B., 3-218
Firestone, David B., 3-138
Fischer, L. Richard, 3-37
Fischer, Louis, 3-337, 3-348
Fiscina, Salvatore Francis, 3-296
Fisher, Bruce D., 3-230
Fisher, Mary L., 2-21
Fisher, Roger, 3-208
Flanagan, John R., 3-176
Flaster, Donald J., 3-297
Folsom, Gwendolyn B., 2-126
Fontana, Vincent J., 3-194
Foster, Lynn, 2-33
Fox, Vernon B., 3-95
Franks, Maurice R., 3-119
Frels, Kelly, 3-338
Fried, Charles, 3-73
Friedman, Lawrence M., 3-231
Friedman, Leon, 2-44
Friedman, Paul R., 3-158
Friedman, Ronald M., 3-327
Frost, Martin L., 3-101
Furcalo, Foster, 3-232

Gadow, Sandy, 3-326
Gale, Alice T., 3-300
Gammage, Alan Z., 3-103
Garber, Lee Orville, 3-339
Gasaway, Laura N., 2-34, 3-177
Geller, Bradley, 3-11
Gentry, Harold W., 3-343
Gerhart, Eugene C., 2-83
Gifis, Steven H., 2-65

Gilbertson, Gerard, 2-80
Gillers, Stephen, 3-18, 3-251, 3-259
Gilmore, Grant, 3-233
Ginger, Ann Fagan, 3-46
Glantz, Leonard H., 3-292
Glassman, Don, 3-178
Glendon, Mary Ann, 3-54
Goehlert, Robert, 2-127
Goldberg, Steven S., 3-340
Goldfarb, Gerald, 3-21
Goldfarb, Ronald L, 3-283
Goldfarb, Sally F., 3-260
Golding, Martin P., 3-190
Goldstein, Gersham, 2-5
Gora, Joel M., 3-26
Gordon, Frank S., 2-66
Gordon, Michael Wallace, 3-54
Gottlieb, Alan M., 3-151
Gottron, Martha V., 3-153
Green, Robin M., 3-120
Greenberg, E. B., 2-133
Gressman, Eugene, 3-43
Grieve, Andrew, 3-370
Gross, Frederic, 3-393
Grow, James R., 3-222

Haavik, Sarah F., 3-159
Haensch, Günther, 2-86
Halloran, Mark E., 3-175
Hamre, Julie P., 3-270
Harbison, Winfred A., 3-59
Hardy, Benjamin A., Jr., 3-213
Harnett, Bertram, 3-234
Harris, Fabia, 2-136
Hartman, Chester, 3-137
Hartman, Susan, 3-173
Harvey, John J., 3-210
Hayden, Trudy, 3-47
Hearn, Edward R., 3-175
Heinz, John P., 3-40
Helburn, Judith, 3-280
Helm, Alice K., 3-235
Hemnes, Thomas M. S., 2-66
Hemphill, Anita M., 3-358
Hemphill, Charles F., Jr., 2-67, 3-103, 3-358
Hemphill, Phyllis D., 2-67
Henke, Dan F., 2-29
Henke, Shirley, 3-104
Henszey, Benjamin N., 3-236, 3-327
Hermann, Phillip J., 3-19
Herr, Stanley S., 3-160
Herskowitz, Mickey, 3-265
Hewman, Susan, 3-393
Hieb, Elizabeth A., 2-87
Hill, John L., 3-68
Hill, Marvin, Jr., 3-211

Hiller, Jeffrey, 3-74
Hodes, W. William, 2-142
Hodson, Thomas S., 3-27
Hoffman, Paul, 3-252
Hollander, Patricia, 3-341
Holzman, Robert S., 3-143, 3-382, 3-383
Honigsberg, Peter Jan, 3-212
Hood, Jack B., 3-213
Hoover, James L., 2-34
Huckaby, Stan, 3-136
Hughes, Theodore E., 3-144
Hull, Kent, 3-161

Inbau, Fred E., 3-105, 3-106
Israel, Fred L., 2-44

Jacobini, H. B., 3-7
Jacobs, Jerald A., 3-78
Jacobstein, J. Myron, 2-143
Jaffe, Frederick S., 3-2
James, A. Everette, 3-298
Jaworski, Leon, 3-265
Jessup, Libby F., 3-168
Johnson, Nancy P., 2-26
Johnston, Donald F., 3-179
Joseph, Joel D., 3-74
Jowitt, William Allen, 2-88
Judicial Conference of the United States, 2-45

Kahan, Stuart, 3-20
Kalisch, Beatrice J., 3-195
Kalvelage, Carl, 3-7, 3-61
Kane, Mary Kay, 3-41
Kanowitz, Leo, 3-359
Kaplan, Melvin J., 3-65
Kaplan, Roger P., 3-215
Kasgulski, Marech, 2-113
Kastner, Carolyn R., 3-121
Katz, Barbara F., 3-292
Katz, Sanford N., 3-122, 3-126
Kavass, Igor, 2-18
Kelly, Alfred A., 3-59
Kennedy, David W., 3-387
Kenny, John J., 3-204
Kersch, Mary Ellen, 3-139
Kiefer, Louis, 3-123
Kindred, Michael, 3-162
Kinnard, Joyce, 3-69
Kinoy, Arthur, 3-266
Kintner, Earl W., 3-79
Kirkemo, Ronald B., 3-182
Kleckner, Simone-Marie, 2-25
Klein, David, 3-144
Klein, Fannie J., 2-134

192 / Author Index

Knight, Richard S., 3-342
Kobetz, Richard W., 3-196
Koren, Edward I., 3-323
Kosel, Janice, 3-33
Kretschman, Karen L., 3-280
Kutten, L. J., 3-30

Laitner, Skip, 3-320
Lambert, Jeremiah D., 3-64
Lammers, Nancy, 3-284
La Morte, Michael W., 3-343
Lane, Marc J., 3-86
Langsley, Donald G., 3-299
Larbalestrier, Deborah E., 3-273
Larson, Richard E., 3-48
Lasnik, Robert S., 3-124
Last, Jack, 3-237
Laudicina, Robert, 3-344
Laumann, Edward O., 3-40
Law, Sylvia, 3-49
Lawrence, William H., 3-315
Lee, Phillip R., 3-2
Levin, Noel Arnold, 3-214
Levin-Epstein, Michael D., 3-205
Levine, Alan, 3-345
Levy, Charlotte L., 3-165
Lewis, Alfred J., 2-144
Lewis, William Draper, 2-56
Libbey, Keith, 3-82
Licata, Tony, 3-256
Lieberman, Jethro Koller, 3-275, 3-277, 3-288
Likavec, Michael A., 3-27
Lindheim, Barbara L., 3-2
Lipman, Ira A., 3-107
Lloyd, David, 2-145
Loeb, Robert H., Jr., 3-197
Loevi, Francis J., 3-215
Looney, J. W., 3-145
Loring, Murray, 3-17
Lovett, William A., 3-38
Lowe, David, 2-146
Lowe, John S., 3-313
Lowell, Cym H., 3-376
Luban, David, 3-276
Lynch, Jane Shay, 3-360

MacNeil, Ian R., 3-75
Maley, Terri S., 3-314
Maloney, John P., 3-197
Mancini, Marguerite R., 3-300
Mandell, Sidney, 3-39
Mann, Stephanie, 3-104
Manville, Daniel E., 3-289
Maraist, Frank L., 3-8
Mariano, William E., 3-306

Marks, Burton, 3-21
Marshall, Edith Paul, 3-324
Martin, Cynthia, 3-125
Martin, Julian A., 2-89
Masters, Richard, 3-154
Matthews, Byron S., 3-311
Matthews, Elizabeth W., 3-287
McCaffrey, Joan F., 3-270
McCarthy, David J., 3-310
McCarthy, Martha M., 3-346
McCue, James K., 2-31
McDaniel, Paul R., 3-384
McDonald, Forrest, 3-60
McDonald, Hugh C., 3-108
McDonald, Laughlin, 3-48
McKenney, Betsy B., 3-237
McNulty, John K., 3-385
Meezan, William, 3-126
Melone, Albert P., 3-7, 3-61
Menninger, Karl A., II, 3-159
Menzel, Harold H., 3-146
Meranus, Leonard S., 3-28
Mermin, Samuel, 3-238
Mersky, Roy M., 2-31, 2-143
Meyers, Charles J., 2-93
Mickens, Kenneth L., 3-308
Milberg, Aaron S., 3-34
Miller, Alan S., 3-316
Miller, Ellen J., 3-332
Miller, Robert D., 3-301
Miller, Vernon X., 3-390
Milligan, W. D., 3-328
Minan, John H., 3-315
Mitchelson, Marvin, 3-127
Moller, Richard Jay, 3-134
Moody, William J., 3-147
Morales-Macedo, Fernando, 2-79
Morawetz, Thomas, 3-191
Morehead, Joe, 2-128
Moss, Elaine, 3-219
Munneke, Gary A., 3-253
Munnell, Alicia H., 3-366
Murphy, Maureen, 3-177
Murray, Paul V., 3-201
Myers, Barry Lee, 3-236

Nabors, Eugene, 2-15
Nader, Ralph, 3-69
Naifeh, Steven W., 2-58, 3-23
Neely, Richard, 3-91, 3-92
Newman, Roger K., 3-331
Nicholas, Ted, 3-80
Noble, June, 3-128
Noble, William, 3-128
Nycum, Susan, 3-29
Nygaard, Gary, 3-371

Oliver, Douglas B., 3-237
O'Neil, Robert, 3-216
Oran, Daniel, 2-68
Orenstein, Alan, 3-336
Osakwe, Christopher, 3-54
Osborn, John J., 3-281
Osborn, Percy George, 2-69
Oxbridge Communications, Inc., 2-32

Padover, Saul K., 3-62
Paenson, Isaac, 2-81
Peck, Robert S., 3-250
Pelton, Robert W., 3-285
Phalan, Reed T., 3-236
Philo, Harry M., 2-159
Polk, Anthony, 3-268
Polking, Kirk, 3-28
Pomroy, Martha, 3-361
Pozgar, George D., 3-302
Pressman, David, 3-180
Price, Barbara Raffle, 3-362
Price, Miles C., 2-147

Quattrochi, Joseph A., 2-148
Quemner, Thomas A., 2-82
Quimby, Charles W., 3-303

Raistrick, Donald, 2-76
Ralph Nader's Conference on Excessive Corporate Legal Fees, 3-81
Ramer, Leonard V., 3-50
Rathbun, Katherine C., 3-304
Ray, Larry, 3-70
Raymond, James C., 3-283
Re, Edward D., 3-42
Reed, Frank C., 3-138
Rein, M.L., 3-115
Remer, Daniel, 3-31
Reynolds, William L., 3-183
Rezny, Arthur A., 2-149
Rhein, David, 3-184
Rice, Jerome S., 3-82
Rice, Michael Downey, 2-90
Richards, Edward P., III, 3-304
Robbins, Richard L., 3-316
Robert, Marilyn McCoy, 3-184
Robertson, John A., 3-111
Robinson, Joan, 2-160
Robinson, Leigh, 3-223
Rockefeller, Edwin S., 3-392
Rogers, Harry Ellis, 3-35, 3-129
Rollo, V. Foster, 3-15
Rombauer, Marjorie Dick, 2-150
Rosengart, Oliver, 3-109
Rosenthal, Douglas E., 3-22

Ross, Susan Deller, 3-363
Roth, George J., 3-261
Rothenberg, I. Herbert, 3-217
Rothenberg, Robert E., 2-70
Rothman, Raymond C., 3-318
Rothstein, Paul F., 3-149
Rubin, David, 3-347
Rudenstine, David, 3-51
Rudovsky, David, 3-323
Rush, George E., 2-91
Russell, L. Mark, 3-163
Russo, Eva Manoff, 3-126
Ruxin, Robert H., 3-372

Sabin, Arthur J., 3-240
Sales, M. Vance, 2-149
Saliwanchick, Roman, 3-181
Sangrey, Dawn, 3-98
Sarshik, Steven, 3-241
Sass, Lauren R., 3-3
Saunders, Charles A., 3-148
Scharf, Charles F., 3-83
Schiller, Margery K., 3-67
Schimmel, David, 3-337, 3-348
Schmeckebier, Lawrence F., 2-129
Schmidhauser, John R., 3-185
Schottland, Charles I., 3-367
Schroeder, Milton R., 3-36
Schuck, Peter H., 3-391
Schultz, Jon S., 2-19
Schwartz, Helene E., 3-267
Schwartz, Mortimer, 2-29
Sen, Biswanath, 2-161
Service, J. Gregory, 3-170
Shain, Henry, 3-34, 3-242
Shanor, Charles A., 3-307
Shapiro, Andrew O., 3-71, 3-72, 3-225, 3-290
Sherick, L. G., 3-152
Shimp, Donna M., 3-218
Shrybman, James A., 3-349
Siegel, David D., 3-6, 3-56
Siegel, Stanley, 3-6
Silverman, Steven B., 3-217
Simon, James F., 3-188
Singer, Gerald M., 3-254
Sinicropi, Anthony, 3-211
Sive, Mary Robinson, 3-140
Sklar, Stanley L., 3-364
Sloan, Irving F., 3-135
Sloan, Irving J., 3-12, 3-198
Sloan, Phillip Samuel, 3-373
Slonim, Scott, 3-224
Smith, Gregory White, 2-58, 3-23
Smith, Herbert H., 3-220, 3-221
Smith, Sara Lyn, 3-360
Smolover, Deborah, 3-70

Author Index

Sobel, Lionel S., 3-374
Sokoloff, Natalie J., 3-362
Speidel, Richard E., 3-53
Speiser, Stuart M., 3-278
Spence, Gerry, 3-268
Spiotto, James E., 3-106
Sprouse, Mary L., 3-386
Sprudzs, Adolf, 2-18
Squillante, Alphonse M., 3-309
Steelman, David C., 3-88
Steffen, Roscoe T., 3-14
Steiner, Barry R., 3-387
Steiner, Gilbert Y., 3-4
Steingold, Fred S., 3-84, 3-243
Stelzer, Leigh, 3-350
Stern, Robert L., 3-43
Stevens, Robert, 3-279
Stewart, James B., 3-255
Stoddard, Thomas B., 3-52
Striker, John M., 3-71, 3-72, 3-225, 3-290
Stromme, Gary L., 2-151
Sussman, Alan N., 3-199
Swiger, Elinor Porter, 3-200
Szykitka, Walter, 3-241

Talbott, John, 3-388
Tarlow, Barry, 2-61
Tatum, Arlo, 3-57
Taylor, Irwin M., 3-172
Tennenhouse, Dan J., 2-163
Terrell, Timothy P., 3-307
Thomas, Ella Cooper, 3-113
Thomas, R. Murray, 3-201
Thomas, William A., 3-316
Tiemann, William H., 3-55
Tierney, Kevin, 3-394
Tompkins, Dorothy Campbell, 2-35
Traumutola, Joseph L., 3-344
Tseng, Henry P., 2-111
Turner, Charles, 3-245
Turow, Scott, 3-262

Ury, William, 3-208
U.S. Department of Justice, 3-110
U.S. Government Printing Office, 2-123

Vanderbilt, Arthur T., 3-263
Vardin, Patricia A., 3-202
Vasan, R. S., 2-92
Very, Donald L., 3-244
Vogt, John A., 3-312

Wade, Jack Warren, Jr., 3-389
Waicukauski, Ronald J., 3-375
Walker, David M., 2-167
Walsh, Clifford, 2-88
Walton, Ralph, 3-245
Waltz, Jon R., 3-150
Ward, Peter D., 2-39
Warden, Dorothy M., 2-34
Warner, Ralph, 3-93, 3-246
Wasserman, Paul, 2-113
Watters, Annette Jones, 2-146
Weber, Charles M., 3-53
Weckstein, Donald T., 3-274
Weeks, Kent M., 3-351
Wehringer, Cameron K., 3-24
Weinerman, Chester S., 3-247
Weistart, John C., 3-376
Weitzman, Lenore J., 3-130
West, Terrell, 3-157
Wheeler, Michael, 3-131
Whisenand, Paul M., 3-95
White, Charles J., 3-250
White, Jay C., 3-16
White, Lawrence, 3-64
Wilkerson, Albert E., 3-203
Williams, Howard R., 2-93
Williams, Phillip, 3-85
Wishard, William R., 3-13
Wolkin, Paul A., 3-25
Wood, William C., 3-321
Woodroof, M. G., III, 3-309
Woodward, Bob, 3-94
Woody, Robert Henley, 3-132
Woolley, Persia, 3-133
Wren, Christopher G., 2-152
Wren, Jill Robinson, 2-152
Wydick, Richard C., 2-124

Young, D. Parker, 3-343
Young, Lawrence R., 3-121
Yudof, Mark, 3-155

Zepke, Brent E., 3-249
Zwirn, Jerrold, 2-130

TITLE INDEX

The Abortion Dispute and the American System, 3-4
Abortion: Freedom of Choice and the Right to Life, 3-3
Abortion Politics: Private Morality and Public Policy, 3-2
Access Points to the Law Library: Card Catalog Interpretation, 3-287
Accounting and Financial Disclosure: A Guide to Basic Concepts, 3-6
Acquisitions, Mergers, Sales, and Takeovers: A Handbook with Forms, 3-83
Admiralty in a Nutshell, 3-8
Adoptions without Agencies: A Study of Independent Adoptions, 3-126
Age Discrimination in Employment Act, ADEA: A Symposium Handbook for Lawyers and Personnel Practitioners, 3-9
Agency-Partnership in a Nutshell, 3-14
The Ages of American Law, 3-233
Alcohol and Drug Abuse and the Law, 3-135
All about Escrow, or How to Buy the Brooklyn Bridge and Have the Last Laugh, 3-326
All about Suing and Being Sued, 3-240
Almanac of the Federal Judiciary, 2-40
Alternative to Fear: A Citizen's Manual for Crime Prevention through Neighborhood Involvement, 3-104
Alternatives: A Family Guide to Legal and Financial Planning for the Disabled, 3-163
The American Bankruptcy Kit, 3-35
American Bar Association Directory, 2-95
The American Bar, the Canadian Bar, the International Bar, 2-49
The American Bench: Judges of the Nation, 2-41
The American Constitution: Its Origins and Development, 3-59

American Indian Legal Materials: A Union List, 2-34
American Jurisprudence: A Modern Comprehensive Text Statement of American Law, State and Federal, 2-115
American Jurisprudence, Desk Book, 2-153
American Law, 3-231
The American Lawyer Guide to Leading Law Firms, 1983-1984, 2-50
An American Legal Almanac: Law in All States: Summary and Update, 2-160
The American Legal System, 3-229
Anglo-Scandinavian Law Dictionary of Legal Terms Used in Professional and Commercial Practice, 2-77
Animal Law, 3-17
Anti-trust Counseling for the 1980s, 3-392
Arbitration and the Federal Sector Advocate, 3-215
Association Law Handbook, 3-78
The Athlete and the Law, 3-373
An Athlete's Guide to Agents, 3-372
Attorneys Medical Deskbook, 2-163
Author's Guide to Journals in Law, Criminal Justice and Criminology, 2-31
Automobile Liability and the Changing Law, 3-309
Aviation Law: An Introduction, 3-15
Avoiding Liability in Architecture, Design, and Construction: An Authoritative and Practical Guide for Design Professionals, 3-63

Ballentine's Law Dictionary, with Pronunciations, 2-63
Bank Officer's Handbook of Commercial Banking Law, 3-36
Banking and Financial Institutions Law in a Nutshell, 3-38
Bankruptcy: Do It Yourself, 3-33

196 / Title Index

Banned Films: Movies, Censors, and the First Amendment, 3-331
The Bar Examiners Handbook, 2-156
Basic Criminal Law, 3-103
Basic Legal Research Techniques, 2-151
Beating the Adoption Game, 3-125
The Belli Files: Reflections on the Wayward Law, 3-264
The Best Lawyers in America, 2-58
Bibliographical Index to the State Reports Prior to the National Reporter System, 2-17
Bibliography of International Law, 2-24
Biographical Dictionary of the Federal Judiciary, 2-43
Biographical Directory of the American Association of Law Libraries, 2-46
Black's Law Dictionary: Definitions of the Terms and Phrases of American and English Jurisprudence, Ancient and Modern, 2-64
Book Publishers' Legal Guide, 3-330
The Brethren: Inside the Supreme Court, 3-94
Brief Writing and Oral Argument, 3-42

The California Divorce Kit, 3-129
The California Notary Law Primer, 3-317
Capitol Hill Manual, 2-155
Cases: A Resource Guide for Teaching about the Law, 3-201
Censorship, Libraries, and the Law, 3-286
Changes and Choices: Legal Rights of Older People, 3-11
Chicago Lawyers: The Social Structure of the Bar, 3-40
Child Abuse: Governing Law and Legislation, 3-198
Child Abuse and Neglect: An Annotated Bibliography, 3-195
Child Snatching: The Legal Response to the Abduction of Children, 3-122
Children's Rights: Contemporary Perspectives, 3-202
CIS Abstract/Index, 2-10
CIS U.S. Congressional Committee Hearings Index, 2-11
Citizen's Arrest: The Law of Arrest, Search and Seizure for Private Citizens and Private Police, 3-99
Citizen's Guide to Nuclear Power, 3-320
The Citizen's Guide to Planning, 3-220
The Citizen's Guide to Zoning, 3-221
Civil Procedure in a Nutshell, 3-41
Civil Rights Directory, 2-96
The Civil Rights of Students, 3-348

Clean Slate: A State-by-State Guide to Expunging an Arrest Record, 3-97
Clear Understanding: A Guide to Legal Writing, 3-283
Combined Catalog, Anglo-American Law Collections, University of California Law Libraries, Berkeley and Davis, with Library of Congress Class K Added, 2-29
Commercial Paper in a Nutshell, 3-53
Comparative Legal Traditions in a Nutshell, 3-54
Comparative Statutory Sources, 2-19
The Complete Condo and Co-op Information Book, 3-324
Computer Buyer's Protection Guide: How to Protect Your Rights in the Computer Marketplace, 3-30
Confession and Avoidance: A Memoir, 3-265
Conflicts in a Nutshell, 3-56
Congress and Law-Making: Researching the Legislative Process, 2-127
Congressional Index, 2-12
Congressional Publications: A Research Guide to Legislation, Budgets, and Treaties, 2-130
Congressional Quarterly's Guide to the U.S. Supreme Court, 2-132
A Constitutional History of the United States, 3-60
Consultation with a Divorce Lawyer, 3-117
Consumer Dispute Resolution: Exploring the Alternatives, 3-70
Contract as Promise: A Theory of Contractual Obligation, 3-73
Copyright Handbook, 3-179
Corpus Juris Secundum: A Complete Restatement of the Entire American Law as Developed by All Reported Cases: 1658 to Date, 2-116
Court Organization and Administration: A Bibliography, 2-35
Crime Prevention Handbook for Senior Citizens, 3-110
The Crime Victim's Book, 3-98
Criminal Justice Abstracts, 2-1
The Criminal Justice Periodical Index, 2-2
The Criminal Justice System and Women, 3-362
Criminal Law for the Layman: A Guide for Citizen and Student, 3-105
Crisis at the Bar: Lawyers' Unethical Ethics and What to Do about it, 3-275
CSI Federal Index, 2-13

Current Law Index, 2-3
Current Treaty Index, 2-18
The Custody Handbook, 3-133
The Custody Trap, 3-128
Cutting Legal Costs for Business: Proceedings of Ralph Nader's Conference on Excessive Corporate Legal Fees, May 18, 1981, Washington, D.C., 3-81

The Defendant's Rights Today: 3-102
Democracy and Distrust: A Theory of Judicial Review, 3-89
Dictionary Catalog of the Columbia University Law Library, 2-28
Dictionary of Criminal Justice, 2-91
Dictionary of Criminal Justice Data Terminology: Terms and Definitions Proposed for Interstate and National Data Collection and Exchange, 2-85
Dictionary of Current American Legal Citations, 2-73
Dictionary of International Relations and Politics, 2-86
Dictionary of Legal Abbreviations Used in American Law Books, 2-74
Dictionary of Legal Terms: A Simplified Guide to the Language of Law, 2-65
The Dictionary of Practical Law, 2-67
Dictionary of Sigla and Abbreviations to and in Law Books before 1607, 2-75
Dictionnaire juridique francais-anglais [anglais-francais], 2-82
A Diplomat's Handbook of International Law and Practice, 2-161
Directory of Juvenile and Adult Correctional Departments, Institutions, Agencies, and Paroling Authorities, United States and Canada, 2-97
Directory of Law Libraries, 2-98
Directory of Law Teachers, 2-47
Directory of Law-Related Education Projects, 2-99
Directory of Lawyer Referral Services, 2-100
The Directory of Legal Aid and Defender Offices in the United States, 2-101
Directory of Legal Employers, 2-135
Directory of the Legal Profession: Major Firms, Specialty Firms, and Corporate Legal Departments, 2-51
Displacement: How to Fight It, 3-137
Dissolution: No-Fault Divorce, Marriage, and the Future of Women, 3-118
Divided Children: A Legal Guide for Divorcing Parents, 3-131

Divorce or Marriage: A Legal Guide, 3-115
Divorce without Defeat: A Survival Handbook, 3-120
Do I Really Need a Lawyer?, 3-20
Do It My Way or You're Fired: Employee Rights and the Changing Role of Management Prerogatives, 3-207
Do You Need a Lawyer?, 3-19
A Documentation System for Teacher Improvement or Termination, 3-338
Due Process in Special Education, 3-349
Due Process in Special Education: On Going to a Hearing, 3-336
Duties and Liabilities of Public Accountants, 3-5

The Educator in the Law Library, 2-149
Effective Legal Research, 2-147
Effective Legal Writing: A Style Book for Law Students and Lawyers, 3-282
Emergency Care and the Law, 3-300
Employee Benefit Plans: A Glossary of Terms, 2-87
Encyclopedia of Crime and Justice, 2-117
English-French-Spanish-Russian Manual of the Terminology of Public International Law (Law of Peace) and International Organizations, 2-81
Environmental Law for Non-Lawyers, 3-138
Environmental Law Handbook, 2-154
Environmental Legislation: A Sourcebook, 3-140
Estate Planning for Farmers, 3-145
Estate Planning: The New Golden Opportunities, 3-143
Everybody's Guide to Small Claims Court, 3-93
Everyday Law Made Simple, 3-237
Everything a Woman Needs to Know to Get Paid What She's Worth, 3-355
The Eviction Book for California, 3-223
Evidence in a Nutshell: State and Federal Rules, 3-149
Evidence in Arbitration, 3-211

The Family Guide to Crime Prevention, 3-101
A Family Guide to Estate Planning, Funeral Arrangements, and Settling an Estate after Death, 3-144
The Family Legal Advisor: A Clear, Reliable and Up-to-Date Guide to Your Rights and Remedies under the Law, 3-235
Fear of Filing: A Beginner's Handbook on Record Keeping and Federal Taxes for Performers, Visual Artists, and Writers, 3-380

198 / Title Index

Federal and State Court Systems—A Guide, 2-134
Federal Court Directory, 2-102
Federal Income Taxation of Individuals in a Nutshell, 3-385
Federal Regulatory Directory, 2-103
Federal Tax Articles: Income, Estate, Gift, Excise, Employment Taxes, 2-4
Federal Tax Research, 2-148
Federal Yellow Book, 2-104
Fedfind: Your Key to Finding Government Information, 2-125
Fighting Back: How to Cope with the Medical, Emotional, and Legal Consequences of Rape, 3-333
Finding the Law: A Guide to Legal Research, 2-145
Finding the Law: A Workbook on Legal Research for Laypersons, 2-138
Fundamentals of Legal Research, 2-143
The Future of Social Security, 3-366

Gerry Spence: Gunning for Justice, 3-268
Getting Custody: Winning the Last Battle of the Marital War, 3-132
Getting into America: The United States Visa and Immigration Handbook, 3-167
Getting to Yes: Negotiating Agreement without Giving In, 3-208
Glossary of Real Estate Law, 2-84
The Good Lawyer: Lawyers' Roles and Lawyers' Ethics, 3-276
Government Publications and Their Use, 2-129
Great American Lawyers, 2-56
Grievance Guide, 3-209
The Guide to American Law: Everyone's Legal Encyclopedia, 2-118
A Guide to Business Law, 3-76
A Guide to Municipal Leasing, 3-312
Guide to State Legislative Materials, 2-21
Guide to the Federal Courts: An Introduction to the Federal Courts and Their Operation, Includes Explanation of Litigation Process, 3-90
Guidelines for Federal Campaign Compliance, 3-136
Guidelines for Fiduciaries of Taft-Hartley Trusts: An ERISA Manual, 3-214

Handbook for Conscientious Objectors, 3-57
Handbook of Mineral Law, 3-314

Handbook of Modern Construction Law, 3-64
A Handbook on Historic Preservation Law, 3-164
Harrap's German and English Glossary of Terms in International Law, 2-80
Health and the Law, 3-294
Help Me, I'm Hurt: The Child Abuse Handbook, 3-192
Holzman's New Guide to the Accumulated Earning Tax, 3-382
Hotel-Motel Law: A Primer on Innkeeper Liability, 3-170
How Courts Govern America, 3-91
How to Avoid Probate—Updated!, 3-141
How to Be a Witness, 3-394
How to Become a Citizen of the United States, 3-168
How to Brief a Case: An Introduction to Legal Reasoning, 3-258
How to Do Business with the IRS: The Complete Guide for Tax Professionals, 3-378
How to Do Your Own Bankruptcy, 3-34
How to Draw Up Your Own Legal Separation, Property Settlement, or Cohabitation Agreement without a Lawyer, 3-114
How to Fight City Hall: A Guide for Citizen and Environmental Action, 3-139
How to File for "Chapter 11" Bankruptcy Relief from Your Business Debts, with or without a Lawyer, 3-32
How to Find the Law, 2-140
How to Form Your Own Corporation without a Lawyer for under $50.00, 3-80
How to Form Your Own Illinois Corporation before the Inc. Dries!, 3-85
How to Get Your Creditors off Your Back without Losing Your Shirt, 3-65
How to Go Directly into Solo Law Practice without Missing a Meal, 3-254
How to Live—and Die—with Texas Probate, 3-148
How to Make It through Law School, 3-257
How to Prepare Patent Applications, 3-176
How to Probate an Estate: A Handbook for Executors and Administrators, 3-147
How to Protect Your Health at Work, 3-218
How to Protect Yourself against Cops in California and Other Strange Places, 3-96
How to Protect Yourself from Crime: Everything You Need to Know to Guard Yourself, Your Family, Your Home, Your Possessions, and Your Business, 3-107

How to Register a Copyright and Protect Your Creative Work, 3-173
How to Save 50% or More on Your Income Tax—Legally, 3-377
How to Use the Freedom of Information Act (FOIA), 3-152
How to Win Custody, 3-123
How You Can Sue without Hiring a Lawyer: A Guide to Winning in Small Claims Court, 3-290
Hugo Black and the Judicial Revolution, 3-187
The Human Body and the Law: Legal and Ethical Considerations in Human Experimentation, 3-165
Human Rights Organizations and Periodicals Directory, 2-105

I'd Rather Do It Myself: How to Set up Your Own Law Firm, 3-251
In the Best Interest of the Child; A Guide to State Support and Paternity Laws, 3-121
Independent Journey: The Life of William O. Douglas, 3-188
Index to Federal Tax Articles, 2-5
Index to Legal Citations and Abbreviations, 2-76
Index to Legal Periodicals, 2-6
Index to Periodical Articles Related to Law, 2-7
Index to the Code of Federal Regulations, 2-14
Index to U.S. Government Periodicals, 2-8
Inside the Law Schools: A Guide by Students, for Students, 3-260
The Insurance Bar: A Directory of Eminent Lawyers and the Selective Digest of the Law of Insurance and Related Topics, 2-52
Insurance Law in a Nutshell, 3-171
International Directory of Bar Associations, 2-106
International Legal Bibliography, 2-25
Interstate Compacts and Agencies, 3-154
Introduction to Basic Legal Principles, 3-236
Introduction to Criminal Evidence, 3-150
Introduction to Criminal Justice, 3-95
An Introduction to International Law, 3-182
Introduction to Law and the Legal Process, 3-226
Introduction to the Legal System, 3-230
An Introduction to the Legal System of the United States, 3-228

Introduction to United States International Taxation, 3-384
Introduction to United States Public Documents, 2-128
Intruder in Your Home, 3-353

Joint Property: Everything You Must Know to Save Time, Trouble, and Money on Your Jointly Owned Property, 3-325
Journalists' Handbook to Ohio Courts, 3-27
Jowitt's Dictionary of English Law, 2-88
Judges and Justices: The Federal Appellate Judiciary, 3-185
Judges of the United States, 2-45
Judicial Process in a Nutshell, 3-183
Judicial Review and the National Political Process: A Functional Reconsideration of the Role of the Supreme Court, 3-87
The Justices of the United States Supreme Court, 1789-1969: Their Lives and Major Opinions, 2-44
Juvenile Justice Administration, 3-196

Kime's International Law Directory, 2-107

Labor Arbitration—What You Need to Know, 3-206
Labor Unions: How to Avert Them, Beat Them, Out-Negotiate Them, Live with Them, Unload Them, 3-217
Land Use Controls in the United States: A Handbook on the Legal Rights of Citizens, 3-219
Landlords and Tenants: Your Guide to the Law, 3-224
Latin Worlds and Phrases for Lawyers, 2-92
Law and Amateur Sports, 3-375
Law and Business Directory of Corporate Counsel, 2-53
Law and Business Directory of Major U.S. Law Firms, 1984-85, 2-54
Law and International Law: A Bibliography of Bibliographies, 2-23
Law and Legal Information Directory, 2-113
The Law and Legislation of Elderly Abuse, 3-12
Law and the Legal System; An Introduction, 3-238
The Law and the Teacher in Missouri: A Handbook for Teachers, Administrators, and School Board Members, 3-339

200 / Title Index

Law and the Writer, 3-28
The Law and You, 3-200
Law Books, 1876-1981: Books and Serials on Law and Its Related Subjects, 2-37
Law Books in Print: Books in English Published throughout the World and in print through 1981, 2-36
Law Books Published, 2-38
Law Dictionary for Non-Lawyers, 2-68
Law Dictionary: Technical Dictionary of the Anglo-American Legal Terminology, English-German, 2-78
A Law Enforcement Guide to United States Supreme Court Decisions, 3-100
Law Enforcement Vocabulary, 2-89
Law for Non-Lawyers, 3-249
Law for Physical Educators and Coaches, 3-371
Law for the Medical Practitioner, 3-303
Law for You, 3-232
Law, Lawyers, and Laymen: Making Sense of the American Legal System, 3-234
The Law of Financial Privacy: A Compliance Guide, 3-37
The Law of Insurance, 3-172
The Law of Libel and Slander and Related Action, 3-113
Law of Self-Defense, 3-352
The Law of Sports, 3-376
Law School: Briefing for a Legal Education, 3-263
Law School: Legal Education in American from the 1850s to the 1980s, 3-279
The Law Schools of the World, 2-111
The Law, the Supreme Court, and the People's Rights, 3-46
Laws Governing Banks and Their Customers, 3-39
Lawsuit, 3-278
Lawyer and Client: Who's in Charge?, 3-22
Lawyering, 3-267
The Lawyer's Almanac 1984: A Cornucopia of Information about Law, Lawyers, and the Profession, 2-157
Lawyers' Desk Book, 2-158
Lawyer's Desk Reference: Technical Sources for Conducting a Personal Injury Action, 2-159
Lawyer's Medical Cyclopedia of Personal Injuries and Allied Specialties, 2-119
Lawyer's Register by Specialties and Fields of Law; A National Directory of Lawyers Listed by Fields of Law, 2-55
The Layman's Guide to Legal Terminology and Documents, 2-133
Legal Agreements in Plain English, 3-74

Legal and Law Enforcement Periodicals: A Directory, 2-32
The Legal Aspects of Athletics, 3-370
Legal Aspects of Certification and Accreditation, 3-299
Legal Aspects of Health Care Administration, 3-302
Legal Aspects of Solar Energy, 3-315
The Legal Assistant's Handbook, 3-270
Legal Care for Your Software: A Step-by-Step Guide for Computer Software Writers, 3-31
Legal Deskbook for Administrators of Independent Colleges and Universities, 3-351
Legal First Aid: Your Complete Basic Guide to the Law (in Understandable Language), 3-242
A Legal Guide for Gay and Lesbian Couples, 3-44
The Legal Guide for the Family, 3-244
Legal Guidebook in Mental Health, 3-306
Legal Handbook for Educators, 3-341
Legal Handbook for Nonprofit Organizations, 3-86
Legal Looseleafs in Print, 2-30
Legal Master Guide for Small Business, 3-84
Legal Medicine, with Special Reference to Diagnostic Imaging, 3-298
Legal Novels: An Annotated Bibliography, 3-280
A Legal Perspective for Student Personnel Administrators, 3-344
Legal Problem Solving: Analysis, Research, and Writing, 2-150
Legal Protection for Computer Programs, 3-177
Legal Protection for Microbiological and Genetic Engineering Inventions, 3-181
Legal Research: A Self-Teaching Guide to the Law Library, 2-142
Legal Research: How to Find and Understand the Law, 2-141
Legal Research and Education Abridgment; A Manual for Law Students, Paralegals, and Researchers, 2-137
Legal Research for Educators, 2-146
Legal Research in a Nutshell, 2-139
The Legal Research Manual: A Game Plan for Legal Research and Analysis, 2-152
Legal Thesaurus, 2-94
The Legal Word Book, 2-66
Legality of Student Disciplinary Practices, 3-335
Legislative History: Research for the Interpretation of Laws, 2-126

Legislative Reference Checklist: The Key to Legislative Histories from 1789-1903, 2-15
The Lemon Book, 3-69
Let the Buyer Beware: Consumer Rights and Responsibilities, 3-67
Librarians' Affirmative Action Handbook, 3-210
Lions of the Eighties: The Inside Story of the Powerhouse Law Firms, 3-252
The Litigious Society, 3-288
Living Together, 3-127
The Living U.S. Constitution, 3-62
Local Government: How to Get into It. How to Administer It Effectively, 3-311
Local Government Law in a Nutshell, 3-310
Looking at Law School: A Student Guide from the Society of American Law Teachers, 3-259
Loony Laws . . . You Didn't Know You Were Breaking, 3-285

Making the Law Work for You: A Guide for Small Businesses, 3-82
Malpractice: A Guide to the Legal Rights of Patients and Doctors, 3-297
The Maltreated Child: The Maltreatment Syndrome in Children: A Medical, Legal, and Social Guide, 3-194
Marijuana; Your Legal Rights, 3-134
The Marriage Contract: Spouses, Lovers, and the Law, 3-130
Martindale-Hubbell Law Directory, 2-57
Medical Law for the Attending Physician: A Case-Oriented Analysis, 3-296
Medical Risk Management, 3-304
Men of the Supreme Court: Profiles of the Justices, 2-42
Mental Health and the Law, 3-305
The Mentally Retarded Citizen and the Law: President's Committee on Mental Retardation, 3-162
Milestones! 200 Years of American Law: Milestones in Our Legal History, 3-277
Military Law in a Nutshell, 3-307
Modern Legal Systems Cyclopedia, 2-120
Monthly Catalog of United States Government Publications, 2-22
Multilingual Law Dictionary: English, Francais, Espanol. Deutsch, 2-79
Musician's Guide to Copyright, 3-175

The National Directory: Law Enforcement Administrators, Prosecutions, Correctional Institutions, and Related Agencies, 2-108
National Directory of Criminal Lawyers, 2-61
The National Directory of State Agencies, 2-109
National Legal Bibliography: Recent Acquisitions of Major Legal Libraries, 2-39
Nelson's Law Office Directory, 2-59
New Credit Rights for Women, 3-66
The New Social Contract: An Inquiry into Modern Contractual Relations, 3-75
New York City Tenant Handbook: Super Tenant: Your Legal Rights and How to Use Them, 3-225
Notary Public Practices and Glossary, 3-318
Nuclear Safety: Risks and Regulation, 3-321

Obstetrics/Gynecology and the Law, 3-295
Odometer Law, 3-308
Oil and Gas Law in a Nutshell, 3-313
Oil and Gas Terms: Annotated Manual of Legal Engineering Tax Words and Phrases, 2-93
On What the Constitution Means, 3-58
One L., 3-262
Osborne's Concise Law Dictionary, 2-69
Overcoming Legal Uncertainties about Use of Solar Energy Systems, 3-316
The Oxford Companion to Law, 2-167

The Paper Chase, 3-281
The Paralegal, 3-272
The Paralegal and the Lawyer's Library, 3-271
Paralegal Practice and Procedure: A Practical Guide for the Legal Assistant, 3-273
A Parent's Guide to Adoption, 3-124
Parker Directory of California Attorneys, 2-60
The Partners: Inside America's Most Powerful Law Firms, 3-255
Patent It Yourself! How to Protect, Patent, and Market Your Inventions, 3-180
The People's Law Review, 3-246
Perfectly Legal: 300 Foolproof Methods for Paying Less Taxes, 3-387

202 / Title Index

Philosophy of Law, 3-190
The Philosophy of Law: An Introduction, 3-191
Physical Education and the Law, 3-368
Pilots and Aircraft Owners Legal Guide, 3-16
Plain English for Lawyers, 2-124
The Plain-Language Law Dictionary, 2-70
Power Plays: How to Deal Like a Lawyer in Person-to-Person Confrontations and Get Your Rights, 3-71
Powers of Congress, 3-284
The Practical Guide to Michigan Law, 3-243
Practical Law: A Layperson's Handbook, 3-247
The Practical Lawyer's Manual on Lawyer-Client Relations, 3-25
A Practical Tax Guide for the Horse Owner, 3-388
Prentice-Hall Dictionary of Business, Finance, and Law, 2-90
Primer of Equal Employment Opportunity, 3-205
Primer of Labor Relations, 3-204
Primer on Constitutional Law, 3-61
A Primer on the Law of Deceptive Practices: A Guide for Businesses, 3-79
Prisoners' Self-Help Litigation Manual, 3-289
Probation and Parole Directory, 2-110
Problems in Hospital Law, 3-301
Professional Responsibility in a Nutshell, 3-274
Professional Sports and the Law, 3-374
Protective Security Law, 3-106
Providing Legal Services for Prisoners: A Tool for Correctional Administrators, 3-322
Psychology and American Law, 3-329

Quote It! Memorable Legal Quotations: Data, Epigrams, Wit, and Wisdom from Legal and Literary Sources, 2-83

Rape: Preventing It; Coping with the Legal, Medical, and Emotional Aftermath, 3-334
Reader's Digest Family Legal Guide: A Complete Encyclopedia of Law for the Layman, 3-239
Real Estate Law, 3-327
Real Estate Law, 3-328
Reason in Law, 3-189
Regulation: Process and Politics, 3-153
Research Essentials of Administrative Law, 3-7

The Right to Participate: The Law and Individuals with Handicapping Conditions in Physical Education and Sports, 3-157
The Right to Silence: Privileged Clergy Communication and the Law, 3-55
Rights and Advocacy for Retarded People, 3-160
The Rights of Aliens, 3-166
The Rights of Americans: What They Are—What They Should Be, 3-45
The Rights of Children: Emergent Concepts in Law and Society, 3-203
The Rights of Doctors, Nurses, and Allied Health Professionals: A Health Primer, 3-292
The Rights of Ex-Offenders, 3-51
The Rights of Gay People, 3-52
The Rights of Government Employees, 3-216
The Rights of Gun Owners, 3-151
The Rights of Hospital Patients, 3-291
The Rights of Lawyers and Clients, 3-18
The Rights of Mentally Retarded Persons, 3-158
The Rights of Physically Handicapped People, 3-161
The Rights of Prisoners, 3-323
The Rights of Racial Minorities, 3-48
The Rights of Reporters, 3-26
The Rights of Students, 3-345
The Rights of Students and Teachers: Resolving Conflicts in the School Community, 3-337
The Rights of Suspects, 3-109
The Rights of Teachers, 3-347
The Rights of Tenants, 3-222
The Rights of the Critically Ill, 3-111
The Rights of the Elderly and Retired: A People's Handbook, 3-13
The Rights of the Mentally Retarded—Developmentally Disabled to Treatment and Education, 3-156
The Rights of the Poor, 3-49
The Rights of Veterans, 3-393
The Rights of Women, 3-363
The Rights of Women, 3-357
The Rights of Young People; The Basic ACLU Guide to a Young Person's Rights, 3-199
Rights on Trial: The Odyssey of a People's Lawyer, 3-266

Say It Safely: Legal Limits in Publishing, Radio, and Television, 3-112

Sexuality, Law, and the Developmentally Disabled Person: Legal and Clinical Aspects of Marriage, Parenthood, and Sterilization, 3-159
Shana Alexander's State-by-State Guide to Women's Legal Rights, 3-354
Shepard's Acts and Cases by Popular Names: Federal and State, 2-162
Shepard's Law Review Citations: A Compilation of Citations to Law Reviews and Legal Periodicals, 2-9
Shoplifting: What You Need to Know about the Law, 3-364
Slaying the Law School Dragon, 3-261
The Social Security Program in the United States, 3-367
Social Security Today and Tomorrow, 3-365
Sources of Compiled Legislative Histories: A Bibliography of Government Documents, Periodical Articles, and Books, 1st Congress-94th Congress, 2-26
Special Education Law: A Guide for Parents, Advocates, and Educators, 3-340
Sports and the Courts, 3-369
State Constitutional Conventions: from Independence to the Completion of the Present Union, 1776-1959: A Bibliography, 2-20
Stopping Sexual Harassment: A Handbook, 3-356
Students' Legal Rights and Responsibilities, 3-343
Students' Rights: Issues in Constitutional Freedoms, 3-342
Style Manual, 2-123
Subject Compilations of State Laws: Research Guide and Annotated Bibliography, 2-33
Suing Government: Citizen Remedies for Official Wrongs, 3-391
Super Threats: How to Sound Like a Lawyer and Get Your Rights on Your Own, 3-72
The Supreme Court, 2-131
Supreme Court of the United States, 1789-1980: An Index to Opinions Arranged by Justice, 2-16
Supreme Court Practice, 3-43
Survival, 3-108
A Survival Kit for Taxpayers: Staying on Good Terms with the I.R.S., 3-383
Surviving the First Year of Law School, 3-256
Surviving Your Role as a Lawyer: A Program to Reduce Stress and Increase Productivity, 3-269

Taking Care of Strangers: The Rule of Law in Doctor-Patient Relations, 3-293
Tax Shelters for the Not-so-Rich, 3-379
Tax Shelters in Plain English, 3-381
Taxable You: Every Woman's Guide to Taxes, 3-386
Teachers Have Rights, Too: What Educators Should Know about School Law, 3-350
Texan's Guide to Consumer Protection, 3-68
Texas Business Kit for Starting and Existing Businesses, 3-77
Texas Law in Layman's Language, 3-245
Texas Law Review Manual on Style, 2-121
The Texas Notary Law Primer, 3-319
Trademark Problems and How to Avoid Them, 3-174
Traffic Court Procedure and Administration, 3-88

Under 21: A Young People's Guide to Legal Rights, 3-193
Understanding the Law: A Handbook on Educating the Public, 3-250
The Unemployment Benefits Handbook, 3-212
A Uniform System of Citation, 2-122
Union List of Legislative Histories, 47th Congress, 1881-93rd Congress, 1974, 2-27
United Nations Juridical Yearbook, 2-164
United States Court Directory, 2-112
United States Government Manual, 2-165
United States Lawyers Reference Directory, 2-62
United States Supreme Court Reports, Lawyers' Edition, Second Series Desk Book, 2-166
Using American Law Books, 2-144

Video: A Guide for Lawyers, 3-332

The Washington Want Ads: A Guide to Legal Careers in the Federal Government, 2-136
The Ways of a Judge: Reflections from the Federal Appellate Bench, 3-186
Webster's Legal Speller, 2-71
What Every Client Needs to Know about Using a Lawyer, 3-23
What Every Man Should Know about Divorce, 3-116
What Every Woman Needs to Know about the Law, 3-361

What Legally Constitutes an Adequate Public Education: A Review of Constitutional, Legislative, and Judicial Mandates, 3-346
What Some People Ought to Know about Personal Injury Law, 3-390
When and How to Choose an Attorney, 3-24
When Government Speaks: Politics, Law, and Government Expression in America, 3-155
When You Owe the IRS, 3-389
Who's Who in American Law, 2-48
Why Courts Don't Work, 3-92
Winning Custody, 3-119
Winning with Your Lawyer, 3-21
Without a Lawyer, 3-241
Womanlaw; A Guide to Legal Matters Vital to Women, 3-358
A Woman's Choice, 3-1
Women and the Law: The Unfinished Revolution, 3-359
Women in the Judiciary: A Symposium for Women Judges, 3-184
The Women's Guide to Legal Rights, 3-360
Words and Phrases, 2-72
Worker's Compensation and Employee Protection Laws in a Nutshell, 3-213
World Legal Dictionary, 2-114
Write Your Own Will and Avoid Probate, 3-146
Writers' and Artists' Rights: Basic Benefits and Protections to Authors, Artists, Composers, Sculptors, Photographers, Choreographers, and Moviemakers under the New American Copyright Law, 3-178

You and the Law, 3-248
You Can't Take It with You, 3-142
Your Complete Guide to IRAs and Keoghs, 3-169
Your Computer and the Law, 3-29
Your Introduction to Law, 3-227
Your Legal Rights as a Minor, 3-197
Your New Lawyer: The Legal Employer's Complete Guide to Recruitment, Development, and Management, 3-253
Your Rights over Age 50, 3-10
Your Rights to Privacy, 3-47
Your Sexual Rights: An Analysis of the Harmful Effects of Sexual Prohibitions, 3-50

ABOUT THE AUTHORS

Bernard D. Reams, Jr., is Professor of Law and Director of the Law Library at the Freund Law Library, School of Law, Washington University in St. Louis. He holds the B.A. degree from Lynchburg College in Virginia, the M.S. degree from Drexel University's Graduate School of Library and Information Science, the J.D. degree from the University of Kansas, and the Ph.D. degree from Saint Louis University. Reams is the author of many books and articles on law and library science.

James M. Murray is Director of the Law Library and Assistant Professor at Gonzaga University School of Law. He holds the B.A. and J.D. degrees from Gonzaga University and the M. L. Libr. degree from the University of Washington. Murray is a former editor of the Book Appraisals Column in the *Texas Bar Journal* and author of numerous book reviews and bibliographies.

Margaret H. McDermott is Assistant Law Librarian for Reference Services at Washington University's Freund Law Library. She holds the B.A. degree from Barat College, the M.S. degree in Library Science from the University of Illinois, and the M.A. degree in Political Science from the University of Missouri-St. Louis.

LIBRARY USE ONLY
DOES NOT CIRCULATE